TERRITORY, THE STATE AND URBAN POLITICS

Territory, the State and Urban Politics

A Critical Appreciation of the Selected Writings
of Kevin R. Cox

Edited by

ANDREW E. G. JONAS
University of Hull, UK

ANDREW WOOD
University of Kentucky, USA

Routledge
Taylor & Francis Group

LONDON AND NEW YORK

First published 2012 by Ashgate Publishing

2 Park Square, Milton Park, Abingdon, Oxon OX14 4RN
711 Third Avenue, New York, NY 10017, USA

Routledge is an imprint of the Taylor & Francis Group, an informa business

First issued in paperback 2016

British Library Cataloguing in Publication Data
Territory, the state and urban politics : a critical
 appreciation of the selected writings of Kevin R. Cox.
 1. Cox, Kevin R., 1939- 2. Political geography. 3. State,
 The. 4. Municipal government. 5. Capitalism.
 I. Jonas, Andrew E. G., 1961- II. Wood, Andrew, 1964-
 320.1'2-dc23

Library of Congress Cataloging-in-Publication Data
Jonas, Andrew E. G., 1961-
 Territory, the state, and urban politics : a critical appreciation of the selected writings of
Kevin R. Cox / by Andrew Jonas and Andrew Wood.
     p. cm.
 Includes bibliographical references and index.
 ISBN 978-0-7546-7998-1 (hbk)
 1. Political geography. 2. State, The. 3. Municipal government. 4. Capitalism.
 5. Cox, Kevin R., 1939- I. Wood, Andrew, 1964- II. Title.

 JC319.J665 2012
 320.1'2--dc23

                                                                               2012029572

ISBN 978-0-7546-7998-1 (hbk)
ISBN 978-1-138-26800-5 (pbk)

Contents

PART III: STATE, TERRITORY AND DIFFERENCE

REJOINDER

List of Illustrations

Notes on Contributors

Delphine Ancien lectures in urban geography at the School of Geography, Planning and Environmental Policy at University College Dublin. Since completing her PhD at The Ohio State University, her research trajectory has been shaped by interests in the politics underlying the production and reproduction of uneven geographies of development. A particular focus of her work has been on the complex and multi-scalar political geographies of global cities and, increasingly, the variety of neoliberal contexts within which these unfold.

Allan Cochrane is Professor of Urban Studies at the Open University. He writes and researches on issues of urban and regional politics and policy, with a particular interest in the ways in which cities, regions and localities are made up, defined and governed. He is the author of *Urban Policy: A Critical Approach* (Blackwell 2007) and joint editor of *Security: Welfare, Crime and Society* (Open University Press 2009).

Kevin R. Cox is Distinguished University Professor of Geography at The Ohio State University. His interests include historical geographical materialism, the politics of local and regional development and South Africa. He is the author of numerous books including *Political Geography: Territory, State and Society.*

Kim England is Professor of Geography and Adjunct Professor of Gender, Women and Sexuality Studies at the University of Washington in Seattle. She is an urban social and feminist geographer who focuses on care work, critical social policy analysis, labor markets, economic restructuring, and inequalities in North America.

Alistair Fraser's work cuts across political, economic, and cultural geography. He has conducted research on land reform in South Africa and connecting this to broader processes of agrarian change in the contemporary period. His current work builds on these interests by examining Ireland's place within the global food economy. He has also published work on scalar practices, music, and fieldwork. He is a lecturer in the Department of Geography at the National University of Ireland Maynooth.

Mark Goodwin is Professor of Human Geography and Dean of the College of Life and Environmental Sciences at the University of Exeter. He has extensive research interests in the areas of local government, local politics and the local state, and has directed several research projects on these themes for a variety of funders. He is the author of many books and papers on these issues, including *The Local State and Uneven Development* (1988, with Simon Duncan) and *Rescaling the State* (2012, with Martin Jones and Rhys Jones).

Jamie Gough was employed in economic and employment policy in the Greater London Council before its abolition. He has subsequently taught geography and urban planning at Sydney, Northumbria and Sheffield Universities. He has written on local industry dynamics, labour processes and geography, geographies of economic cycles, urban and regional political economy and governance since the 1970s, neoliberalism and its contradictions, and dialectical theorisation of society and space. His latest book, with Aram Eisenschitz, is *Spaces of Social Exclusion* (Routledge).

Ron Johnston is a Professor in the School of Geographical Sciences at the University of Bristol. He has been researching in electoral geography since 1970, his interest in the subject being awakened by Kevin Cox's 1969 essay in *Progress in Geography*. With Charles Pattie he has co-authored many books (including *Putting Voters in their Place* in 2006) and papers in electoral studies.

Andrew E. G. Jonas is Professor of Human Geography at the University of Hull. After completing his PhD in Ohio under the supervision of Kevin Cox, he taught at Clark University and the University of California at Riverside before moving back to the United Kingdom. His research interests are encompassed by the broad theme of territory, the state and urban politics. He co-edited *The Urban Growth Machine: Critical Perspectives Two Decades Later* (1999, SUNY Press) and *Interrogating Alterity* (2010, Ashgate).

Jeff McCarthy is Programme Director at the Centre for Development and Enterprise, Johannesburg. He was appointed Honorary Professor at the University of Witwatersrand in Johannesburg 1989, and served as Professor and University Fellow at the University of KwaZulu-Natal for extended periods in the 1990s and early 2000s.

Charles Pattie is a Professor in the Department of Geography at the University of Sheffield. He has written on various aspects of political behaviour. Much of that research, carried out with Ron Johnston, has focussed on issues of electoral geography and party campaigning.

Kevin Ward is Professor of Human Geography and director of cities@manchester (www.cities.manchester.ac.uk). His current research is exploring the assembling of urban politics through the circuits, networks and webs in and through which policies are constituted and moved.

Andrew Wood is an Associate Professor in the Department of Geography at the University of Kentucky. As an economic, urban and political geographer his research interests are in three related areas: urban and regional governance; the politics of local economic development; and issues relating to competition and collaboration between firms. He has published over forty articles and book chapters on these themes and is co-author (with Susan Roberts) of *Economic Geography: Places, Networks and Flows* published by Routledge.

Preface

Following its rise to prominence in the 1980s and 1990s, work on territory, the state and urban politics continues to be a vibrant and dynamic area of academic concern. However, as yet there has been little attempt to take stock and reflect on how the field has developed, to examine the major influences in its evolution, and to assess the prospects for future work in this area. The rationale for this book is to begin the process of reflection and assessment. In order to do so we focus heavily on the work of one key influential figure in the development of the field – Kevin R. Cox.

Since his graduate education in the United States in the 1960s, British-born Kevin Cox has been a major figure in the development of urban and political geography on both sides of the Atlantic. A central force in the development of behavioural and quantitative geography, Kevin Cox has also been a pioneer of Marxist geography. Whilst we do consider Cox's earlier contributions to the study of voting behaviour and locational conflict, it is his more recent work on territory, the state and urban politics that provides the central theme of this volume. Since the 1980s, Kevin's theoretical approach has been inspired by critical realism (for example, the writings of Doreen Massey and Andrew Sayer) and historical materialism (David Harvey). An abiding theme running throughout his work is an interest in the conceptualisation of space. For Kevin, space is more than a container for social processes; rather space is constitutive of capitalism, its processes of accumulation, and ensuing struggles around the distribution of the social product. He is especially wary of spatial fetishism – that is, the view that the spatial can be examined separately from the social – and that certain processes operate at specific spatial scales seemingly to the exclusion of others. An interest in the critical theorisation of space and territory can be read into much if not all of Kevin's work over the years.

In 2008, we organised two panel sessions in honour of Kevin at the Association of American Geographers' Annual Conference in Boston, Massachusetts. These sessions were designed to draw together a range of scholars whose work broadly reflected Kevin's own interests. The sessions were well attended and, without exception, the presentations were thoughtful, insightful and well received. Building on the success of these sessions, we submitted a proposal to Ashgate to put together an edited volume which would provide a robust critical assessment of Kevin's contributions over the years. The resulting book draws together a collection of urban scholars to reflect on the development and state of field and to establish a research agenda for future work.

Overall, the book has three principal aims. The first is to bring together cutting-edge contributions on the conceptualisation of territory, the state and urban politics. The various chapters address a range of methodological, conceptual and philosophical issues, including questions of abstraction and empirical specification. The second aim is a somewhat narrower one – to highlight and reflect on the work of Kevin Cox in particular and assess his influence on the field. The chapters explore his various contributions to important debates on electoral geography, territory, the state, local economic development, urban politics, the 'situatedness' of everyday life, inequality, development, comparative analysis and globalisation. Thirdly, the book is designed to advance a research agenda for further theoretically-informed work on territory, the state and urban politics, drawing insights from influential theorists working at the cutting edge of contemporary human geographical research.

Andy Jonas and Andy Wood

Acknowledgements

First and foremost, we would like to thank Kevin Cox for his enthusiasm and willingness to engage with this project. We are grateful to the chapter contributors for producing such thoughtful reflections on Kevin's contributions. We would also like to thank everyone who participated in the sessions and events organised at the Association of American Geographers Annual Conference in Boston in 2008 in honour of Kevin, including Bob Lake, Martin Jones, Gordon MacLeod, Mark Boyle, Bae-Gyoon Park, Murray Low, and Mike and Felicity Sutcliffe. Finally, thanks to faculty, staff, graduate students and friends in the Department of Geography at The Ohio State University for contributing to a stimulating learning environment in which many of the concepts and ideas explored in this book were first aired.

Andy Jonas and Andy Wood
May, 2012

INTRODUCTION

Chapter 1

Territory, the State and Urban Politics in Critical Perspective

Andrew E. G. Jonas and Andrew Wood

This book is centered on how capitalist societies organize state territory, why ensuing struggles often converge around the urban scale, and how geographical difference can be incorporated into abstract knowledge of processes of capitalist development. These considerations can be condensed into the single overarching theme of 'territory, the state and urban politics'. In thinking around this theme, we have chosen to highlight the work of British-born geographer Kevin R. Cox. His work stands out both in terms of its analytical rigor and enduring spatial sensibility. On a more personal level, Kevin was our academic supervisor when we undertook doctoral dissertation research at The Ohio State University in the late 1980s and early 1990s. We – along with the contributors to this volume – have been profoundly influenced by Kevin's critical approach to questions of territory, the state and urban politics. Yet to provide a comprehensive review of Kevin's insights and contributions over the years would be an impossible task. Instead, the theme of territory, the state and urban politics offers a useful way of focusing the book and bringing coherence to what are quite diverse individual chapter contributions. Before we get into the contents of the book, we offer a brief summary and interpretation of the main theme.

Alongside such concepts as space, place and scale, the analysis of territory occupies an important position in the social division of geographical knowledge (Jessop et al. 2008). From the vantage point of urban political geography, territory is usually taken to reference the ways in which human society organizes and controls space. The state is often instrumental in the political organization of territory, and hence our interest in connecting territory to struggles around the state. Nonetheless, the term territory itself has a rich and complex history which cannot be reduced solely to questions of state sovereignty and control (Elden 2009). Moreover, our use of the term territory is not to be confused with territoriality, although the former usually presupposes the latter (see, for example, Sack 1986; Cox 2002, 1-6). As Delaney (2005, 15) puts it, whereas territory is a "…bounded meaningful space", territoriality draws attention to "…the relationship between territories *and some other social phenomena*" [emphasis in original]. We are certainly not advocating an ecological perspective on territoriality. Even if at some basic level nature and human labor are co-dependent there is nothing natural about the way societies organize themselves into territories. From our perspective territorial organization reflects and embodies the dominant social relations, struggles and actions of powerful social agents at a given moment of history. The time period which concerns us here is the period from World War II to the first decade of the twenty-first century, which broadly covers the transition from monopoly capitalism to advanced or late capitalism.

Throughout his academic career Kevin has sought to understand how capitalist society organizes territory and to account for the political interests and social processes adhering to particular spaces of capitalism and the state. An important theme running throughout this work is how the state, under capitalism, becomes enrolled in the politics of territorial organization. Through its territorial structure (by which we mean the allocation of powers and responsibilities to different levels and branches of the state), the state is a key player in how capitalist social relations and power struggles are expressed in a territorial manner. The state can be both the object of political struggle as well as an agent of territorial organization in its own right. We are especially interested in those conflicts and struggles which occur around state territorial structures that are more or less at the urban scale, recognizing that the urban is one among a number of state hierarchies, social networks and power structures. With respect to the wider spatial context, the book also speaks to debates about geographical scale and the politics of globalization, debates to which Kevin has been a significant contributor.

The remainder of this chapter provides a brief introduction to Kevin's work on state, territory and urban politics and sets the context for the contributions that follow. The book is divided into three main sections, which broadly correspond to the evolution of Kevin's work and provide a structure for grouping individual contributions around key conceptual ideas. In the first section (Part I) we show how Kevin's initial contributions to knowledge of state, territory and urban politics came through his pioneering work on elections and locational conflict in the 1960s and 1970s. Here we also get a sense of how Kevin's philosophical and epistemological treatment of space evolved, embracing such diverse methods as quantitative analysis and, in due course, critical realism. As we shall see, Kevin eventually came to the conclusion that realism had certain limitations when it came to historical-geographical explanation. Nevertheless it was formative of his approach to questions of territory, the state and urban politics.

The second section (Part II) examines Kevin's work on urban politics and local economic development. The concept of local dependence, which he developed with Andrew Mair, proved highly influential in theorizing local material interests and the strategies deployed by growth coalitions to ensure conditions conducive to local economic development. This section also examines how the urban question led to Kevin's key interventions on scale and the politics of globalization. The third and final section (Part III) puts Kevin's work in a broader, comparative context and considers how his ideas have been translated to settings outside North America and Europe. For Kevin and many of his students, South Africa's apartheid system and racial labor control policies brought into sharp focus the importance of geographical difference, identity and social context in explaining how capitalism develops and produces inequality. This section also touches on Kevin's response to post-structuralist and feminist critiques of Anglo-American Marxist geography. In the final chapter, Kevin offers a rejoinder to a number of critical issues raised by the respective contributors to the book.

Conceptualizing Space and Territory: From Quantitative Geography to Historical-Geographical Materialism

In the first section of the book, we contextualize the underlying theme of territory, the state and urban politics by situating it in relation to wider disciplinary concerns about space. In recent years there has been a marked turn away from bounded notions of territory towards a relational understanding of space which seeks to unbound spatial theorization. This means, for example, that the urban is no longer to be examined as if it were a discrete and bounded political space; instead the urban political arena represents a territorial assemblage of processes, institutions and policies many of which originate from beyond the jurisdictional boundaries of the city. Thanks to important interventions by Doreen Massey (2005), amongst others, critical thinking about space continues to preoccupy discussion in human geography, suggesting that it is very much work in progress (Malpas 2012). The conceptualization of space has been very central to the evolution of Kevin Cox's approach to questions of territory, the state and urban politics. For Kevin, space is more than a contingent effect or container of social processes; rather space is actively constitutive of capitalism, its mechanisms of accumulation, and the political interests attached to particular territorial configurations. We therefore start by tracing the development of Kevin's critical approach to space: from his formative interests in voting behavior to subsequent work on the local state and the urban question.

In the 1960s, when Kevin left the United Kingdom to undertake his graduate training in the United States, human geography was becoming influenced by quantitative methods. Explanation was based on the identification of statistical relationships between dependent and independent variables. Strong correlations between spatially-situated variables commonly indicated the presence of a causal relationship; typically the task of explanation in geography involved the identification of empirical regularities of a spatial nature. As Ron Johnston and Charles Pattie point out in Chapter 2, Kevin initially honed his critical thinking skills on the analysis of voting behavior before turning to the study of welfare and locational conflict. It might therefore be suggested that at this point in time Kevin's work was more about state and territory than urban politics. Specifically, he was interested in measuring and accounting for patterns in local and regional voting behavior, and deployed regression analysis to identify associations between variables of a spatial nature, as in his early studies of British elections (Cox 1968; 1969; 1970). As Johnston and Pattie suggest, the geographical dimension in electoral studies was often treated "...as either epiphenomenal (i.e. illustrating the outcome of deeper, non-spatial, processes) or residual rather than intrinsic to the explanation of observed patterns". However, Kevin injected a stronger sense of spatial causation into the analysis of voting patterns, which became even more apparent in his influential work on the identification of neighborhood effects in voting behavior (1972a). This work pointed to role of spatial proximity in influencing the voting decision. As Johnston and Pattie argue, Kevin "...showed that geographers could offer much more than mapping of certain aspects of electoral behaviour and electoral practice. Geography – and its key concepts of place and space – is situated at the heart of understanding elections."

Examining space and the geographic constitution of social life has been a constant in Kevin's work. His 1973 book, *Conflict, Power and Politics in the City*, sought to develop a specifically geographical framework for examining the city and its politics. Space and spatial concepts – such as locational externalities – provide the tools for examining political conflict in the city. Furthermore, the problematic of securing positive externalities while avoiding the negative was sufficiently powerful to enable analysis to shift between geographical scales. Kevin's discussion moves from the fiscal disparity between central city and suburb that structured the well-being of the US city to a focus on differences within jurisdictions as selected neighborhoods organize in order to secure positive spatial outcomes. While the book had a significant bearing on the discipline it also marked a transitional period in Kevin's own work. Nonetheless, his pioneering studies of the neighborhood effect and, subsequently, jurisdictional fragmentation suggested that 'space' was not a contingent variable; instead space and territorial structure seemed to have causal effects, in this case on people's voting behavior or patterns of fiscal redistribution by the state.

Kevin eventually became frustrated with the limitations of quantitative methods in terms of their ability to explain social processes, behavior and conflict. There was a brief encounter with the behavioral approach to urban locational problems but in the event this too proved unsatisfactory (Cox and Golledge 1969; Cox 1972b). In the late 1970s, Kevin turned to the writing of radical geographers such as David Harvey and Doreen Massey, both of whom in different ways had introduced human geography to Marxist theories of capital accumulation and uneven spatial development. In applying these theories to problems of welfare and locational conflict in the city, Kevin became interested in wider questions concerning the relationship between society and space. Notably, he was intrigued with the question of whether space could be said to possess its own properties or instead was the contingent expression of general social processes, namely, capital accumulation and social reproduction. This led to a formative engagement with critical realism which as Mark Goodwin points out in Chapter 3 heavily influenced Kevin's subsequent writings on the local state and urban politics.

Critical realism has its origins in the work of the philosophers Roy Bhaskar and Rom Harré. It was brought to the attention of critical human geographers by Andrew Sayer. Sayer (1984) sought to translate critical realist ontology into a workable and practical set of methods which could be applied to empirical research of concrete events and outcomes. One of the reasons why realism was attractive to radical geographers such as Kevin Cox was because it offered a critique of empirical generalization as a mode of explanation. Another factor was the assumption of a similarity between the realist method and Marxist ontology, an assumption which Kevin now believes to be erroneous.

Realism's approach to causal analysis could be distinguished from that of positivism on the basis of the former's emphasis on social relations, internal mechanisms and their conditions of activation. Abstract research seeks to identify the relations that structure social processes and provide social objects with different powers and liabilities. Concrete research is about the ways in which these powers and liabilities are expressed contingently to produce actual processes and outcomes. This means that the causes of spatial patterns and events cannot be inferred directly from their observed patterns of occurrence. Therefore any attempt empirically to model spatial patterns and derive general laws of spatial behavior is likely to obscure rather than reveal causal mechanisms and processes. In these respects, realism seemed to offer a viable alternative to the methods of positivist spatial science.

However, realism raised troubling questions about the ontological status of space. From a realist perspective, space can be approached in terms of its necessary social properties, which in turn must be identified and isolated through the method of rational abstraction. Space, in turn, takes on many different concrete forms; and these forms can make a difference to the ways in which causal mechanisms are activated. Therefore knowledge of spatial form must be incorporated into concrete research; but space itself can be ignored at the level of abstract research. As Sayer (1985, 54) argued:

> Abstract social theory need only consider space insofar as necessary properties of objects are involved, and this does not amount to very much. It must acknowledge that all matter must have spatial extension and hence that processes do not take place on the head of a pin and that no two objects can occupy the same (relative) place at the same time…Hence, while it is important for abstract theory to be aware of the existence of space, the claims that can be made about it are inevitably rather indifferent ones …

Whilst broadly sympathetic to the realist method of rational abstraction, Kevin was nonetheless eager to work through its strengths and weaknesses, a task which he initially undertook in the 1980s and continues with the discussion in Chapter 4. His particular concern is with the ontological status of space. Is space merely a container or contingent effect of general social processes which can be identified without reference to the spatial context? Or can space be said to have properties which influence and shape how causal mechanisms work in practice? In other words, does capitalism generate particular spatial forms and do these forms have emergent social properties and causal powers?

Working with his graduate students, Kevin Cox initially sought answers to these questions through the lens of research on the local state and urban politics. The debate about locality studies in the 1980s became an important outlet for the development of many of these ideas. The locality debate emerged from criticisms of an ESRC (Economic and Social Research Council)-funded interdisciplinary research program in the United Kingdom known as the Changing Urban and Regional System (CURS). The CURS project was designed to interrogate wider propositions about the restructuring of the UK space economy at a time of rapid economic, social and political change (Cooke 1987). It generated quite a fractious debate in scholarly journals. Neil Smith (1987), for one, accused researchers working under the CURS banner as engaging in empiricism: each team of locality researchers seemed to be preoccupied with the detailed characteristics of the specific places they were examining (six British case studies were chosen) rather than with interrogating wider theoretical propositions about the capitalist space economy and the changing nature of state spatial policy. At issue was the status of 'theory' vis-à-vis 'empirics', with the charge that in the case of locality research theorization was often playing second fiddle to empirical analysis. In short, locality researchers were seen to be guilty of empirical generalization.

Although there were various nuances to the locality debate, Kevin Cox made several interventions which in many respects define his approach to territory, the state and urban politics. In one paper published with Andrew Mair in *Antipode*, Cox and Mair (1989a) argued the case for approaching locality studies from the vantage of different levels of abstraction. In a related paper, Cox (1991a) deployed levels of abstraction to criticize the claim that urban political regimes are structurally predisposed towards promoting capital accumulation at the expense of social reproduction, suggesting that this relationship is socially necessary yet contingent in form. The notion of levels of abstraction disrupts the idea that the 'empirical' and the 'theoretical' are opposite sides of the ontological coin; indeed, as realism suggests all observations about social forms are dependent on the conceptual tools which are brought to bear upon them. Instead of reducing space to the level of the concrete, the method of abstraction allows for different layers of historical and geographical specificity to be introduced into concrete analysis of a given spatial problem. At a more abstract level, it is possible to identify the necessary conditions for capital accumulation but this tells us very little about the precise spatial form of these conditions. At a lower level of abstraction, it becomes possible to specify the particular spatial assemblages required for accumulation in a given place. For example, it seems that capital requires fixed spatial investments, which in turn constrain the activities of individual capitalists and impose conditions on how accumulation plays out in given spatial contexts.

In order to suggest how space can make a difference to processes of capital accumulation, Cox and Mair (1988; 1989b) offered the intermediate level abstraction of 'local dependence'. The concept of local dependence draws upon Harvey's (1982) theorization of the tension between the spatial fixity and mobility of capital: capital must first produce space (e.g., transport infrastructure, office buildings, housing, etc.) in order to accumulate and send into circulation money, profits and investment funds. In so producing space there is an ever-present threat of devaluation to capital invested therein. This tension creates a stake in how the local economy develops for, respectively, firms, workers and local states (Cox and Mair 1988). For firms it might be a case of seeking to develop local markets; for workers it could be supply of adequate housing and education; for local states it is the local tax base. There can be many different 'localities' depending on the nature of the material interests involved; but only when these local interests are identified is it possible to explain why some 'localities' are proactive in seeking to facilitate economic development and others are not.

A second question that follows from this conceptualization of space relates to the theorization of territory. In confronting problems of local dependence, locally based actors (e.g., firms, local governments, etc.) might draw upon powers and resources beyond their particular territories of operation. Thus for Kevin territory is not simply a matter of the state exercising its authority within, say, a local or 'urban' jurisdiction; territory is socially constructed and contested at and through different geographical scales. This consideration led Kevin to think through what might be called the 'politics of scale' whereby, in order to protect and reproduce local material interests, it might be necessary to draw down extra-local powers and resources. Following Massey's (1984) insights about how capital organizes through spatial divisions of labor, Cox and Mair (1991) argued that the state likewise has a scalar division of labor. This division of labor arises from how the state allocates its different administrative functions, investments and operational branches across its territory. An important aspect of this is how powers are allocated between various branches or levels of the state. Here Kevin has often referred to the differences between the federal system of the United States and more centralized states such as the UK; differences which in turn might account for the presence or absence of organized urban growth coalitions or the pattern of territorial expenditures endorsed by elected politicians, for instance. Therefore struggles at or around the 'urban' are sometimes premised upon establishing new scalar divisions of labor within the state; divisions which might well extend far beyond the limits of the 'urban' as defined in a local jurisdictional sense.

In a very influential paper in *Political Geography*, Cox (1998) elaborated on this theme and drew a distinction between 'spaces of dependence' and 'spaces of engagement'. Spaces of dependence refer to material interests and attachments to place. Spaces of engagement are the territorial structures and institutional arrangements drawn upon by locally based actors in order to reproduce their spaces of dependence. This insight is important to this book's theme in two respects. First, it demonstrates that the organization of territory is often about establishing new territorial divisions of responsibility and power that differ from the jurisdictional limits of the locality itself. Second, by showing how the material reproduction and political identity of the local often depends on marshalling extra-local powers, networks and resources, it anticipates subsequent relational thinking about territory and urban politics.

In Chapter 3, Mark Goodwin argues that it was Kevin Cox's work with Andrew Mair on the concept of local dependence which helped better to identify the material interests and processes surrounding local development politics. Goodwin traces the moves that Kevin made between the concepts of 'local dependence', 'spaces of dependence' and 'spaces of engagement' in order to shed light on the relation between different sorts of politics and the territorial organization of the state. Kevin's work opened up a research agenda focused around the key intersections of state, territory, space and power – an agenda which Goodwin suggests is still as pertinent today as it ever was.

In Chapter 4, Kevin Cox takes up the story and discusses the influence of critical realism and historical materialism in geography in the 1980s, noting that initially there appeared to be some compatibility between these two approaches to the analysis of capitalist socio-spatial forms. He examines these philosophical traditions in order to shed light on the urban question and how it has been examined by geographers such as Harvey and Massey. The question being asked at the time was whether or not the urban could be said to have some irreducible social significance or whether social theory could ignore the city. Reflecting upon these early spatial explorations, Kevin argues that his research sometimes went down blind alleys but at other times resulted in productive engagements across disciplinary and methodological boundaries. In hindsight, he feels that historical materialism offers a much more convincing way of thinking about capitalist territoriality and the urban condition. But he also argues that some of critical realism's concepts especially those of social structure and causal mechanisms can be usefully assimilated into historical materialism. However, a major proviso for Kevin is that they need to be "purged of their pluralistic baggage". He further draws attention to the ontological differences (rather than the presumed similarities) between critical realism and Marxism, noting that the latter's dynamic, totalizing and non-reductionist view of social change contrasts markedly with the pluralizing, flat and reductionist perspective of the former.

Urban Politics and Local Economic Development in Territorial Context

The second main section of the book explores Kevin's investigations into urban politics and local economic development in more depth, and introduces some new approaches to investigating these processes and forms. As we have already indicated, much of Kevin's early work sought to understand voting behavior and conflict around the urban living place and this soon encouraged him to explore the urban question in greater depth (see, for instance, Cox and Johnston 1982; Cox 2001). As Chapter 4 reveals, Kevin has always striven to unite knowledge of urban politics with a more abstract appreciation of the changing geographies of capitalism and the state. Certainly an important development was the work with Andy Mair on local dependence and levels of abstraction in the 1980s, and with Andy Wood in the 1990s on local economic development networks (Cox and

Wood 1994; 1997). Kevin has since gone on to question whether urban politics can be said to have an autonomous existence apart from, say, struggles around the territorial structure of the state at large. Critical urban scholars have likewise sought to unbound notions of urban politics, recognizing that something important is happening to urban economies and power structures which demands that critical attention turns to the wider role of the state, processes of economic globalization and, ultimately, a consideration of the power relations, flows and networks between cities as well as within them.

Towards the end of the 1980s, critical urban scholarship in North America and Western Europe became acutely interested in the regulatory transition of capitalism from Fordism to a flexible regime of accumulation. Researchers wanted to know what this shift in modes of societal regulation might entail *inter alia* for urban management, the form of the local state and the politics of urban development (see, for example, the chapter contributions in Lauria 1997). In one significant paper, Harvey (1989) described a shift in urban government from Keynesian managerialism to an entrepreneurial form. He noted that urban managers and élites in many if not most North American and European cities were pursuing similar strategies of urban regeneration, often competing for the same flagship regeneration projects, and in doing so were incentivized by their national governments (see Jessop et al. 1999). The emergence of urban entrepreneurialism dovetailed with the work of political scientists on urban regimes (Stone 1989; 1993) and sociologists on the urban growth machine (Logan and Molotch 1987), albeit each of these approaches had its own priority in terms of what the competition for jobs and inward investment entailed for urban institutions and power structures. Increasingly frustrated by the localistic focus of much of this work, critical contributions by geographers began to examine the broader state-regulatory processes underlying the purported shift in urban governance from Keynesian to neo-liberal institutional and political forms (see Lauria 1997; Jonas and Wilson 1999). Kevin's work was formative in these debates.

In order to focus critical attention on such intellectual developments, Cox (1991b; 1993; 1995) chose to draw together the different contributions under the theme of the New Urban Politics (NUP). One way in which the NUP stood out from earlier work on the local state was the desire to locate urban politics in the wider setting of capital mobility and economic globalization. From this, he argued, it was possible to infer two quite different territorial logics. On the one hand, the spatial logic of capital investment knows no urban political boundaries, which means that cities must compete to attract investment. On the other hand, the logic of electoral politics dictates that urban politicians and policy makers must find ways of isolating their revenue enhancing activities from local electoral interests and pressures. The effect of these potentially contradictory logics is to force cities increasingly to follow a neo-liberal development pathway and devise new institutional structures which draw capital investment into their localities. The NUP often came to the conclusion that the pursuit of redistributive urban policies is neither politically necessary nor structurally possible; it assumed that inter-urban competition results in an inevitable 'race to the bottom' with disastrous consequences for the working class and the urban poor.

Kevin suggested that the NUP had engaged in empirical overgeneralization; it had a poor grasp of social structures, necessary relations and contingent conditions. Moreover, it was often silent on the role of class relations and struggles around collective consumption and social provision. Cox and Jonas (1993) argued that urban politics must at some level reflect a contradictory relation between the creation of conditions conducive to economic development, on the one hand, and social reproduction through the provision of public services and environmental amenities in the living place (e.g., housing, schools, parks, open space), on the other. The question then was how the apparent separation of economic development from social welfare and collective consumption at the urban scale had come about. This, Cox and Jonas suggested, could only be explained with reference to concrete circumstances based on a detailed knowledge of urban development trajectories in a given context. Here we see how Kevin's abiding interest in the politics of the urban living place and electoral geography allowed him to temper claims about the purported shift towards a politics of urban development at the expense of social reproduction.

Subjecting these sentiments to further critical scrutiny, in Chapter 5 Allan Cochrane argues that social theorists and geographers have for some time struggled to identify the intrinsic nature of the 'urban'. For a while the answer seemed to lie in studies of collective consumption and social welfare in the city. But this has often meant imposing rigid conceptual boundaries around the urban; boundaries which do not exist in practice. Cochrane proceeds to broaden the focus away from the urban as a welfare-distributional politics to examine processes of urban economic development. Here we see Cochrane's commitment to exploring relational notions of urban politics through an examination of how particular assemblages of power (including those powers and policies orchestrated around the state) help to construct the urban as a semi-coherent structure of social relations and networks if not always as an autonomous political arena. Whilst noting Kevin's contribution, Cochrane introduces a critique of hierarchical concepts of territory and scale, deploying concepts of topology and assemblage to explain how power is expressed in a territorial (urban or regional) context.

Writing from a Marxist perspective in Chapter 6, Jamie Gough takes up some of the claims made by Kevin about the processes of urban and regional development in capitalism and subjects them to critical scrutiny. Gough claims that Kevin has often privileged how capitalists and growth coalitions tend to pursue a 'high road' to growth rather than engage in a 'race to the bottom'. The alternative 'low road' was discussed by Cox (1999, 23-4) in a critique of the NUP in the following terms:

> Workers and residents in different localities are placed in competition with one another resulting in a so-called "race to the bottom." It is capital that gains. This includes: the firms looking for sites for branch plants or back offices; the membership of the growth coalition who will benefit from expansion of the local

economy's basic sector; and those firms in that sector that would have trouble relocating and are willing to accept any regulatory or fiscal relief that comes their way.

Kevin's apparent reluctance to take seriously the possibility of a 'low road' creates in Gough's view a one-sided view of the politics of urban and regional development. He argues that Kevin underestimates the power of capital to discipline labor through, for instance, wage restraint and intensification of work; in other words, Kevin does not fully explore the limits of 'high road' growth strategies. Gough's answer is to relocate class struggle more centrally in what he refers to as a dialectical analysis of regional development. For Gough, labour remains a political agent of regional change rather than a dupe of the urban growth coalition.

Unpacking the dialectical spatial and political logics of economic globalization is central to Kevin's more recent explorations of capitalist development trajectories. For example, in his edited collection on *Spaces of Globalization* (1997a), Kevin was eager to criticize claims that globalization represents the latest phase of capitalist development and that, accordingly, nation states have tended to follow a neo-liberal free-trade regime regardless of political tensions and divisions inside the state. Focusing on distributional struggles around the state, he shows how different forms of globalization can engender different regulatory and political responses (Cox 1997b). Rather than representing a uniform advanced stage in the development of capitalism, these different forms of globalization are constructed around different territorial politics.

Pursuing a similar line of argument in Chapter 7, Delphine Ancien reintroduces notions of social regulation and politics in a critical analysis of the concept of the global city. Taking London as her case study, she explores how the contradictions of globalization have played out in struggles around the provision of housing in the city. In doing so, Ancien offers a Coxian critique of the global city idea: the problematic of engaging in empirical generalizations about the characteristics of the global city given that each place engenders its own distinct politics of social reproduction and state intervention.

In the final chapter in this section, Kevin Ward examines an important yet often overlooked theme in the analysis of urban politics, namely, how urban managers and politicians in different cities learn from each other and the attendant mechanisms by which urban policies transfer from one city to another. Ward shows how the analysis of urban policy mobility requires a different way of thinking about urban social relations; namely, it puts emphasis on the social relations and networks stretching out between urban places rather than within them. He further examines the 'transfer agents' involved in the translation of Business Improvement Districts (BIDs) from the USA to the UK. A BID involves downtown property and business owners collaborating to make a collective financial contribution to the retail and commercial development and marketing of the district. By unbounding the urban in this manner, Ward provides a neat twist on the 'localities' debate. If Kevin Cox examined localities in terms of their social relations of spatial fixity, Ward shows how policies fixed in one place can in effect be taken from one context and applied to another. The net result is a particular form of mobile urbanism, namely, the spatial transfer of urban policy knowledge and practice.

State, Territory and Geographical Difference

Whilst the main focus of the book is territory, the state and urban politics in western capitalist societies, we recognize that there are important differences in the ways in which capitalist development processes play out concretely not only within the state territories of advanced economies but also in non-western contexts. In the third section, we look beyond the realm of the urban condition as imagined by Anglo-American urban theorists and consider other forms and contexts in which the tensions and contradictions within capitalism are expressed.

We begin by noting that problems of inequality, distribution and identity have always been at the heart of Kevin's intellectual project, going back to his earliest work on voting behavior, his contributions to the political geography of welfare, and subsequently his interest in the politics of globalization (see Cox 1979; 1997b; 2002). He is well aware that questions of class, race and identity feature centrally in struggles around the distribution of the social product in capitalism. One important insight is how the state sets the context for political geographies of difference and uneven development in capitalism. For some social theorists these differences seem to be disappearing. Thus in commenting on urban trends across Europe, Brenner (2009, 129) has recently argued that "...the reorientation of state spatial strategies from nationally redistributive modalities towards urban-centric, competitiveness-oriented forms of locational policy still appears quite pervasive across the EU [European Union]." Kevin believes that such claims about the empirical generality of certain processes (i.e., that in light of growing similarities between places an appreciation of geographical difference is not as important as it once was) need to be subject to critical scrutiny.

In a recent paper, Cox (2009) considers arguments to the effect that there is a generalized 'hollowing out' or 'rescaling' of the state. He suggests that observations to the effect that economic development powers are being redistributed downwards in the state hierarchy fail to explain why and it what concrete forms regulatory processes become territorialized in such a manner. He is much more interested in how territorial politics shape wider processes of regulation and state rescaling than in the opposite tendency: could it be that political processes of a 'bottom up' rather than 'top down' nature are responsible for the reallocation of powers and responsibilities inside the state? One of Kevin's former graduate students, Bae-Gyoon Park (2008) has investigated this question in some depth. Park demonstrates how territorial politics have indeed been important in framing the ways in which the Korean state has embraced city-regionalism and inter-urban competition. He argues that such attempts to set up new city-regional state spaces reflect and embody longstanding central-local tensions inside the Korean state.

In developing his own ideas about difference, territorial politics and capitalist development, Kevin has been profoundly influenced by the situation in post-colonial South Africa. Indeed, the first two chapters in this section examine the formative influences of South Africa – and South African geographers – on Kevin's thinking. In Chapter 9, Jeff McCarthy traces how Kevin was profoundly influenced by the starkly racialized geographies of apartheid. Kevin first visited South Africa in 1982 and was struck by both the similarities and differences in the country's spatial patterns of racial segregation as compared to the USA. In approaching the development of capitalism in South Africa, Kevin and his South African colleagues have gone on to study the role of influx control, labour migration and gender relations in shaping urbanization processes and resulting geographies of inequality (Cox and Henson 2008; Cox et al. 2004). In South Africa, as Alistair Fraser (Chapter 10) argues, Kevin "...has discovered a wide range of tantalizing geographical patterns, such as the country's unique urban geography ..." Fraser, on the other hand, became interested in the rural development context. He was inspired by Kevin's critical thinking to examine the land question from the vantage of the 'local knowledge' held by South African banks and other lenders. Here we see how abstract concepts developed in the urban context of North America can judiciously be applied to a very different setting, rural South Africa, albeit recognizing that concrete circumstances create unique outcomes.

Taking difference seriously is a theme that runs through much work in contemporary human geography especially where it engages with post-colonial contexts. Part of this can be attributed to a certain degree of dissatisfaction with structuralist forms of explanation and, in particular, crude varieties of Marxist theorization. Here the work of feminist and post-structuralist geographers has been influential in drawing attention to questions of gender and patriarchy in capitalism, and seeking to uncover the diverse social practices underpinning local economies in different contexts (Gibson-Graham 1996). Drawing upon her research in the North American context, including a detailed examination of US welfare reform, Kim England (Chapter 11) reflects on feminist geographers' engagement with these questions through works on welfare, care and household relations in advanced capitalist economies. In a revealing reflection on her graduate studies under Kevin's tutelage, she shows how the "unhappy marriage of Marxism and feminism" led her to question some of the assumptions informing Kevin's work on place, politics and the situatedness of everyday life in the city. Despite these differences of viewpoint, she notes how Kevin has become increasingly open to taking on board some of the insights of feminist and post-structuralist thinkers, all the while adhering to the view that class is *the* overarching determinant of power relations and systems of oppression in capitalism.

Conclusion

The central focus of the book is on Kevin Cox's approach to territory, the state and urban politics. But the theme should encourage us to reflect on wider disciplinary concerns to which Kevin has made a significant contribution over the years. Human geography has gone through several phases – or paradigm shifts – in which foundational concepts of place, region, territory and scale have been worked and reworked, often separately but increasingly together, in order to shed light on significant social and political questions (Jessop et al. 2008). At times this means that concepts (and their proponents!) get rejected or ignored along the way. We have already noted this in respect of locality studies; and scale is another deeply contested idea in human geography (Marston, Jones and Woodward 2005; Jonas 2006; Herod 2011). But perhaps what stands out is a willingness within the discipline to subject such spatial concepts to critical scrutiny, to take nothing at face value, and above all to reject empiricist thinking. Here Kevin's critical acumen stands out as exemplary in terms of how to think critically not just about spatial concepts and ideas but with and through them as well.

In terms of critical thinking about space and territory, it is clear that Kevin's ideas have moved forward with the times. Notions of territory that refer to bounded spatial units (e.g., the 'urban' as a discrete political arena) are being challenged by the relational viewpoint. Part of this has to do with how the debates about urban politics, scale and locality have informed work on capitalist territoriality. Relational thinkers are justified in wanting to distance themselves from bounded representations of urban territory and overly hierarchical thinking around the state. Here Kevin's work has been influential.

Hopefully we have shown that a consistent theme in Kevin Cox's work and those influenced by it is to try to think relationally about territory and urban politics. For Kevin relational thinking involves the analysis of social relations and their necessary properties. In his rejoinder (Chapter 12), he seeks to reconnect relational critical thinking to its foundations in historical-geographical materialism (HGM). HGM locates urban politics and state territoriality at the nexus of tensions between fixity and flow in capitalism (Harvey 1985). This is an abstract idea but Kevin has consistently shown how it is possible to proceed from this to the concrete level and examine the actions and strategies of those agents, actors and interests which constitute the urban polity, focusing on their respective spaces of dependence and engagement. In this final chapter, Kevin advances the discussion by reflecting on four key ideas addressed in the various contributions to this book: (1) the concept of local dependence; (2) the territorial structure of the state; (3) the role of comparison; and (4) the question of method.

We conclude our introduction with a suggestion that future work on territory, the state and urban politics needs to hold onto the idea that certain, social economic and political interests continue to be expressed in a territorial fashion. If in this respect questions of territory and political identity are to remain at the forefront of human geographical inquiry, then we need to hold onto a relational perspective akin to that deployed by Kevin. His approach to the analysis of state, territory and urban politics offers a well defined set of methods and conceptual tools with which to approach this task. We anticipate that it will inform future progress on the relationship between capitalism and questions of economic globalization, state territoriality and the urban condition.

Acknowledgments

We are very grateful to Kevin Cox for commenting on an earlier draft of this chapter. We alone are responsible for any remaining errors, obscurities and inconsistencies.

References

Brenner, N. (2009), 'Open questions on state rescaling', *Cambridge Journal of Regions, Economy and Society* 2, 123-39.

Cooke, P. (1987), 'Clinical inference and geographic theory', *Antipode* 19, 69-78.

Cox, K. R. (1968), Suburbia and voting behaviour in the London metropolitan area. *Annals of the Association of American Geographers*, 58, 111-27.

Cox, K. R. (1969), The voting decision in a spatial context, in *Progress in Geography Volume 1*, edited by C. Board, R. J. Chorley, P. Haggett and D. R. Stoddart (London, Edward Arnold, 83-117).

Cox, K. R. (1970), Geography, social contexts and voting behaviour in Wales, 1861-1951, in *Mass Politics: Studies in Political Sociology*, edited by E. Allardt and S. Rokkan (New York, The Free Press), 117-59.

Cox, K. R. (1972a), The neighborhood effect in urban voting response surfaces, in *Models of Urban Structure*, edited by D. C. Sweet (Lexington MA, Lexington Books), 159-76.

Cox, K. R. (1972b), *Man, Location and Behavior: an Introduction to Human Geography* (New York, John Wiley).

Cox, K. R. (1973), *Conflict, Power and Politics in the City: A Geographic View* (New York, McGraw Hill).

Cox, K. R. (1979), *Location and Public Problems: A Political Geography of the Contemporary World* (Chicago, Maaroufa Press).

Cox, K. R. (1991a), 'Questions of abstraction in studies in the New Urban Politics,' *Journal of Urban Affairs* 13, 267-80.

Cox, K. R. (1991b), 'The abstract, the concrete, and the argument in the New Urban Politics,' *Journal of Urban Affairs* 13, 299-306.

Cox, K. R. (1993), 'The local and the global in the New Urban Politics: a critical view', *Environment and Planning D: Society and Space* 11, 433-48.

Cox, K. R. (1995), 'Globalisation, competition and the politics of local economic development', *Urban Studies* 32, 213-24.

Cox, K. R. (ed.) (1997a), *Spaces of Globalization: Reasserting the Power of the Local* (New York, Guilford Press).

Cox, K. R. (1997b), 'Globalization and the politics of distribution', in K. R. Cox (ed.), *Spaces of Globalization: Reasserting the Power of the Local* (New York, Guilford Press), 115-36.

Cox, K. R. (1998), 'Spaces of dependence, spaces of engagement and the politics of scale; or, looking for local politics', *Political Geography* 17, 1-24.

Cox, K. R. (1999), 'Ideology and the growth coalition', in A. E. G. Jonas and D. Wilson (eds) *The Urban Growth Machine: Critical Perspectives Two Decades Later* (Albany, NY, State University Press of New York), 21-36.

Cox, K. R. (2001), 'Territoriality, politics and the urban', *Political Geography* 20, 745-62.

Cox, K. R. (2002), *Political Geography: Territory, State, and Society* (Oxford, Blackwell).

Cox, K. R. (2009), "Rescaling the state' in question', *Cambridge Journal of Regions, Economy and Society* 2, 107-21.

Cox, K. R. and Golledge, R. G. (eds), (1969), *Behavioral Problems in Geography: A Symposium* (Evanston IL, Northwestern University, Department of Geography, Studies in Geography 17).

Cox, K. R. and Hemson, D. (2008), 'Mamdani and the politics of migrant labor in South Africa: Durban dockworkers and the difference that geography makes', *Political Geography* 27, 194-212.

Cox, K. R., Hemson, D. and Todes, A. (2004), 'Urbanization in South Africa and the changing character of migrant labour', *South African Geographical Journal* 86, 7-16.

Cox, K. R. and Johnston, R. J. (eds) (1982), *Conflict, Politics and the Urban Scene* (London, Longman).

Cox, K. R. and Jonas, A. E. G. (1993), 'Urban development, collective consumption and the politics of metropolitan fragmentation,' *Political Geography* 12, 8-37.

Cox, K. R. and Mair, A. (1988), 'Locality and community in the politics of local economic development,' *Annals of the Association of American Geographers* 78, 307-25.

Cox, K. R. and Mair, A. (1989a), 'Levels of abstraction in locality studies', *Antipode* 21, 121-32.

Cox, K. R. and Mair, A. (1989b), 'Urban growth machines and the politics of local economic development', *International Journal of Urban and Regional Research* 13, 137-46.

Cox, K. R. and Mair, A. (1991), 'From localised social structures to localities as agents', *Environment and Planning A* 23, 197-213.

Cox, K. R. and Wood, A. (1994), 'Local government and local economic development in the United States,' *Regional Studies* 28, 640-45.

Cox, K. R. and Wood, A. (1997), 'Competition and cooperation in mediating the global: the case of local economic development,' *Competition and Change* 2, 65-94.

Delaney, D. (2005), *Territory: A Short Introduction* (Oxford, Blackwell).

Elden, S. (2009), *Terror and Territory: The Spatial Extent of Sovereignty* (Minneapolis, University of Minnesota Press).

Gibson-Graham, J. K. (1996), *The End of Capitalism (As We Knew It): A Feminist Critique of Political Economy* (Cambridge MA, Blackwell).

Harvey, D. (1982), *The Limits to Capital* (Oxford, Basil Blackwell).

Harvey, D. (1985), 'The geopolitics of capitalism', in D. Gregory and J. Urry (eds), *Social Relations and Spatial Structures* (London, Macmillan), 128-63.

Harvey, D. W. (1989), 'From managerialism to entrepreneurialism: the transformation in urban governance in late capitalism', *Geografiska Annaler* 71B, 3-17.

Herod, A. (2011), *Scale* (London, Routledge).

Jessop, B., Brenner, N. and Jones, M. (2008), 'Theorizing sociospatial relations', *Environment and Planning D: Society and Space* 26, 389–401.

Jessop, B., Peck, J. A. and Tickell, A. (1999), 'Retooling the machine: economic crisis, state restructuring, and urban politics', in A. E. G. Jonas and D. Wilson (eds), *The Urban Growth Machine: Critical Perspectives Two Decades Later* (Albany, NY, State University Press of New York), 141-59.

Jonas, A. E. G. (2006), 'Pro scale: further reflections on the 'scale debate' in human geography', *Transactions of the Institute of British Geographers New Series* 31, 399-406.

Jonas, A. E. G. and Wilson, D. (eds) (1999), *The Urban Growth Machine: Critical Perspectives Two Decades Later* (Albany, NY, State University of New York Press).

Lauria, M. (ed.) (1997), *Reconstructing Urban Regime Theory: Regulating Urban Politics in a Global Economy* (Thousand Oaks, CA, Sage Publications).

Logan, J. and Molotch, H. (1987), *Urban Fortunes: The Political Economy of Place* (Berkeley and Los Angeles, University of California Press).

Malpas, J. (2012), 'Putting space in place: philosophical topography and relational geography', *Environment and Planning D: Society and Space* 30, 226-42.

Marston, S. A., Jones III, J. P. and Woodward, K. (2005), 'Human geography without scale', *Transactions of the Institute of British Geographers NS* 30, 416-32.

Massey, D. (1984), *Spatial Divisions of Labor* (London, Macmillan).

Massey, D. (1985), 'New directions in space', in D. Gregory and J. Urry (eds), *Social Relations and Spatial Structures* (London, Macmillan), 9-19.

Massey, D. (2005), *For Space* (London, Sage Publications).

Park, B-G. (2008), 'Uneven development, inter-scalar tensions, and the politics of decentralization in South Korea', *International Journal of Urban and Regional Research* 32, 40-59.

Sack, R. (1986), *Human Territoriality: Its Theory and History* (Cambridge, Cambridge University Press).

Sayer, A. (1984), *Method in Social Science: A Realist Approach* (London, Hutchison).

Sayer, A. (1985), 'The difference that space makes', in D. Gregory and J. Urry (eds), *Social Relations and Spatial Structures* (London, Macmillan), 49-66.

Smith, N. (1987), 'Dangers of the empirical turn: the CURS initiative', *Antipode* 19, 59-68.

Stone, C. N. (1989), *Regime Politics: Governing Atlanta, 1946-1988* (Lawrence, KS, University of Kansas Press).

Stone, C. N. (1993), 'Urban regimes and the capacity to govern: a political economy approach', *Journal of Urban Affairs* 15, 1-28.

PART I
CONCEPTUALIZING
SPACE AND TERRITORY:
FROM QUANTITATIVE
GEOGRAPHY TO HISTORICAL-
GEOGRAPHICAL MATERIALISM

Chapter 2

Kevin Cox and Electoral Geography[1]

Ron Johnston and Charles Pattie

Few social scientists can justifiably claim to have been one of a small group of prime movers in the establishment of a sub-discipline, authoring a seminal paper which set the agenda for work over the subsequent four decades and exemplifying this in a series of pioneering empirical studies. Kevin Cox is in that category, however. His publications in the late 1960s and early 1970s – especially his *Progress in Geography* essay (Cox 1969a; Pattie et al. 1998) – were major foundations in the creation of electoral geography: he was not the first geographer to study spatial aspects of voting patterns, but he was certainly among the first – and the most influential – to give that sub-discipline a rationale and theoretical foundation. He showed that geographers could offer much more than mapping of certain aspects of electoral behaviour and electoral practice. Geography – and its key concepts of place and space – is situated at the heart of understanding elections. Having established that he then switched his interests, leaving a legacy on which we continue to build.

Although he never made a case for a separate electoral geography, Kevin Cox was thus highly influential in challenging views (such as Prescott's, 1973) that a spatial science approach had little to offer the sub-discipline. Following a brief outline of Kevin's early career and the context within which his own and his contemporaries' work in electoral geography emerged, subsequent sections of this essay discuss Cox's theoretical foundation for electoral studies in which geography was intrinsic, and the two types of empirical analyses that he conducted within that framework. We then turn to an overall assessment of his impact on the sub-discipline whose emergence he played such a major part in preparing.

Kevin's Early Career and the Origins of Electoral Geography

After graduating from the University of Cambridge in 1961, Kevin undertook graduate work at the University of Illinois (MA, 1963; PhD, 1966). This was the era of rapidly spreading interest in quantitative methods through American

---

1 We are grateful to those who helped us reconstruct the prehistory of electoral geography, including John Agnew, Clark Archer, Ross Barnett, Andrew Bodman, Bill Clark, Colin Flint, Rex Honey, Kelvyn Jones, John Mercer, John O'Loughlin, John Orbell, David Reynolds, Fred Shelley, Peter Taylor – and, of course, Kevin Cox.

geography departments. Illinois joined early with Ronald Boyce (one of the Seattle 'space cadets' and working at Illinois's Community Research Center) offering quantitative courses in a department whose mission was 'that excellence in graduate training must rest upon great technical competence' (Fellmann 1974, 21). Boyce's wide-ranging and enthusiastically-delivered one-semester course provided the initial self-confidence to undertake quantitative work but, as Bill Clark (2007) – also a graduate student there at the time – notes, there was a great deal of collective self-education among the students.[2] Kevin chose as his doctoral thesis topic 'Regional anomalies in the voting behaviour of the population of England and Wales: 1921-1951'. The original stimulus came from a graduate seminar in which he regressed electoral returns against data on urban characteristics from Moser and Scott's (1961) book and mapped the residuals to identify areas where Labour support was under- and over-predicted.[3] This approach was extended in the thesis, which was supervised by an economic geographer, Howard Roepke. Kevin also acknowledges the assistance of Dennis Sullivan, a political scientist who later moved to Dartmouth College and specialised in political psychology; he taught a course on political behaviour in the sociology minor that Kevin took as a graduate student, which provided a grounding in the relevant literature.

Kevin joined the Department of Geography at Ohio State University in 1965, one of a distinguished group of quantitatively-inclined geographers recruited by Ned Taaffe (Gauthier 2002).[4] He published a sequence of papers over the next decade which – more than those by any other single individual or group – established a role for geography in electoral studies, which until then had attracted little attention. He never, however, promoted a separate sub-discipline of electoral geography; he just applied the concepts and methods of spatial science to the study of elections.[5] Elections, in Peter Taylor's (1978, 153) words, are a positivist's dream because they provide large volumes of data that can be mapped and analysed. Early geographical analyses involved establishing correlations between patterns of support for various political parties and the socio-economic characteristics of the local population – as in the classic French studies by Siegfried (1913, 1949)

---

2   Kevin (personal communication) records that Bill first encouraged his interest in quantitative methods – having himself been exposed to them at the University of Canterbury by Reg Golledge and Les King. Kevin's career trajectory might have been very different otherwise – his appointment at Ohio State was because he was a 'quantifier', as they were known then.

3   Kevin was a Labour supporter and concerned about the party's future as discussed in Abrams and Rose's *Must Labour Lose?* (1960).

4   Others included John Arnfield, Larry Brown, Emilio Casetti, George Demko, Howard Gauthier, Reg Golledge, Les King, Harold Moellering, and John Rayner.

5   He was not the first. Thomas (1968) draws on a 1952 unpublished paper by Harold McCarty at the University of Iowa – 'McCarty on McCarthy: the spatial distribution of the McCarthy vote' – which tested Key's 'friends-and-neighbours' model using multiple regression and the mapping of residuals to show that Senator McCarthy got greater support close to his home town in Wisconsin than in other rural parts of the state.

and an early British study which concluded that 'it is evident that geographical or natural factors have contributed very materially in creating the conditions which determine political predilections; and that a multitude of artificial [sic] factors have done likewise' (Krehbiel 1916, 432). The correlations deduced were not statistical, of course, but geography's quantitative revolution had not been long in progress when the possibility of statistical analyses of voting patterns and their correlates was realised (as in Roberts and Rummage 1965, and Lewis and Skipworth 1966). These lacked any firm geographical (or spatial) theoretical base, however: as Agnew (1990, 18) later expressed it, geography in such studies was treated as either epiphenomenal (i.e. illustrating the outcome of deeper, non-spatial, processes) or residual rather than intrinsic to the explanation of observed patterns: such electoral studies lacked a 'geographically informed social theory appropriate for addressing the various objectives of the field' (p. 20).[6]

Kevin Cox provided that theoretical base, as we discuss here. But he was not alone. A parallel stream of electoral work was established at the University of Iowa, where the key individual was David Reynolds, whose PhD at Northwestern University was on the US-Canada border (examined by four of the 'quantitative revolution's' leaders – Bill Garrison, Duane Marble, Michael Dacey and Ed Thomas). While at Indiana before his move to Iowa he developed his interests in mathematical modelling in political science – first stimulated by his coursework at Northwestern and then by Coleman's (1964) book. Drawing on some of the same political science influences as Cox – notably V. O. Key Jr. who published several seminal studies of American politics involving geographical analyses (e.g. Key 1949, 1955, 1966) – he published three papers (Reynolds 1969a, 1969b, 1974) applying spatial interactional models to voting pattern analysis. (Cox's, 1968a, first paper in electoral geography was also entitled 'A spatial interactional model for political geography'.)

Reynolds included the study of elections in his graduate political geography course at Iowa[7] and, with then graduate student Clark Archer (Reynolds and Archer 1969), sought a particular geographical approach to electoral study – consistent with Agnew's later case. According to their argument, cartographic analysis and correlation may be sufficient to account for spatial variations in voting behaviour

---

6   John Agnew was a graduate student at Ohio State University in the mid-1970s, having been attracted there by Kevin's electoral work (John studied geography and politics as an undergraduate at the University of Exeter: OSU was recommended to him by an American visiting lecturer), but Kevin had by then moved on and John did his dissertation with him on an urban topic, returning to electoral study later in his career. Andrew Bodman was also attracted to study elections with Kevin at OSU (from Cambridge, on Dick Chorley's recommendation: Dick was the link which led to Kevin's seminal theoretical paper – 1969a – appearing in *Progress in Geography*): Kevin supervised Bodman's 1973 MA thesis on 'National and local components of a voting response surface' but not his subsequent PhD (see Bodman 1982, 1983, 1985).

7   Entitled 'Locational analysis of political behavior' that course was co-taught for some years in the early 1970s with John Mercer.

– 'the process or processes which generate(s) a voting response surface(s) are exogenous to the spatial system. If this assumption is valid, such factors as distance, direction, and relative location could exert no proximate and independent effect upon the form which these surfaces take' (p. 3). In such a situation, geography would be epiphenomenal. But if it can be shown that spatial variables are important in the generation of voting patterns, then geography is intrinsic and a case can be made for a viable electoral geography in which local context and diffusion are key concepts. An empirical study of voting at an Indianapolis mayoral election (also reported in Reynolds 1974) sustained their argument that intrinsic geographic factors were involved, leading them to conclude that 'electoral geography can rest on a more sound theoretical and operational footing if it supplements an areal approach with a more spatial approach' (p. 31).

The development of electoral geography at Iowa was further stimulated when Peter Taylor was a visitor during 1970-1971.[8] His expertise in classification and regionalisation and the use of factor analysis was deployed in two ways. In the first, he developed Key's (1955) work on critical elections and sectionalism with Clark Archer, leading to a major monograph which placed long-term trends in US Presidential voting on a firm political economy theoretical foundation (Archer and Taylor 1981: this work was followed up in Archer et al. 1988; Archer and Shelley 1986).[9] And in the second he used the same technical base to develop work on redistricting, which he initially encountered in Bunge's (1966a) paper on gerrymandering and geography; while in Iowa he experienced gerrymandering at first hand as the state was being redistricted during his visit – hence the use of Iowa examples in his work (e.g. Taylor 1973). This research culminated in both a further major monograph on the seats: votes relationship (Gudgin and Taylor 1979) and seminal work on the modifiable areal unit problem (Taylor and Openshaw 1981). Other graduate students at Iowa – including Ross Barnett and Fred Shelley (e.g. Barnett 1973; Shelley 1988) – also undertook work on elections with Dave Reynolds, John Mercer and Rex Honey, with added stimuli from political scientists such as David Ranney.[10] Not all did dissertations with an electoral focus, however; some worked on various aspects of urban political economy and organisation, including electoral components (as exemplified in Archer and Reynolds 1976).

These two separate, but far from independent, strands (Cox and Reynolds collaborated on a conference and book project, for example: Cox, Reynolds and Rokkan 1974) were the foundations of the contemporary electoral geography sub-

---

8   The Iowa department was looking for a one-year replacement while Michael McNulty was on leave. Pete was recommended to Clyde Kohn by Kevin on the basis of his 1969 comment on Kevin's paper on voting in London (Cox 1968; Taylor 1969).

9   One of Cox's (1969b) earliest papers took a very similar approach, but not set in the context of Key's (1955) argument.

10   Ross Barnett initially went from New Zealand to Indiana, to work with Norman Pounds, but moved on to Iowa where the approach to electoral study was more to his liking: Kevin Cox suggested that he go to OSU, but Ross preferred Iowa.

discipline, very different in its nature from that proclaimed by Prescott (1959) a decade earlier. After briefly discussing the small number of electoral studies by geographers, Prescott set his framework for electoral geography clearly within the regional tradition established by Hartshorne (1950): electoral cartography can be used to identify political regions, 'territorial variation of the way in which people think about certain, usually secular, matters...providing the criterion for the regional division of the state' (Prescott 1959, 304), and that division can be used to assess the state's internal cohesion. A decade later, soon after the first appearance of statistical analyses of voting patterns, Prescott (1969) critiqued the approach, and followed this up with a chapter on electoral geography in an introductory textbook on political geography, stating that (Prescott 1972, 75):

> The responsibility of the political geographer is to describe the pattern of votes cast in elections and plebiscites, and to explain, as far as he is able, why that particular pattern developed.

This was written soon after Cox's initial publications and Reynolds and Archer's (1969) appeared, offering what Prescott termed a 'new spatial approach' whose conclusions he considered 'very tentative', making it premature to assess its potential. Nevertheless, he felt that (pp. 86-87):

> If geographers follow the advice of Reynolds and Archer and Cox and concentrate on these spatial processes, they will be abandoning a road of proven reliability for a track which may lead into regions of sociology where they are ill-equipped to survive.

His reliable road involved cartographic correlations of voting patterns and population characteristics – identifying areas where one party predominates and others where the situation is more competitive, or 'maps of electoral regions'. For him, in 1972 (p. 87):

> It will need many more studies of larger areas than a suburb or a city, over a number of elections, to signpost the way, before the analysis of spatial processes becomes a major part of electoral geography...My own experience in talking to individuals about the way they voted in particular elections, is that many do not know exactly why they voted as they did. Certainly in rationalizing their decision no one has ever explained their vote in terms of the flow of information or the political complexion of the area in which they live.

This view was partly shared by an English geographer – Alan Taylor – who completed a PhD on voting patterns at the University of Southampton in 1971. He argued that statistically-based geographical studies of voting patterns (such as Roberts and Rumage 1965, and Rowley 1971) achieved 'little beyond the repetition of several well-known truisms concerning voter motivation...They produce no more subtle explanations, and no new explanations' (Taylor 1972a, 3). He identified potential in Cox's information-flow model, which he characterised as 'social processes which modify the direct effect of the other aspects of the local social context on electoral behaviour' (p. 4) but concluded that 'A strictly spatial electoral geography would be limited to studies of the effect of remoteness and innovation waves on election results' and 'Cox is much too willing to claim that an effect is due to a spatial process: the effect may not even exist' (p. 6).[11] Taylor wrote several other pieces on aspects of voting patterns (e.g. Taylor 1973a), including seminal notes on distance to the polling station and turnout (Taylor 1973b) and the impact of local campaigning (Taylor 1972b) both of which illustrated the potential of a spatial approach. He left academic life in the mid-1970s, however,[12] and so was not involved in the creation of an electoral tradition in the UK, led by Peter Taylor and Ron Johnston and firmly set in the moulds formed at Ohio State and Iowa (Taylor and Johnston 1979).[13]

The Voting Decision in a Spatial Context

The most comprehensive theoretical statement underlying Cox's work on electoral geography is provided by his 1969 *Progress in Geography* paper which sought (as its title suggested) to place 'the voting decision in a spatial context' (Cox 1969a). In it, he conceptualised the environment within which voting decisions are made as a network through which information is passed and processed, subject to identifiable biases. There is a clear affinity here with contemporaneous research on information networks and diffusion (see, for instance, Haggett 1965; Bunge 1966b; Hägerstrand 1965), especially that of Kevin's Ohio colleague Larry Brown (e.g. Brown 1968), whose advice is acknowledged in a number of his papers. Individuals, households and both formal and informal groups are conceptualised as nodes in this network. Political information circulates through the network

---

11   The last point was based on Taylor's argument that, in his London study, Cox studied the wrong dependent variable by looking at the percentage of the votes cast won by each party rather than his favoured percentage of the total electorate (Taylor 1974).

12   One consequence of this may have had great significance for how British electoral geography developed. In 1975 David Rossiter, having decided that he wanted to do a PhD on electoral geography, approached the University of Southampton, being aware of Alan Taylor's work. He was told that they had nobody who might supervise such a thesis and was advised to apply to Sheffield, to work with Ron Johnston. He did: the rest is (electoral geography) history!

13   A precursor of this was Busteed's (1975) short book in which he claimed that geography 'can add an entirely new dimension to the study of elections. The geographer brings a characteristic emphasis on spatial location, distribution, and spatial interrelationships to the study of electoral behaviour, aspects not normally considered by other disciplines' (p. 3). His three chapters covered districting and the aggregate and behavioural approaches to voting studies.

along the various links between these nodes (via conversations with other voters, reading political communications, attendance at political meetings, and so on) – though how easily information might flow depends upon the nature of the link between them.

The nodes (voters etc.) in this network can perform a number of different roles. They can be senders of information (for instance, political parties put out campaign messages; the media carries news stories with a political dimension; voters talk to their friends, relations and colleagues about their political opinions; and so on).[14] Some information senders are likely to be more effective than others, however, whether because of the greater authority with which they speak or because of the wider range of individuals their messages reach. In making this observation, Cox was influenced by the 'two-step' model of political influence current in US political science at the time: this argued that parties' messages were picked up by politically interested and knowledgeable individuals, who then acted as authoritative sources of advice and information for their less knowledgeable or partisan friends and acquaintances (e.g. Campbell et al. 1960). Furthermore, he hypothesised that the greater the partisan bias within a network (i.e. the greater the propensity for individual nodes sending information to favour one political party or position over another), the greater the pressure on those receiving this information to agree with it.

The obvious corollary to nodes as senders of information is that they are also recipients of information: all those conversations require conversation partners, all those media stories and campaign messages imply an audience. But again, some individuals are better information recipients than others: strongly partisan individuals will be more likely to discount information which does not accord with their pre-existing opinions than will the relatively non-partisan, for instance.

Finally, voters are not passive nodes within the network, simply receiving and transmitting information. Rather, they are active processors of that information, weighing up and evaluating the messages they receive and deciding what information they wish to pass on to others, and how. As before, just how adept individuals are at this will depend on their personal resources and on their circumstances.

But what sort of information flows between nodes in the network, and with what effect, depends not only on the nodes themselves (for instance, on how partisan they are) but also on the nature of the links between the nodes. Cox hypothesises four different sorts of bias which might influence how likely links are to form within a network, and how well (or badly) they are likely to perform in transmitting politically relevant information.

The first, the geographical distance bias, is perhaps the most familiar to geographers trained in the spatial science tradition – and links Kevin's work with his colleague Larry Brown's. It describes the tendency for links to be formed

---

14   We might note that this formulation could have been written 30 years later in actor network theory terms.

between individuals or groups which are relatively close together rather than between those which are further apart. This is Tobler's (1970, 236) first law of geography (that 'everything is related to everything else, but near things are more related than distant things') applied to voting behaviour. To the extent that a distance decay function typifies the spread of politically relevant information (such that sources near at hand are more noticed and more influential than sources far away), the geographical distance bias contributes to the neighbourhood effect, whereby voters in a neighbourhood tend be disproportionately influenced by the local majority view.[15] Cox speculates, however, that this bias will have more effect on the voting decisions of the less well educated than on those of the better educated.

Cox's second source of bias is the acquaintance circle bias. Put simply, we are more likely to swap information with, and we are more likely to be influenced by, people we know rather than total strangers. Members of the same organisations, for instance, are likely to develop the same opinions. But the extent to which acquaintance circles generate homogeneous opinions depends on how open or closed those circles are. More open groups of acquaintances are more likely to encounter divergent views and hence are less likely to agree with each other (Granovetter 1973: Huckfeldt & Sprague 1995; Huckfeldt et al. 2004). A neighbourhood effect is more likely to arise via the acquaintance circle bias, therefore, where residents' main interactions are with others in the same neighbourhood than where neighbourhood social networks are weak and people's acquaintance circles are widely spread and heterogeneous.

Forced field biases form the third means by which links may be affected. In these, the individual (group, party) sending political information is in a position of power over the recipient and hence can coerce the receiver into agreement. For instance, prior to the introduction of the secret ballot, employers could not only exhort their employees to vote for their favoured candidates but they could also see who did so and who did not (and hence know who to punish and who reward). Public voting produced conditions under which coercion might operate.

Finally, reciprocity biases occur where relations exist between nodes such that the influence of one on the other is matched by the reciprocal influence. A possible example might occur between couples: their mutual influence on each other makes them likely to share the same views.

Overall, the theory described how co-location might affect both the spread of political information and political influence, therefore. But, importantly, it neither assumed that only distance mattered, nor did it assume that all voters were equally open to influence. And it took care to specify just what sorts of effects might be predicted from the theory. This was a sophisticated, not a simplistic, application of spatial science thinking.

---

15   For a discussion of the extent to which distance biases still operate in an era of much greater mobility and ease of communication, see Johnston and Pattie (2010).

Establishing an Electoral Geography

The theoretical basis set out in that classic essay underpinned Kevin's empirical chapters in his PhD and also the studies inaugurated when he moved to Ohio State in 1965. Those papers each have a theoretical introduction emphasising that part of the larger whole relevant to the specific issue being addressed (Cox 1969e, reworks the material on acquaintance circle biases, for example), but the main concerns are with hypothesis-testing. In this, some of the methods employed were relatively new to the geographical literature: in evaluating the new theories he was bringing to human geography Kevin was also making seminal contributions to its (quantitative) practices.[16]

Ecological (or Aggregate) Analyses

Much electoral geography – and all geographical studies of elections conducted prior to Cox – relies on aggregate data, in most cases election results for defined areas (such as precincts and constituencies); these are often combined with census or other data for the same areas. Cox's early published work – drawn from his PhD thesis – followed that tradition, but employed more sophisticated analytical methods.

A first example of this aggregate (or ecological) approach was a paper on voting in London (Cox 1968b; a revised version appeared as Cox 1969c).[17] It was based on research which showed that US urban areas were electorally polarised between left-wing central cities and right-wing suburbs, a difference that reflected not only the particular socio-economic and demographic characteristics of residents in the two areas (with the geography being epiphenomenal), exacerbated by patterns of selective migration of right-wing-tending voters to the suburbs, but also by a contagion effect, suggesting that whatever their individual backgrounds and characteristics, suburban residents are more likely to vote Republican as a consequence of their interactions with Republican supporters who form the majority in their local social networks. Cox examined this intrinsically geographical hypothesis – which implies the operation of spatially-structured information flows – with data for Greater London, using factor analysis to generate the independent variables in causal models of both Conservative voting and turnout. (This was one of the first papers by a geographer to employ causal modelling as developed by Blalock 1964.) He concluded that suburban location was related to voting behaviour not only through influencing the social class, age and commuting

---

16   Kevin's first paper (Cox 1965) was also a pioneering technical piece on linear programming, unrelated to his electoral studies. The first journal to which it was submitted rejected it as 'not geography' (a not uncommon response in those days: Berry 1993), despite favourable referees' reports.

17   An earlier version of the 1968 paper was awarded first prize in the Illinois Geographical Essay Awards competition in 1965.

characteristics of local populations – which stimulated both higher turnout and Conservative support – but also independently. Conservative support was greater in the suburbs than anticipated from knowledge of features of the local population, providing circumstantial support (all that was feasible with aggregate data) for the contagion effect hypothesis.

This paper was the subject of two published critiques. Kasperson (1969) – author of an earlier study of links between Chicago's electoral geography and public policy there (Kasperson, 1965) – questioned whether ecological analysis was the best strategy for testing behavioural hypotheses and doubted the viability of the conversion-by-contagion argument, among other points – in an argument which frequently elided American and UK material.[18] He concluded that although there was 'much of merit' in Cox's paper, 'even the most sophisticated of analyses is still no better than the care which is exercised in selecting valid basic data, the clarity in the formulation and testing of hypotheses, and the maximum use of prior research' (Kasperson 1969, 411). In reply, Cox (1969d) accepted the desirability of testing the hypotheses using survey data,[19] but argued that his use of aggregate data established the existence of empirical regularities consistent with his hypotheses – drawn from a wide literature on neighbourhood effects that Kasperson largely ignored. Taylor's (1969) comment was methodological, identifying problems with Cox's causal modelling, which Cox (1969d) responded to, sustaining his argument that the results gave tentative support to his intrinsic geographical hypotheses.[20]

Another major study emanating from Kevin's PhD thesis was an analysis of voting patterns in Wales, originally presented at a meeting of the International Political Science Association and then published in a volume of essays on political sociology (Cox 1970a). Much of the analytic work in this used aggregate data – as with a factor analysis, similar to that in the London study – to identify the country's voting regions in 1951. He then undertook an historical analysis of the differing socio-economic and political milieux in those regions over the preceding century, clearly differentiating urban from rural Wales and their separate political contexts, with liberalism emerging as the opposition to the Conservative squirearchy in the latter areas and socialism as the opposition to capitalist industrialists in the former. The chapter ended with a short first combination of aggregate with survey data, allowing him to show that, for example, class was a much more important determinant (correlate) of voting behaviour in urban (or 'modern') than rural (or 'traditional') Wales.

Survey and aggregate data were also combined in a paper that, like the London analyses, sought to establish that parties got greater support than expected

---

18   Rowley (1969, 399) made a similar point, associating Cox's paper with 'the development of disturbing trends within electoral geography that derive essentially from unsatisfactory knowledge of research areas'.

19   This was later done by Walks (2005), with results that sustained Cox's arguments.

20   The revised version of the original paper (Cox, 1969c) made no changes to the reported models in the light of Taylor's points.

where the local population was favourably inclined towards them, because of an assumed neighbourhood effect (Cox 1971), which operated separately from social and locational components. Thus in Paris support for the Parti Communiste was greater than anticipated in areas with large percentages of ouvriers in their population, and in Columbus areas that were strongly Democratic at the 1960 Presidential election were even more so in 1964. (This analysis was extended in Cox 1972a.) The neighbourhood effects were assumed to be a product of spatially-structured social networks, which data from a small study of farmers in Sweden conducted by Kevin's OSU colleague Larry Brown provided some validation for (Cox 1969e).[21]

The Spatial Analysis of Survey Data

Kevin's use of aggregate data to test hypotheses derived from his spatial theories of voting behaviour was in the vanguard of spatial analyses at the time. Even more pioneering – but disappointingly so, given the lack of others who followed his lead – was his work integrating survey and aggregate data in the evaluation of arguments that – as Kasperson (1969) had argued – could not be assessed with aggregate data alone.

The potential of this approach was demonstrated briefly in the final section of Cox's (1970a) chapter on voting in Wales, but it was fully realised soon after his arrival at Ohio State University. A political scientist there – John Orbell; a New Zealander who did a PhD at the University of North Carolina on black college student protests – had a National Science Foundation grant to study the 'impact of neighborhood conditions of social and political behavior'.[22] Kevin joined him in the enterprise – although they did not publish anything together; Orbell's survey data were combined with census tract data that Kevin had compiled for Columbus, thereby allowing the investigation of individual behaviour in its neighbourhood context.[23] (Orbell's papers deriving from this combined data set include Orbell 1970; Orbell and Sherill 1969; Orbell and Uno 1972.)

The value of analyses using such amalgamated data was initially demonstrated in Kevin's first published paper in electoral geography (Cox 1968a) – a contribution to a journal special issue in which he cited Bunge (1966b, 267) that 'political geography is a subject rich in mathematical applications' to sustain

---

21 One other study using aggregate data (Cox 1969b) indicated links to the later work on sectionalism that emanated from the 'Iowa stable': factor analyses of voting data over time were used to identify regions with different trajectories of support for American political parties.

22 See http://polisci.uoregon.edu/profiles/vitae/John_Orbell.pdf.

23 This innovative approach has never been followed up by American electoral geographers and it was 30 years before an opportunity was grasped in the UK to develop a similar approach based on the definition of census-based 'bespoke neighbourhoods' for individual survey respondents (MacAllister et al. 2001; Jones et al. 2007).

his case that, as Haggett and Chorley (1967) had shown for urban and economic geography, there was also much potential for 'mathematization of political geography' (Cox 1968c, 2).[24] In it, he used data on whether survey respondents varied in their voting behaviour according to the political orientation of the precinct in which they lived, whether they had local friends there, whether they discussed politics with their friends, and whether they belonged to locally-focused voluntary organisations to test for neighbourhood effects. One of the main findings was that members of locally-focused organizations were much more likely to illustrate voting patterns consistent with the neighbourhood effect argument than those who were members of organizations with much wider membership bases.

Further testing of this spatial interactional model was reported in a second essay included in the volume on social science quantitative applications (Cox, 1969f). In addition to the variables included in the earlier paper, Cox added recency of residence in an area, arguing that the contextual effects of a new milieu on individual behaviour may be greater than those on individuals who had resided there much longer. Again he found that the strongest support for the hypothesis occurred with respondents who were members of locally-focused voluntary organisations (such as parent-teacher associations and church groups). Level of political involvement was added as a further variable, with similar findings. (These analyses were further developed in Cox 1970b.)

A major conclusion from this body of work (set out in Cox 1969f, 182-185) was that formal networks – especially those focused on local voluntary organizations – were much more likely to generate neighbourhood effect-consistent voting patterns than informal friendship networks, and that some space-searching was involved in creating the conditions for such influence by an area's new residents. But Cox noted (as also in Cox 1970b) that despite the quality of the data another hypothesis could equally well account for his findings: homopolitical selectivity – whereby individuals select the people they interact with and the places they live in according to their political preferences. This is the classic endogeneity problem identified by many economists: do places structure attitudes, or do attitudes structure places – or both? The foundation was laid for a major continuing research programme.

But Kevin did not build on it – and nor did other US political-electoral geographers (and those based in the UK came to it only two decades later, when data became available: Johnston and Pattie 2006). Kevin did no more work in electoral geography – although he did briefly contribute to two debates about voting patterns (Cox 1987a, 1987b).[25] Furthermore, Kevin not only changed

---

24   Interestingly, neither Cox (1968a) nor Cox (1968c) is listed in his cv!

25   Intriguingly, in one of them he concluded that 'community strategies as a means of mobilizing support for political parties are rapidly losing their validity. Local community as distinctive is a pale shadow of what it was. Place competition homogenizes...' (Cox 1987b, 32). The UK experience has shown exactly the opposite over the last two decades as political mobilisation becomes increasingly place focused (Johnston and Pattie 2006).

the focus of his research but he also appeared to marginalise electoral studies within his emerging urban political economy and political geography interests. Thus electoral behaviour got no mention at all in either his textbook on human geography as spatial science – published at the end of his 'electoral career' (Cox 1972b) – or his general text on political geography (Cox 2002).

Prospect and Retrospect

Kevin Cox thus provided a strong theoretical and empirical basis for a sub-discipline of electoral geography. The theory was spatial: it did not deny the importance of those theories that dominated political science, but nor did it place spatial theory in a secondary role – it was integral to the enterprise of analysing voting patterns. Furthermore, he established his case among political scientists; he attended a number of their meetings – including organising a special session at the American Political Science Association meetings in New York in 1969 (which also involved Larry Brown and Dave Reynolds) – and published in their journals and edited collections.[26] He provided a very firm foundation for the study of elections by geographers. But he didn't promote electoral geography, and did no work on other aspects – notably redistricting – on which some geographers since have focused (following Sauer's, 1918, lead). Others (notably Taylor 1978; Taylor and Johnston 1979) provided a broader structure for the sub-discipline, and Reynolds (1990) argued that alongside the 'compelling case' for deploying concepts related to place in accounting for voting patterns there was a need for 'deeper historical analyses of the exercise of power and social struggles against it in particular places during periods of significant social change' – as in Burghardt's (1963, 1964) studies of Austria and Agnew's early work on Scotland (Agnew 1984; Mercer and Agnew 1988) and later studies of Italy (e.g. Shin and Agnew 2008). But Kevin's interests were by then elsewhere, having been encouraged by Ned Taaffe to develop an interest in urban political economy through an invitation to write *Conflict, Power and Politics in the City* (Cox 1973) which was an early exemplar of the new line of work being established by David Harvey, Julian Wolpert, Michael Dear and others.

The foundations laid by Kevin and at Iowa have formed the core of work in electoral geography not only in North America but also in the UK – with Peter Taylor being the principal agent in their transatlantic transmission. The theoretical base has been substantially enhanced, by greater exploration of the ways in which political actors use place as an arena – a cause advanced in particular by John Agnew's theoretically-based writings (Agnew 1987, 1989) and exemplified by his studies of Italian politics (Agnew 2002; Shin and Agnew 2008). That latter work also illustrates the continued use of sophisticated methods of spatial analysis

---

26   The initial contact was with Stein Rokkan, to whom Kevin sent a copy of his thesis.

in voting pattern studies, as does that of John O'Loughlin and his collaborators (O'Loughlin et al. 1994; O'Loughlin 2000, 2001: see also O'Loughlin 2003).[27]

But the structures built on those foundations have varied. More of Cox's agenda – and especially his pioneering integration of aggregate and survey data – has been followed through in the UK (as synthesised in Johnston and Pattie 2006) than in North America, where analyses based on survey data (including the secondary analysis of major social and other surveys, first noted by Rowley 1969) are rare (Johnston 2005). And British electoral geographers have become very active members within the political science sub-community concerned with electoral studies, whereas after the initial contacts made by Cox American electoral geographers appear to have kept their distance. Much has been done by electoral geographers in and on the United States – although mainly on the Iowa rather than the Cox agenda (emphasising redistricting, for example, and sectional voting patterns). Cox's arguments remain powerful and need testing – as Walks (2004, 2005, 2006) is currently doing in Canada and the UK.

In 1998, Kevin Cox's (1969a) paper on 'The voting decision in a spatial context' was selected as a 'Classic in human geography' by the editors of *Progress in Human Geography*. In responding to what the commentators identified as 'the first published work in modern electoral geography', advancing an 'innovative and even iconoclastic' framework in a 'fresh and compelling voice' (Pattie et al. 1998, 410-411), Cox (p. 413) stated that:

> My main concern…is that the study of voting patterns should not be seen as an end in itself. My 1969 article assumed that it could be. My realization that this was intellectually unsatisfying led me to move away from voting studies…I could not see how they could be related satisfactorily to political geography as a whole.[28]

Kevin was teaching political geography at OSU, but felt that electoral studies did not provide a satisfactory focus for the course (and in any case felt that he had exhausted the potential of the spatial approach he had been promoting). His new-found interest in urban political economy did, however – an interest that coincided with the Marxist critique of spatial science with which he sympathised.[29]

---

27   John O'Loughlin did a PhD at Penn State University on racial gerrymandering. His first academic post was at Illinois, where he read Kevin's thesis and was stimulated to follow it up.

28   Ross Barnett (personal communication) similarly saw it then as a 'dead end'. It was also the case – as Kevin and others have appreciated – that electoral geography was always going to be a very small enterprise within geography, especially compared to the contemporary booming interest in urban and economic studies. Despite shared methodological interests within spatial science, electoral geographers were likely to be isolated from the mainstream at all scales, and perhaps especially within the daily milieux of their academic departments.

29   Kevin had first encountered Marxism at school when he read Christopher Hill's work, and then from Maurice Dobb in Cambridge's Socialist Club.

Two others who have also written much in electoral geography are of a similar opinion. According to Flint and Taylor (2007, 195):

> It is not at all clear where electoral geography has been leading. The goal of most studies seems to be nothing more than understanding the particular situation under consideration. The result has been a general failure to link geographies of elections together into a coherent body of knowledge. In short, we have a bitty and uncoordinated pattern of researches, which has produced a large number of isolated findings but few generalizations.[30]

Their own work integrating electoral geographies into a wider political economy uses research results to underpin arguments about the geography of power and how and where it is exercised through the democratic process, illustrating how electoral geography can be presented as part of political geography. The key theme underpinning work in both is the role of place as the locale within which the structuration of attitudes and behaviour is mobilised, as illustrated by several projects emanating from the 'Iowa School' (e.g. Archer and Reynolds 1976; Barnett and Mercer 1973; Mercer and Barnett 1975), including Reynolds' (1999) work on rural school consolidation.

But that need not be its only use; electoral geography can be considered – as Cox originally presented it – as an illustration of how space is used by a range of political actors to promote specific interests, and also how space can be a constraint to such action (Johnston and Glasmeier 2007). And the sphere within which this theme can be examined is much wider than just neighbourhood effects in voting patterns (Cox's original contribution) and redistricting, as in the pioneering studies of the 1970s and 1980s. While these themes still dominate electoral geography, others – such as the activities of parties over space in the mobilisation of support, both long- and short-term – have been added to the electoral geographers' portfolio. And there are many benefits to be gained from inserting a geographical perspective into electoral studies, where political scientists dominate but – in some countries at least – the spatial perspective has been adopted as an important component in the understanding of how elections operate in democratic societies. There may be – in electoral geography as in other parts of the academic enterprise – papers that appear to be isolated, addressing a particular issue without any more general conclusions being drawn (which is not to say that they cannot be). But most of them can be used in building a larger body of knowledge to be deployed in a variety of ways.

Kevin Cox, along with a few other pioneers, showed the way, illustrating that geography is not merely epiphenomenal in the study of elections; it is an integral

---

30   This statement has appeared in every edition of that textbook, in virtually the same form, since the first in 1985. The 2007 edition contains only a few references to recent electoral work – all of it North American, with Agnew's major contributions in the 'suggested reading' section only!

component in that study, because space is a resource that is necessarily manipulated in the contests for power within democratic polities – the best electoral strategists are good geographers. He – like most of the other pioneers in this small corner of the geographical enterprise – moved away from the spatial scientific study of elections but others have built on the foundations that he provided, in a vibrant enterprise that illustrates some of human geography's key arguments within the social sciences – space and place matter.

References

Abrams, M. and Rose, R. (1960), *Must Labour Lose?* (London, Penguin).
Agnew, J. A. (1984), 'Place and political behaviour: the geography of Scottish nationalism', *Political Geography Quarterly*, 3, 191-206.
Agnew, J. A. (1987), *Place and Politics: the Geographical Mediation of State and Society* (Boston, Allen and Unwin).
Agnew, J. A. (1989), 'The devaluation of place in social science', in J. A. Agnew and J. S. Duncan (eds), *The Power of Place* (Boston, Unwin Hyman), 9-29.
Agnew, J. A. (1990), 'From political methodology to geographical social theory? A critical review of electoral geography 1960-1987', in R. J. Johnston, F. M. Shelley and P. J. Taylor (eds), *Developments in Electoral Geography* (London, Croom Helm), 15-21.
Agnew, J. A. (2002), *Place and Politics in Modern Italy* (Chicago, University of Chicago Press).
Archer, J. C. and Reynolds, D. R. (1976), 'Locational logrolling and citizen support of municipal bond proposals: the example of St. Louis', *Public Choice* 27, 21-39.
Archer, J. C. and Shelley, F. M. (1986), *American Electoral Mosaics* (Washington DC, Association of American Geographers).
Archer, J. C., Shelley, F. M., Taylor, P. J. and White, E. R. (1988), 'The geography of US Presidential elections', *Scientific American* 259, 44-51.
Archer, J. C. and Taylor, P. J. (1981), *Section and Party: a Political Geography of American Presidential Elections from Andrew Jackson to Ronald Reagan* (Chichester, John Wiley).
Barnett, J. R. (1973), 'Scale components in the diffusion of the Danish Communist Party, 1920-63', *Geographical Analysis* 5, 35-44.
Barnett, J. R. and Mercer, J. H. (1973), *Urban Political Analysis and New Directions in Political Geography* (Iowa City IA, University of Iowa, Department of Geography, Discussion Paper 22).
Berry, B. J. L. (1993), 'Geography's quantitative revolution: initial conditions, 1954-1960: a personal memoir', *Urban Geography* 14, 434-41.
Blalock, H. M. (1964), *Causal Inferences in Nonexperimental Research* (Chapel Hill NC, University of North Carolina Press).

Bodman, A. R. (1982), 'Measuring political change', *Environment and Planning A* 14, 33-48.

Bodman, A. R. (1983), 'The neighbourhood effect: a test of the Butler-Stokes hypothesis', *British Journal of Political Science* 13, 243-49.

Bodman, A. R. (1985), 'Recent trends in electoral support in Britain, 1950-1983', *The Professional Geographer* 37, 288-95.

Brown, L. A. (1968), *Diffusion Processes and Location: a Conceptual Framework and Bibliography* (Philadelphia, Regional Science Research Institute).

Bunge, W. (1966a), 'Gerrymandering, geography and grouping', *Geographical Review* 56, 256-63.

Bunge, W. (1966b), *Theoretical Geography* (Lund, C. W. K. Gleerup, Lund Studies in Geography, C1).

Burghardt, A. F. (1963), 'Regions and political party support in Burgenland (Austria)', *The Canadian Geographer* 7, 91-8.

Burghardt, A. F. (1964), 'The bases of support for political parties in Burgenland', *Annals of the Association of American Geographers* 54, 372-90.

Busteed, M. A. (1975), *Geography and Voting Behaviour* (Oxford, Oxford University Press).

Campbell, A., Converse, P., Miller, W. and Stokes, D. (1960), *The American Voter* (New York, John Wiley).

Clark, W. A. V. (2007), 'Reflections on a changing world and a changing discipline', in L. J. King (ed.), *North American Explorations: Ten Memoirs of Geographers from Down Under* (Victoria BC, Trafford Publishing), 1-17.

Coleman, J. S. (1964), *Introduction to Mathematical Sociology* (New York, Free Press of Glencoe).

Cox, K. R. (1965), 'The application of linear programming to geographic problems', *Tijdschrift voor Economische en Sociale Geografie* 56, 228-36.

Cox, K. R. (1968a), 'A spatial interactional model for political geography', *East Lakes Geographer* 4, 58-76.

Cox, K. R. (1968b), 'Suburbia and voting behaviour in the London metropolitan area', *Annals of the Association of American Geographers* 58, 111-27.

Cox, K. R. (1968c), 'Guest editor's comments', *East Lakes* Geographer 4, 1-4.

Cox, K. R. (1969a), 'The voting decision in a spatial context', in C. Board, R. J. Chorley, P. Haggett and D. R. Stoddart (eds), *Progress in Geography Volume 1* (London, Edward Arnold), 83-117.

Cox, K. R. (1969b), 'On the utility and definition of regions in comparative political sociology', *Comparative Political Studies* 2, 68-98.

Cox, K. R. (1969c), 'Voting in the London suburbs: a factor analysis and a causal model', in M. Dogan and S. Rokkan (eds), *Quantitative Ecological Analysis in the Social Sciences* (Cambridge MA, The MIT Press), 343-69.

Cox, K. R. (1969d), 'Comments in reply to Kasperson and Taylor', *Annals of the Association of American Geographers* 59, 411-15.

Cox, K. R. (1969e), 'The genesis of acquaintance field spatial structures: a conceptual model and empirical tests', in K. R. Cox and R. G. Golledge (eds),

Behavioral Problems in Geography: a Symposium (Evanston IL, Northwestern University, Department of Geography, Studies in Geography 17), 146-68.

Cox, K. R. (1969f), 'The spatial structuring of information flow and partisan attitudes', in M. Dogan and S. Rokkan (eds), *Quantitative Ecological Analysis in the Social Sciences* (Cambridge MA, The MIT Press), 157-85.

Cox, K. R. (1970a), 'Geography, social contexts and voting behaviour in Wales, 1861-1951', in E. Allardt and S. Rokkan (eds), *Mass Politics: Studies in Political Sociology* (New York, The Free Press), 117-59.

Cox, K. R. (1970b), 'Residential relocation and political behavior: conceptual model and empirical tests', *Acta Sociologica* 13, 40-53.

Cox, K. R. (1971) 'The spatial components of urban voting response surfaces', *Economic Geography* 47, 27-35.

Cox, K. R. (1972a), 'The neighborhood effect in urban voting response surfaces', in D. C. Sweet (ed.), *Models of Urban Structure* (Lexington MA, Lexington Books), 159-76.

Cox, K. R. (1972b), *Man, Location and Behavior: an Introduction to Human Geography* (New York, John Wiley).

Cox, K. R. (1973), *Conflict, Power and Politics in the City: a Geographic View* (New York, McGraw Hill).

Cox, K. R. (1987a), 'The 'individual', the 'social' and reconceptualising contextual effects', *Political Geography Quarterly* 6, 41-3.

Cox, K. R. (1987b), 'Comments on 'Dealignment, volatility, and electoral geography'', *Studies in Comparative International Development* 22, 26-34.

Cox, K. R. (2002), *Political Geography: Territory, State, and Society* (Oxford, Blackwell).

Cox, K. R., Reynolds, D. R. and Rokkan, S. E. (eds), (1974), *Locational Approaches to Power and Conflict* (New York, Halsted Press).

Fellmann, J. D. (1974), 'Geography at Illinois: the discipline and the department, 1967-1974', available at http://www.geog.psu.edu/hog/depthistory_files/Illinois.pdf [accessed: 22 September 2009].

Flint, C. and Taylor, P. J. (2007), *Political Geography: World-Economy, Nation-State and Locality* (Harlow, Pearson).

Gauthier, H. L. (2002), 'Edward 'Ned' Taaffe (1921-2001)', *Annals of the Association of American Geographers* 91, 573-83.

Gudgin, G. and Taylor, P. J. (1979), *Seats, Votes and the Spatial Organization of Elections* (London, Pion).

Granovetter, M. (1973), 'The strength of weak ties', *American Journal of Sociology* 83, 1420-43.

Hägerstrand, T. (1965), 'A Monte Carlo approach to diffusion', *European Journal of Sociology* 6, 43-67.

Haggett, P. (1965), *Locational Analysis in Human Geography* (London, Edward Arnold).

Haggett, P. and Chorley, R. J. (1967), 'Models, paradigms and the new geography', in R. J. Chorley and P. Haggett (eds), *Models in Geography* (London, Methuen), 19-42.

Hartshorne, R. (1950), 'The functional approach in political geography', *Annals of the Association of American Geographers* 40, 95-130.

Huckfeldt, R. and Sprague, J. (1995), *Citizens, Politics and Social Communication* (Cambridge, Cambridge University Press).

Huckfeldt, R. Johnson, P. E. and Sprague, J. (2004), *Political Disagreement: the Survival of Diverse Opinions within Communication Networks* (Cambridge, Cambridge University Press).

Johnston, R. J. (2005), 'Anglo-American electoral geography: same roots and same goals, but different means and ends?' *The Professional Geographer* 57, 580-87.

Johnston, R. J. and Glasmeier, A. (2007), 'Neo-liberalism, democracy and the state: temporal and spatial limits to globalisation', *Space and Polity* 11, 1-33.

Johnston, R. J. and Pattie, C. J. (2006), *Putting Voters in their Place: Geography and Elections in Great Britain* (Oxford, Oxford University Press).

Johnston, R. J. and Pattie, C. J. (2010), 'Social networks, geography and neighbourhood effects', in J. Scott and P. Carrington (eds), *The SAGE Handbook of Social Network Analysis* (London, Sage).

Jones, K., Johnston, R. J., Propper C. and Burgess, S. (2007), 'Region, local context, and voting at the 1997 general election in England', *American Journal of Political Science* 51, 640-54.

Kasperson, R. E. (1965), 'Towards a geography of urban politics: Chicago, a case study', *Economic Geography* 41, 95-107.

Kasperson, R. E. (1969), 'On suburbia and voting behavior', *Annals of the Association of American Geographers* 59, 405-11.

Key, V. O. Jr. (1949), *Southern Politics in State and Nation* (New York, Alfred A. Knopf).

Key, V. O. Jr. (1955), 'A theory of critical elections', *Journal of Politics* 17, 3-18.

Key, V. O. Jr. (1966), *The Responsible Electorate: Rationality in Presidential Voting 1936-1960* (Cambridge MA, Belknap Press).

Krehbiel, E. (1916), 'Geographic influences in British elections', *The Geographical Review* 2, 419-32.

Lewis, P. W. and Skipworth, G. E. (1966), *Some Geographical and Statistical Aspects of the Distribution of Votes in Recent General Elections*. Hull, University of Hull, Department of Geography, Miscellaneous Series 3).

MacAllister, I., Johnston, R. J., Pattie, C. J., Tunstall, H., Dorling, D. and Rossiter, D. J. (2001), 'Class dealignment and the neighbourhood effect: Miller revisited', *British Journal of Political Science* 31, 41-60.

Mercer, J. H. and Agnew, J. A. (1988), 'Small worlds and local heroes: the 1987 general election in Scotland', *Scottish Geographical Magazine* 104, 138-45.

Mercer, J. H. and Barnett, J. R. (1975), 'Spatial modifications to models of the urban policy process', *Policy Studies Journal* 3, 320-25.

Moser, C. A. and Scott, W. (1961), *British Towns: A Statistical Study of their Social and Economic Differences* (Edinburgh, Oliver and Boyd).

O'Loughlin, J. (2000), 'Can King's ecological inference method answer a social scientific puzzle: who voted for the Nazi party in Weimar Germany?' *Annals of the Association of American Geographers* 90, 592-601.

O'Loughlin, J. (2001), 'The regional factor in contemporary Ukrainian politics: scale, place or bogus effect?' *Post-Soviet Geography and Economics* 42, 1-33.

O'Loughlin, J. (2003), 'Spatial analysis in political geography', in J. A. Agnew, K. Mitchell, and G. O Tuathail (eds), *A Companion to Political Geography* (Oxford, Blackwell), 30-46.

O'Loughlin, J., Flint, C. and Anselin, L. (1994), 'The geography of the Nazi vote: context, confession and class in the Reichstag election of 1930', *Annals of the Association of American Geographers* 84, 351-80.

Openshaw, S. and Taylor, P. J. (1981), 'The modifiable areal unit problem', in N. Wrigley and R. J. Bennett (eds), *Quantitative Geography: A British View* (London, Routledge & Kegan Paul), 60-70.

Orbell, J. M. (1970), 'An information-flow theory of community influence', *Journal of Politics* 32, 322-38.

Orbell, J. M. and Sherrill, K. S. (1969), 'Racial attitudes and the metropolitan context: a structural analysis', *Public Opinion Research Quarterly* 33, 46-54.

Orbell, J. M. and Uno, T. (1972), 'A theory of neighborhood problem-solving: political action vs residential mobility', *American Political Science Review* 66, 471-89.

Pattie, C. J., Archer, J. C. and Cox, K. R. (1998), 'Classics in human geography revisited', *Progress in Human Geography* 22, 407-13.

Prescott, J. R. V. (1959), 'The function and methods of electoral geography', *Annals of the Association of American Geographers* 49, 296-304.

Prescott, J. R. V. (1969), 'Electoral studies in political geography', in R. E. Kasperson and J. V. Minghi (eds), *The Structure of Political Geography* (London, University of London Press), 376-83.

Prescott, J. R. V. (1972), *Political Geography* (London, Methuen).

Reynolds, D. R. (1969a), 'A 'friends-and-neighbors' voting model as a spatial interactional model for electoral geography', in K. R. Cox and R. G. Golledge (eds), *Behavioral Problems in Geography* (Evanston IL, Northwestern University, Northwestern Studies in Geography 17), 81-100.

Reynolds, D. R. (1969b), 'A spatial model for analyzing voting behaviour', *Acta Sociologica* 12, 122-30.

Reynolds, D. R. (1974), 'Spatial contagion in political influence processes', in K. R. Cox, D. R. Reynolds and S. Rokkan (eds), *Locational Approaches to Power and Conflict* (New York, Halsted Press), 233-73.

Reynolds, D. R. (1990), 'Whither electoral geography?' in R. J. Johnston, F. M. Shelley and P. J. Taylor (eds), *Developments in Electoral Geography* (London, Croom Helm), 22-35.

Reynolds, D. R. (1999), *There goes the Neighborhood: Rural School Consolidation at the Grass Roots in Early Twentieth-Century Iowa* (Iowa City IA, University of Iowa).

Reynolds, D. R. and Archer, J. C. (1969), *An Inquiry into the Spatial Basis of Electoral Geography* (Iowa City IA; University of Iowa, Department of Geography, Discussion Paper 11).

Roberts, M. C. and Rumage, K. W. (1965), 'The spatial variations in urban left-wing voting in England and Wales in 1951', *Annals of the Association of American Geographers* 55, 161-78.

Rowley, G. (1969), 'Electoral behavior and electoral behaviour: a note on certain recent developments in electoral geography', *The Professional Geographer* 21, 398-400.

Rowley, G. (1971), 'The Greater London Council elections of 1964 and 1967: a study in electoral geography', *Transactions and Papers of the Institute of British Geographers* 53, 117-31.

Sauer, C. O. (1918), 'Geography and the gerrymander', *American Political Science Review* 12, 403-26.

Shelley, F. M. (1984), 'Spatial effects on voting power in representative democracies', *Environment and Planning A*, 16, 401-5.

Shin, M. E. and Agnew, J. A. (2008), *Berlusconi's Italy: Mapping Contemporary Italian Politics* (Philadelphia, Temple University Press).

Siegfried, A. (1913), *Tableau Politique de la France de l'Ouest* (Paris, A. Colin).

Siegfried, A. (1949), *Géographie Électorale de l'Ardèche sous la IIIème République* (Paris, A. Colin).

Taylor, A. H. (1972a), *The Place of Geography in Electoral Study* (Southampton, University of Southampton Department of Geography, Research Series in Geography, 7), 3-31.

Taylor, A. H. (1972b), 'The effect of party organization: correlation between campaign expenditure and voting in the 1970 election', *Political Studies* 20, 329-31.

Taylor, A. H. (1973a), 'Variations in the relationship between class and voting in England 1950 to 1970', *Tijdschrift voor Economische en Sociale Geografie* 64, 164-8.

Taylor, A. H. (1973b), 'Journey time, perceived distance, and electoral turnout: Victoria Ward, Swansea', *Area* 5, 59-62.

Taylor, A. H. (1974), 'Measuring movements of electors using election results', *Political Studies* 22, 204-9.

Taylor, P. J. (1969), 'Causal models in geographic research', *Annals of the Association of American Geographers* 59, 402-4.

Taylor, P. J. (1973), 'Some implications of the spatial organisation of elections', *Transactions of the Institute of British Geographers* 60, 121-36.

Taylor, P. J. (1978), 'Political geography', *Progress in Human Geography* 2, 153-62.

Taylor, P. J. and Johnston, R. J. (1979), *Geography of Elections* (London, Penguin).

Thomas, E. N. (1968), 'Maps of residuals from regression', in B. J. L. Berry and D. F. Marble (eds), *Spatial Analysis: a Reader in Statistical Geography* (Englewood Cliffs NJ, Prentice-Hall), 326-52.

Tobler, W. R. (1970), 'A computer movie simulating urban growth in the Detroit region', *Economic Geography* 46, 234-40.

Walks, R. A. (2004), 'Place of residence, party preferences and political attitudes in Canadian cities and suburbs', *Journal of Urban Affairs*, 26, 269-85.

Walks, R. A. (2005), 'City-suburban electoral polarization in Great Britain, 1950-2001', *Transactions of the Institute of British Geographers*, NS30, 500-517.

Walks, R. A. (2006), 'The causes of city-suburban political polarization? A Canadian case study', *Annals of the Association of American Geographers* 96, 390-414.

Chapter 3

The Local State and Urban Politics

Mark Goodwin

Introduction

This chapter explores the work of Kevin Cox on the local state and, in particular, looks at his concern to "argue through the relations between a Marxist concept of the state and space" (Cox n.d., 2). It will argue that this concern still confronts us some thirty years after Kevin first began his research on the local state. Concentrating on the period between two of Kevin's seminal papers (Cox and Mair 1988; Cox 1998), the chapter will pull out three aspects of his ongoing attempt to argue through these relations – the first epistemological, the second conceptual and the third empirical. Epistemologically it will show how Kevin's grounding in critical realism led him to emphasise issues of abstraction and contingency. Conceptually, it will trace the moves that he made between the concepts of 'local dependence', 'spaces of dependence' and 'spaces of engagement'. At each point along this conceptual continuum the articulations he traces between state and space become subtly different, but the shifting connections between state, territory, space and power are constantly drawn. In particular, the chapter will highlight how Kevin has analysed the relation between different sorts of politics and the territorial organisation of the state. Finally, the chapter will look at how these conceptual concerns have been interrogated through a range of empirical work which looks beyond state institutions to explore the wider social, economic and cultural contexts that these institutions are both situated within and contribute to. The chapter argues that by exploring these interlinked epistemological, conceptual and empirical concerns, we can see how Kevin Cox's work opened up a research agenda focused around the key intersections of state, territory, space and power – an agenda which is still as pertinent today as it ever was.

In the late 1970s when Kevin first began to work on these issues, most academic research on local politics and sub-national government was carried out in political science departments, and thus lacked an explicit engagement with the concepts of space and territory. Indeed, to a large degree such work could be labelled as 'aspatial'. For many political scientists the focus was on the institutions and personalities of politics, rather than on the territories and spaces in which they took place. Emerging work on local politics in urban sociology also downplayed the spatial, emphasising a deterritorialised concern with the generic concept of collective consumption (Castells 1978). In contrast, Kevin's work on the local state, from its earliest days, was fired by an indelible geographical imagination.

Place, space and territory were placed at the heart of his investigations into local politics. For those of us starting out on academic careers at the end of the 1970s and beginning of the 1980s, this was an important validation of our own interests in the geography of local politics, and confirmation that such work could be undertaken in Geography Departments as well as in Political Science. In passing, it also helps to explain why Kevin's own department at The Ohio State University became the destination for many postgraduate students from the UK, including the two editors of this volume. For many of those interested in analysing and understanding local politics at this time, Ohio State seemed a natural destination given Kevin's presence. In a set of papers, some of which were written with these graduate students, Kevin sought to develop a theoretically informed account of the local state and local politics. The first task of this chapter is to trace that development, beginning with his epistemological concerns.

Realism, Abstraction and Urban Politics

Kevin was one of the first political geographers to explicitly engage with a realist epistemology. In doing so he would shape the way that he, and many others, approached the study of urban politics. In contrast to an emphasis on statistical description which had dominated much of political science research on urban politics in the 1960s and 1970s (especially studies of voting behaviour and local public spending), critical realism advocated a causal process of explanation (see Sayer 1992). In this view, the search for an explanation of urban political events requires the discovery of relations between different phenomena, and an uncovering of the mechanisms that relate. In order to pursue this line of enquiry, realism uses the process of abstraction – isolating in thought particular aspects of the object under study. This is done both to simplify some of the complexities of the social world being studied, but also in order to identify key or critical linkages and relationships within that world. However, this necessarily isolates in thought a partial or one-sided aspect of a social object. As Sayer puts it "what we abstract *from* are the many other aspects which together constitute *concrete* objects, such as people, economies, nations, institutions, activities and so on" (1992, 87). In this sense we might abstract – or isolate in thought – particular elements of the city, in order to understand its politics. Once we have done so, we can then combine these abstractions "so as to form concepts which grasp the concreteness of their objects" (ibid.).

Using a realist-informed approach Kevin was concerned to ensure that the abstract and the concrete were brought together in appropriate ways – as he put it:

> concrete study and abstract theorizing, therefore, have to proceed in tandem. It is through concrete study that the utility of more abstract categories can be checked and their content redefined. On the other hand, it is only through higher level concepts that more concrete observations can be interpreted. This suggests

that a field of investigation needs to run the gamut from more abstract work to concrete study and to carefully maintain their balance and reciprocity (Cox 1991a, 277).

Two key elements of Kevin's approach to the study of urban politics flowed from this – firstly the need to identify appropriate theoretical concepts at different levels of abstraction, and second the need to use case study research to identify the way these abstractions are combined in any given situation. Each of these points will be explored further in the remainder of the chapter, but this emphasis on conceptual abstraction was relatively unusual in the study of urban politics at this stage.

Kevin explicitly set out these epistemological issues in two papers in the *Journal of Urban Affairs*, which took issue with much of the work then being done within what was labelled as the New Urban Politics (Cox 1991a, 1991b). His main concern was that theoretical abstractions were often overlooked, and where they were used, they were not being deployed with sufficient care. As a result, he "called for greater attention in conceptualising the politics of urban development to structures of necessary social relations, to an emphasis on the relations which connect one social object to another and give them their particular causal properties" (1991a, 278). For Kevin, one consequence of such an approach was a greater emphasis on the social relations of production. As he put it,

> a concept of capital looms large in the new urban politics, but it tends to be one which emphasizes exchange, competition, and distributional struggle rather than capital as a production relation. There is nothing necessarily wrong with this view. It seems, however, to have been adopted by default rather than as a result of careful and critical consideration (Cox 1991a, 279).

This 'default' position partly stemmed from the traditional 'distributional' and allocation concerns of urban politics – 'who gets what, and where' – but even within the new Marxist-inspired work of Castells and the French School of Urban Sociology there was an emphasis on matters of collective consumption. Within Urban Geography, where Marxism was also having a major influence, work on urban politics tended to concentrate on housing, leaving the economy to the separate sphere of economic geography. Against this context, Kevin's emphasis on what might be termed 'the local politics of production' stood out for its originality as well as its insights.

Conceptual Developments: From Local Dependence to Spaces of Engagement

Starting from an avowedly realist position, then, led to a concern with abstraction and conceptualisation, and from there to an interest in the economy and production. The concept that Kevin originally developed to explore these concerns was that of local dependence, which he claimed had the potential "to become a core concept for those studying local areas" whether from an economic, social or political perspective (Cox and Mair 1998, 308). This paper with Andy Mair, published in the *Annals of the Association of American Geographers*, was to become one of the most heavily cited of Kevin's career. Its objective is to explore "the contemporary politics of local economic development, in particular the competition among localities" (1988, 307). Rather than looking for similarities and regularities in urban political behaviour to explain such competition, Cox and Mair looked for the processes behind it, and developed the abstract notion of local dependence to help in this search. Initially, they do this with reference to the capitalist firm, which is said to be locally dependent for a number of reasons: labour markets, supplier networks and consumer markets are often locally based; firms invest in the built environment of a locality, e.g., by building and purchasing factories, offices and retail outlets; issues of trust, brand loyalty, predictability in customer and supplier relations – what Storper (1997) was to later call 'untraded interdependencies' – also tend to occur within particular areal spaces. Through a combination of these factors, firms can find themselves largely dependent on a set of social and economic relations which are geographically circumscribed and non-substitutable at other locations. When this happens, it makes it difficult for these firms to move, and as a consequence Cox and Mair argue that they will seek "to protect, enhance or create a context of exchange linkages that will benefit them" (1988, 309). Often, they do this collectively with other locally dependent firms through local business coalitions, in order to realise their common interests. Crucially, these interests may well be antagonistic to locally dependent firms elsewhere; hence the competition between localities that the paper seeks to examine.

The *Annals* paper then makes two further manoeuvres which broaden the concept of local dependency and opens up the field of local politics. Firstly it points out that "locally dependent firms often attempt to harness the state in their pursuit of a healthy local economy" (1988, 311), and then it notes that "people can also be locally dependent" (1988, 312). The former insight allows an exploration of business-coalitions, public-private partnerships, urban renewal strategies and various other economic development policies, and brings the local state firmly into the orbit of research. However, local states "are by no means neutral institutions that are simply and instrumentally controlled by business coalitions" (1988, 311), for they as well are locally dependent – on a healthy economy and local tax base, but also in some cases on a local electorate. The vast bulk of the local electorate, moreover, will also be locally dependent – as Cox and Mair put it "everyday life is situated" (1988, 312). People tend to work and shop locally and their children attend local schools. They mix with neighbours and take part in local clubs and societies. Given this dependence, firms, states and residents will all find economic restructuring problematic. What this mix of course opens up is the potential for all kinds of local political conflict around local economies, as firms, local communities and local states all seek to resolve the problems of economic change and restructuring in their best interests. After providing examples of such conflicts, the paper closes with two broader points about the relationship between social and spatial structures. The first point relates directly to the underlying realist epistemology of the paper. As Cox and Mair (1988, 322) put it, "while there will necessarily be a politics of local economic development, its precise form is a contingent matter". In other words, the way these different facets of local dependence play out in any particular case will always be a matter for empirical investigation, and cannot be read off from the conceptual developments the paper makes. Sometimes these may be class-based; at other times and in other places they may be based around territorial issues.

The second broad point that the authors make is related to this. "Too often in the literature" they state, "the essential significance of locality, and, in particular, its roots in the material structures of social relations has been missed" (Cox and Mair 1988, 322). The paper thus argues that the scale division of politics, and the motivation activating particular territorially-articulated coalitions of interest, can usefully be understood through an assessment and examination of the places, spaces and scales at which the relevant agents are "locally dependent". While this work obviously drew on David Harvey's ideas of local structured coherence and territorial class alliances (1982, 1985), we can also discern a key concern with the local state – and indeed with interrogating the 'localness' of the local state. What also emerges is the recognition that the democratic state is beset with tensions, having, as the authors put it "a twin local dependence, one part economic, the other electoral" (Cox and Mair 1988, 315). As a result, the local electoral state is always open to contests between local business-led coalitions and more popular democratic movements, with each side trying to impose not just its favoured policies, but also the most strategic institutional arrangements to ensure that these policies are delivered. In many cases this has involved the use of non-elected agencies and institutions, especially in the field of local economic development. This concern with the link between state form – including its territorial arrangements – and state function again remains a key, if still relatively unexplored, problematic.

Kevin then began to refine the concept of local dependence, firstly introducing the idea of spaces of dependence (1993), before reworking it more fully in another seminal paper, published in *Political Geography* in 1998. In this paper he introduced the twin concepts of spaces of dependence and spaces of engagement, which together offered a more fluid and open framework for analysis, allowing us to examine "how different sorts of, spatially-qualified, politics, relate to the state's territorial organization" (Cox 1998, 20). Here we see again the key connections between state, territory, space and power, which Kevin constantly draws. The distinction made in the 1998 paper between spaces of dependence and spaces of engagement is developed in order to explore the connection between the content and form of what Kevin terms "the politics of space" (Cox 1998, 1). He is thus asking a set of questions around how the institutional and territorial form of the state relates to the political issues it attempts to confront – does local government necessarily concern itself with local politics; can there be a local politics without local branches of the state; is a politics which engages with the local state necessarily local; are politics any less local if they engage with regional or national governments; can we conceive of politics within areal or territorial containers, or should we examine instead networks and associations which stretch beyond these?

The notion of spaces of dependence builds on that of local dependence. It signals the "more-or-less localized social relations upon which we depend for the realisation of essential interests and for which there are no substitutes elsewhere" (Cox 1998, 2). These spaces of dependence "define place-specific conditions for our material well-being and our sense of significance" (ibid.). However, such spaces are inserted into broader sets of relationships and processes which may operate at regional, national and international scales, and in order to realise or defend a space of dependence, an individual, say, or community, or firm or state agency, may well have to engage with wider centres of social and economic power. Such engagement constructs and opens up a different form of space, labelled as a space of engagement, and defined in the paper as "the space in which the politics of securing a space of dependence unfolds" (ibid.). Here again Kevin draws on the work of David Harvey, using in particular the idea that the politics of spaces often hinge around the contradiction between the mobility and fixity of capital. Capitalism relies on fixed forms – especially social and physical infrastructures of various kinds – to realise value and generate profits, yet competition between firms constantly threatens to devalue these. Factories close, offices move, new roads are built, IT links are laid, housing estates are built, new educational opportunities open up, all of which will pose a challenge for people and firms left in 'unproductive' areas. As a consequence a politics of space emerges as people, firms and institutions seek to continue the localised conditions that will enable them to, for instance, make a profit, earn a wage, win elections, charge rent, work close to home, save for retirement, remain near to their family and so on.

Kevin then seeks to use the concept of spaces of dependence to explore those relations which are relatively place-bound, and which will therefore be vulnerable to the instability and uncertainty of the capitalist space-economy. These will occur at diverse scales – hence the notion that such spaces are defined by the ability to substitute "one socio(-spatial) relation for another, but beyond which such substitution is difficult if not impossible" (Cox 1998, 5). Firms which need to replace workers will do so within particular journey-to-work areas, people who are seeking to buy or rent another house will usually do so within a particular geographical area, local political parties can seek to substitute one voter for another, but only within a particular jurisdiction, local utility companies may only be franchised to supply certain areas, and can only substitute one customer for another within those, local developers and builders will seek land and development opportunities within a particular area and can only substitute one development opportunity for another within that area. Multinational companies of course have a wider scope of substitution than locally based small firms, and professionals in the finance industry, say, can substitute one job for another over a wider scale than other types of employment. Kevin then goes on to point out that immobilisation within particular spaces of dependence is something which is shared, therefore creating the possibility of local interests, and making it possible to 'identify a set of distinctly local conflicts around (e.g.) labour markets, taxes, local government spending, land use, local economic development and attendant identity formation' (Cox 1998, 6). In this way attempts are made to confront the contradictions which emerge between mobility and fixity, leading to a politics of space, which is played out at different scales and over different territories. Importantly, the ability to realise these local interests 'is critically conditioned by the ability to exercise territorial power. The goal is to control the actions and interactions of others, both within and between respective spaces of dependence: the means is control over a geographic area' (Cox 1998, 7). And crucially for the concerns of this chapter, 'the most obvious candidates for this purpose are the various agencies of the state...the problem then becomes one of influencing state agencies' (ibid.).

The construction and articulation of spaces of engagement facilitates such 'influencing', and the paper uses a set of case studies drawn from the UK, the US and South Africa to explore the different ways in which this might be done. This returns us to the epistemological concerns of realism, which stresses the contingent manner in which different processes combine in practice. Here Kevin works through some of the contingent relations between spaces of dependence and spaces of engagement, using these to draw out a number of broader conclusions about space, politics and the state. Firstly, the studies show how the spatial structure of the state, and the division of responsibilities between its constituent parts, is an important consideration for those seeking to influence state activity, and the appropriate level of the state must be drawn into the space of engagement for that influence to be felt. Sometimes this will be at a local level, sometimes regional and sometimes national, or even international depending on the nature of the state in question. He also points out though that the role of the state is not an exclusive one, and often it will be necessary to pull other agencies into the space of engagement, such as utilities, or corporations, or labour unions. This in turn will make these spaces more complex, and more likely to be mobilised via networks and relations operating well beyond the local scale. It also means that the objectives of what might appear to be a purely 'local' politics may be best realised through wider spheres of activity. Somewhat ironically, Kevin's focus on the scaling of politics leads to the conclusion that it is difficult to slot most political movements and claims into any neatly defined territorial container. And somewhat interestingly, this focus on the exploration of complex political assemblages and connections between different interests operating at different scales predates contemporary concerns with relationality (Goodwin 2012).

Empirical Concerns: Moving Beyond the Town Hall

These epistemological and conceptual concerns led Kevin to undertake a range of empirical work, sometimes on his own, and sometimes with graduate students, which lay outside the traditional remit of urban politics. The other chapters in this collection cover Kevin's own empirical work in some detail, so to avoid overlap I will just draw out some key points in relation to the local state and urban politics. As we noted earlier, previous work on these themes had tended to focus on the institutions, and personnel, of the formal machinery of government, or on distributional struggles around the provision of collective consumption. In contrast, Kevin sought to trace the local politics operating around economic change, and kept to the forefront a concern with class and with class struggles. He always looked beyond the local state as a set of institutions to examine the social, economic and cultural contexts that these institutions are both situated within and contribute to.

For example, in Cox and Mair (1988), Kevin draws on research on local business coalitions in Pittsburgh, Detroit and Ohio, exploring their tactics and political claims around notions of a 'local' interest in competition with other localities for investment and employment. In Cox (1998) the conceptual shift to spaces of dependence and engagement leads to a broadening of empirical concerns. This paper draws on his own work with Andy Wood on local economic development networks in Ohio (Cox and Wood, 1997), and also on other's work on forced residential relocation in South Africa, community builders in the US, and housing development and housing markets in the UK. There is also a consistent thread of comparative work running through Kevin's work – whether between the local politics of different cities in the US, or between urban politics in the US and those in other countries (most notably the UK and South Africa). This stems from his realist approach and Kevin's insistence to explore the way that the same broad processes can give rise to different outcomes in different places, due to the contingent nature of their empirical articulation. Crucially, this work also showed the way in which state agencies at a local level are key players in promoting and underpinning economic, as well as social, development.

Retrospect and Prospect

Although this chapter has been mainly concerned to look back at the ways in which Kevin's work on local politics and the local state evolved, I want to finish by using some of his insights to look forward by thinking about what his work might mean for future work in this area. The first thing to note here is the way in which the evolution of his work opens up an intriguing research agenda which is still ripe for investigation. I write this in the summer of 2011 in the UK, against a backdrop where the Coalition Government has explicitly incorporated 'localism' into its legislative programme by introducing a Localism Bill designed to change not only the relation between central and local government, but also the relation between the local state and its citizens. According to the Government, the Bill is designed "to achieve a substantial and lasting shift in power away from central government and towards local people" (Department for Communities and Local Government 2011, 3). Another context is provided by the riots in August 2011 which took place over a 5-day period in many of the UK's largest cities, when 16,000 police were deployed in London alone in an effort to stem widespread looting and vandalism. Here the only power local youths felt they could wield was laced with violence, and their only relationship with the local state was one of opposition and repression. Questions concerning the relationship between the (local) state, its citizens and local politics are still vital ones.

What Kevin's work does is to open a window on some of the key elements of this relationship. Where is power located, at which levels, and who holds it? How do communities and other 'locally dependent' actors get access to such power? Which 'spaces of engagement' should they deploy to do so? Against a contemporary backdrop where central legislation will alter the powers of local government, and where police from local forces elsewhere are deployed in the UK's major conurbations, can we conceive of local politics as ever being purely local? And when many of those arrested in the riots came from the UK's most economically deprived urban areas, what is the link between the mobility of footloose capital, the fixity of unemployed residents and different forms of local politics? What Kevin's work does is to insist on the centrality of the relation between state, territory, space and power, and analyzing how these four critical elements come together is still a key task for those interested in understanding urban politics. The UK Government's Localism Bill will alter this relationship in one way; the rioters sought to challenge it in another. Quite how this relation plays out will always be a contingent matter, and one that must be subject to empirical investigation.

As part of his own empirical work, Kevin often focused on the coalitions, partnerships and networks which the locally dependent put together in an effort to challenge wider forces of economic and political power. Understanding how these associations and assemblages come together, and over which spaces and territories, to confront and engage which institutions is also a pressing concern. But of course the shape and structure of the state does not remain static, as the Localism Bill reminds us. We should not, of course, be surprised at this territorial restructuring. Neil Brenner has drawn our attention to the ways in which 'historically specific configurations of state space are produced and incessantly reworked' (Brenner 2004, 76). In other words, new geographies of the state, or 'new state spaces' in Brenner's words, are constantly being produced as part and parcel of the shifting nature of state institutions and political strategies. Kevin's own work had, of course, also highlighted the importance of the shifting territorial structure of the state (see, for example, Cox and Jonas 1993). What flows from this in turn is that the social and political forces that are able to gain access to particular parts and branches of the state will also change, as their spaces of engagement with the state are altered. Tracing and analysing this relation between the shifting structures of the state and the shifting form of local political engagement will also be an important challenge. It seems to me that many of the major conceptual and empirical concerns which face today's students of urban politics were prefigured and anticipated in Kevin's work. His legacy is an important one and the spaces of enquiry that he opened up remain vital to an understanding of contemporary urban politics.

References

Brenner, N. (2004), *New State Spaces: Urban Governance and the Rescaling of Statehood* (Oxford, Oxford University Press).

Castells, M. (1978), *City, Class and Power* (London, Macmillan).

Cox, K. (no date), 'Local interests, uneven development and the localness of state institutions' *Unpublished mimeograph.*

Cox, K. (1991a), 'Questions of abstraction in studies in the New Urban Politics', *Journal of Urban Affairs* 13, 267-80.

Cox, K. (1991b), 'The abstract, the concrete, and the argument in the New Urban Politics', *Journal of Urban Affairs* 13, 299-306.

Cox, K. (1993), 'The local and the global in the New Urban Politics: a critical view', *Environment and Planning D: Society and Space* 11, 433-48.

Cox, K. (1998), 'Spaces of dependence, spaces of engagement and the politics of scale, or: looking for local politics', *Political Geography* 17, 1-23.

Cox, K. and Jonas, A. E. G. (1993), 'Urban development, collective consumption and the politics of metropolitan fragmentation', *Political Geography* 12, 8-37.

Cox, K. and Mair, A. (1988), 'Locality and community in the politics of local economic development', *Annals of the Association of American Geographers* 78, 307-25.

Cox, K. and Wood, A. (1994), 'Local government and local economic development the United States', *Regional Studies* 28, 640-45.

Cox, K. and Wood, A. (1997), 'Competition and cooperation in mediating the global: the case of local economic development', *Competition and Change* 2, 65-94.

Department for Communities and Local Government (2011), *A Plain English Guide to the Localism Bill*, Available at http://www.communities.gov.uk/documents/localgovernment/pdf/1923416.pdf.

Goodwin, M. (2012), 'Regions, territories and relationality: Exploring the regional dimensions of political practice', forthcoming in *Regional Studies*.

Harvey, D. (1982), *The Limits to Capital* (Oxford, Basil Blackwell).

Harvey, D. (1985), *The Urbanization of Capital* (Baltimore, Johns Hopkins University Press).

Sayer, A. (1992), *Method in Social Science: A Realist Approach* (London, Routledge).

Storper, M. (1997), *The Regional World: Territorial Development in a Global Economy* (New York, Guilford Press).

Chapter 4

Marxism, Space and the Urban Question

Kevin R. Cox

Context

The question of the relations between society and space has been a central one in human geography at least since the late 1970s. A journal by that title was established in 1983. An important collection edited by Derek Gregory and John Urry that appeared in 1985, *Social Relations and Spatial Structures*, was consumed with it. The interest has clearly continued since then but with less of the fervor of discovery so evident at that time. Yet things remain to be discovered. The initial debate also corresponded with another in human geography, between Marxism on the one hand and critical realism on the other and differences in position were reflected in the contributions to the Gregory/Urry book. Overt contestation was limited,[1] but quite different approaches to the question of space and social theory were on display there. Furthermore, questions were raised then that have never been completely resolved. Noel Castree (2002) recently tried to identify a possible rapprochement between historical materialist views and those of critical realism but, in my view, more needs to be said.

This is because it is difficult if not impossible to achieve some reconciliation of what are very different arguments indeed about space and social theory. This is owing to the fact that they are based on very different beliefs about method in the broad sense: not least, matters of abstraction, totalization, determination and contingency. This does not mean that historical geographical materialists can ignore what critical realism has to say. I believe that some of its concepts can be usefully assimilated so long as they are re-worked and purged of their pluralistic baggage. I am thinking in particular of its concept of structures of social relations and their causal significance. So while a major purpose of this chapter will be to examine the respective claims about space and social theory, I also want to explore the role that a suitably re-tooled critical realist concept of structure might play in historical geographical materialism.

The early 1980s were also a time of intellectual ferment around not so much spatial relations and social theory but a particular ensemble of spatial relations and social theory. The ensemble in question was the urban; and the question being asked was whether or not the urban could be said to have some irreducible social significance or whether social theory could ignore the city. As we will

---

1   See, however, Harvey (1987) and Sayer (1987).

see the notion that social theory did not need to make reference to the city in its claims was very close to Sayer's critical realist conclusions regarding space. Sayer, however, was not the principal protagonist of this viewpoint at that time. Rather it was left to an urban sociologist, Peter Saunders to make the requisite arguments. This he had done in a book appearing in 1982 under the title *Social Theory and the Urban Question*. He then repeated his key arguments in the *Social Relations and Spatial Structures* book referred to above. His key point was that social processes existed, as it were, above space and particular spatial arrangements. All that the latter did was to intensify or weaken social processes. Space in the form of the urban had effects only of a contingent sort. Workers might be more militant in cities in virtue of the co-presence of many other workers and their segregation into occupation-specific neighborhoods. Urban politics might be consumed by land use conflicts but the latter could be found outside cities too; it was just that under urban conditions the fact of proximity resulting from density meant that the effects of land use change were felt more intensely.

The critical riposte came from Harvey in an essay written in 1985. His approach was to build on the idea of the contradiction between fixity and mobility; something very clear in his chapter on the geopolitics of capitalism in the Gregory/Urry collection. Cities represented social and physical resource systems in the reproduction of which workers, capitals and state agencies developed strong interests. They became difficult to substitute for and therefore something to be defended. This was the source of Harvey's relatively autonomous urban politics and the various competitive strategies into which various urban coalitions entered in order to secure that reproduction.

One comment on these competing claims might be their situatedness. The fact of a distinct urban politics and of its rootedness in the fixity-mobility contradiction is much more evident in the US than it is in Great Britain. It is only with great difficulty that conceptions of urban politics like that of Logan and Molotch (1987), which took off from that contradiction, have been transferred across the Atlantic. To what extent, therefore, might one argue that Harvey's paper represented a very American viewpoint while Saunders was simply reflecting his experiences of the British case, and in particular the fact that the sorts of local dependences apparent in American cities are notable more for their absence in the British one? One problem, though, is that even in Great Britain, the urban as a distinct object of policy won't go away. Central government agencies insist on the drawing up of local city plans and scrutinize them for consistency with some notion of national urban policy. There is airport planning, highway and railroad planning, all with a view to the reproduction of particular sets of urban relations. Instead of trying to resolve the urban question in terms of some variable geohistorical applicability, therefore, it needs to be reinterpreted and in ways that avoid the fixity-mobility issue, attractive as it is. Rather what I am going to argue is that a reconstituted concept of structure, reconstituted so that it can be assimilated by historical geographical materialism helps us understand the continuing significance of the urban for social theory.

The Question of Space

Historical Geographical Materialism

I want to consider the way in which historical geographical materialism has tended to view space through the work of its principle interlocuteur, David Harvey. His work in this area goes back to the early 1970s, since when he has put together a quite remarkable oeuvre. It is useful to recall, though, that what a Marxist might make of space was not immediately apparent. Reflecting his urban interests, his early efforts to make the connections focused on urban rent theory. This, however, proved to be far too narrow a foundation and his work on the geography of accumulation turned out to be a much more promising approach: something that was then brought to quite dazzling fruition in the final section of *Limits to Capital*.

One can make several points about his understanding of the matter. The first is that space has to be theorized as an essential aspect of the social process. The most fundamental assumptions of social theories are severely challenged not to say negated when questions of spatial arrangement and connection are taken into account. One of the examples he uses is the assumption of perfect competition in economics; an assumption clearly violated by the scope space affords for monopoly. Similar remarks can be made about sociology. Historically the tendency has been to theorize societies as national, rather than as much messier forms, sometimes bordering on the incoherent and necessarily so given that they are constructed on the basis of a highly variable geography that connects events both within nation states and to points beyond.[2]

As such, and second, space is to be understood in terms of a totalizing social process. At the heart of this totalizing process is production. Social life is organized around production and production conditions social life, circumscribing and facilitating in various ways. Under capitalism production assumes a particular social form: that of the accumulation process. The accumulation process has always been central to Harvey's Marxist work. Capitalism strives to mold geographies to its own needs of accumulation: to abolish space with time so as to speed up the rotation of capital through the construction of highways, railroads, electricity grids, pipelines and the like; and to exploit the productive advantages of scale through the construction of concentrated physical infrastructures – cities, factories, airports, dock facilities (1975; 1985b). At the same time, through

---

2   Although Harvey has been emphatic on this matter, it is curious that space does not enter into the various moments of the social process as he has imagined them on at least two different occasions (1996: Chapter 4; and 2010: Chapter 5).

working, if to a variable degree, with what already exists, it transforms the geography of social infrastructures: the governance systems through which risk can be reduced, exchange lubricated and labor relations stabilized. As production concentrates geographically, so the division of labor can be deepened. Vertical disintegration occurs and constellations of interrelated firms come into being to constitute territorial production complexes. In short, in order to valorize itself, some fraction of capital has to be invested in fixed facilities of long life. Social infrastructures are also required and these have their own forms of fixity owing to the substantial opportunity costs of relocation that they impose, both for firms and for workers.

But, and third, this is a contradictory process and contradictions receive a spatial form. Once appropriated in the money form, for example, capital is free to roam the world in search of profitable investment opportunities. There is no guarantee that it will continue to flow through existing fixed facilities and social infrastructures. Rather it may be embodied in *new* factories, cities, physical infrastructures elsewhere in 'new' industrial spaces or 'newly' industrializing countries which offer competitive advantages over the 'old' – what become, in other words, the various rustbelts and inner cities of the world. And in order to facilitate production in these 'new industrial spaces' new social infrastructures come into being: new ways through which firms relate one to another and to their workforces and which may provide further competitive advantages.

The upshot of this is a competition over space between those who have stakes in the reproduction of existing agglomerations of fixed capital and their associated social infrastructures. Each tries to ensure that, if there is to be devaluation of fixed capital and the imposition of opportunity costs as firms and workers are forced to forsake the advantages provided them by their localized social relations, then it should be somewhere else. Place-based coalitions, often cross-class in character, emerge to defend what Harvey calls elsewhere 'territorial structured coherences.' This they try to do in the only way possible: by guaranteeing a continuing flow of value through local social relations – attracting inward investment, lobbying the state for new investments that will fortify existing advantages or for some sort of regulatory relief and the like. In this way capitalism generates what Harvey called its geopolitics (1985a; 1985c).

In sum, capital seeks to subordinate geography to its own logic of expanded reproduction or accumulation (much as it seeks to subordinate technology, discourse, the state, the family and not least the working class) and it certainly achieves a degree of success in this regard. But at the same time it must, of necessity, revolutionize geography. It must develop new transportation and communication technologies, new products which may shift the balance of advantage between one place and another or result in the creation of entirely new industrial spaces elsewhere. In consequence it invariably creates tensions between fixity and mobility and therefore between the old and the new and between here and there. Capital differentiates itself, not least geographically, in order to solve its contradictions, but this results in a re-posing of them in a new concrete form. In order to be produced, some fraction of capital must be immobilized in fixed forms. But once produced there is no guarantee that it will continue to flow through those fixed forms and permit their amortization.

Critical Realism

Any discussion of a critical realist approach to the question of space has to start with Sayer's much cited chapter in the Gregory/Urry collection entitled "The Difference that Space Makes." In this paper he famously argues that social theory can proceed for the most part as if space did not exist. Only in concrete research does it have to be taken into account. This is the conclusion that has attracted most attention and I certainly think it a questionable one. What has attracted less attention, though, is the way in which his approach secretes a separation of space from social relations that is quite the converse of the Marxist position.

It is useful to reiterate the argument at length here. Space, he argues, is constituted by the objects that compose it. It only exists in and through those objects. Without objects space is nothing. What we refer to as the effects of space are the effects of objects: the so-called 'friction of distance' is the friction of the underlying material surface; likewise, and accordingly, connectivity depends on the configuration of highways with respect to each other. On the other hand, while objects are indeed constitutive of space, space can't be reduced to them. While space is not determinant in the sense of 'producing' or 'changing', it is a condition for the activation of the causal properties of objects and for their actual effects when so activated. People, firms, in other words, exploit relations of proximity and separation in order to achieve useful effects. Firms get close to labor because it facilitates their profitability. More affluent households segregate themselves from the less affluent in order to reduce their tax bills, in order to establish a particular social milieu for their children, in order, in brief, to share out what have been called their 'positive externalities'.

This highlights the fact that social objects like firms, wage workers, state agencies, etc., have causal properties which can be characterized as in part spatial. There are needs and wants and powers that are spatial in character. People need space for their living arrangements. Firms need space for their factories. State agencies need space for highways, parks and schools. Regional malls need to be accessible to large retail markets. Workers need to be accessible to places of work, and soon. Capitalists can disinvest from one location and invest in another. Workers can move around in search of jobs. The crucial question is, though, does this mean that social theory has to be spatial? Sayer is pessimistic. Abstract social theory must indeed incorporate space to the extent that the necessary properties of objects are concerned. But, he says, and quite crucially, this doesn't amount to very much: "To observe that capital must be accessible to property-less workers says very little about the actual spatial form of labor markets, which of course is not surprising, given the contingent nature of this form" (p. 54). The spatial properties of objects, therefore, were of such a general character that they couldn't tell us much about the concrete forms of geographies. In consequence social theory could proceed for the most part as if the world was space-less.

Two comments are warranted here. In the first place, as far as abstract theory and the concrete are concerned, this is an odd argument. While it is true that the spatial aspects of causal properties provide limited purchase on the concrete, this is true of all theory. Nobody expects kinship theory to provide a complete understanding of the family in late capitalist France; and no-one expects stratification theory to be able to grasp the variety of forms in which stratification tends to get expressed in capitalist societies.

In the second place, and what I want to discuss at greater length, is the separation of space and society that is licensed by this view. I do not believe that it is a defensible one. It is an approach vividly on display in the arguments that another person who was identified as critical realist – Doreen Massey – was deploying at that time, including in her chapter in the same Gregory/Urry collection. The language of separation is very clear. In a discussion of the literature on industrial change and spatial change she makes the claim that "(T)he sequence 'production change → spatial change' ignores the crucial impact of spatially-organized locational opportunities (or the lack of them) and of the use of distance and spatial separation themselves" (p. 13). If that might leave the reader wondering exactly what is meant by this, in her book *Spatial Divisions of Labor*, which appeared around about the same time, we are left in no doubt. As she argues there, "... whether or not the adoption of a particular production technique and its constituent labor processes is accompanied by separation of different stages of production will depend on whether or not there are spatially-differentiated labor markets or spatial differentiation of some sort" (p. 54).

On reflection I find this a strange claim. The implication is that without, for example, low wage labor reserves, the sort of branching of deskilled parts of the labor process could not and would not occur. I am reminded here of Marx's discussion of the industrial reserve army in *Capital Volume 1*. As a result of its creation he shows how capital is able to control not only the demand for labor as a result of its impetus to accumulation but also a supply consistent with its needs to make a profit. The same, it can be argued, applies to the question of what Massey called 'locational opportunities': capital creates not just the demand for them but also supplies them in the form of what Dick Walker (1978) called a lumpen geography of places. Capital *has* to create a pool of unemployed and that unemployment is, in virtue of the competitive capacities and vulnerabilities of different sectors and their geographic concentration, invariably uneven geographically.

In short, space or spatial arrangement is always socially produced. It is never, *qua* Sayer, just a spatial arrangement of objects which then trigger off, via their proximity, causal powers and liabilities. As an example we might consider the case of locating a new shopping center. On the one hand there is a profit-seeking corporation that needs appropriate sites; on the other a set of locational possibilities determined by properties of accessibility and the cheapness of the site: in other words, contingent spatial arrangements over which the corporation seemingly has no control. But this contingency, of course, is quite erroneous, not least because capitals, including property development companies, seek to change the map of accessibility. They lobby for new freeway interchanges, sometimes paying for them, themselves. Or they build the housing that will then provide the market for the shopping center. As for the price of the land, they can and do exercise some control over it by land banking: calculating the geographic trends of development so as to know where to buy ahead of development. They then lower their holding costs until the land is 'ripe' by taking advantage of tax rules supposed to benefit farmers and keep land in agriculture.[3] In other words, it is not just spatial arrangement that is at issue but a capitalist spatial arrangement: far more than a contingent condition vis-à-vis property since capital since it was, in various ways, internalized by them. As Harvey and Scott emphasized: "We need to show...how particular contingencies that on first sight *appear* as external and arbitrary phenomena are *transformed* into structured internal elements of the encompassing social logic of capitalism" (1989: 19) (my emphasis).

Discussion

Ontologically critical realism and Marxism are very different. In the first, the world is viewed as differentiated into a variety of objects which, in virtue of their structures, have, of necessity, particular causal properties. States are enabled in virtue of the fact that they have subjects who will pay their taxes and serve in their armies. Capitals have to accumulate in virtue of their competitive relation with other capitals. The division of labor empowers by allowing people to specialize and develop particular skills. And so on. These objects interact in open systems. In consequence, how they are expressed empirically differs from what is called the domain of the real or the domain of structures and causal properties. French capitalism is different from American capitalism as a result of the presence of states with very different structures.

Marxism provides a different world view. This is the world as a totality as discussed earlier but not in a deterministic sense. The concrete trajectory of capital or of any social formation for that matter cannot be reduced to its essential nature in the commonly accepted notion of reduction. Rather, the totality is in a constant state of formation as developments are internalized as aspects of capital. This dynamic, totalizing view is very different from the pluralizing, rather flat one of critical realism. 'Reduction' is not part of the Marxist vocabulary.

Accordingly when we turn to method approaches to abstraction are also at substantial odds with one another. The objective of critical realism is to abstract

---

3   A number of states in the US allow land under agriculture on the urban fringe to be assessed for property tax purposes at its value under agricultural uses and not for its highest and best use, which would be urban, but much higher. Development companies take advantage of this by leasing the land out to a farmer until they are ready to develop.

the real structures which make up the world and then to trace out their contingent effects in conditions produced by the exercise of causal powers entailed by other structures. This has led to an approach which Gunn (1989) has characterized as 'empiricist': it is abstraction *from* particular concrete circumstances. The division of labor can evidently exist without capitalism as can the state, since both precede it. The result is that, as per Sayer's views on the difference that space makes, space tends to get separated from society. Its effects are contingent and not necessary. Human geographies are to be understood as lying at the intersection of what is defined as a general process like capitalism or patriarchy and the contingencies of spatial arrangement.

The Marxist approach to abstraction is quite different. Instead of empiricist ones Marx's abstractions are historical: they are abstractions that can only emerge in the particular circumstances produced by the developing totality; in the context, that is, of particular practices which make them possible and therefore thinkable and which are in turn entailed by a totalizing process of social production. In other words, the abstractions made are ones in which the whole, structured by production, is internalized within the thing. Accordingly, abstracting space means to recognize how it is at the same time a power relation (as in Massey's (1984: Chapter 3) spatial divisions of labor), an institutional relation, a discursive relation as in spatial imaginaries, and all of these as aspects of production. Space is never separate; it is always an aspect of the social relations of production: capitalism, feudalism or whatever. Capitalist space is different: not least it is a space of substitution and of interdependence to a degree unimaginable in other social formations.

Otherwise put, in historical geographical materialism space relations are part of a larger social whole. They are a necessary aspect of a social process with production at its center. Social relations, including their necessary spatial expression, and spatial relations in their necessary social expression, are produced but in a way that allows production to continue and follow whatever social logic governs it in a particular time and place. Under capitalism that means that analysis must start with and return to accumulation. Institutions, power relations, divisions of labor, technologies, imaginaries, geographies, are reproduced and transformed conditions of accumulation.[4] Change is of the essence because of the way in which production encounters contradictions in its own nature, requiring the re-working of the state, discourse and geography too if production as one knows it – capitalist, feudal or some more hybrid form – is to continue. What happens in terms of the creation of new technologies, changes in urban form, in modes of organizing production, or discursive shifts can indeed, as in critical realist understandings, be explained in terms of cause and effect relations: the strategies of property capital, for example. This though is to miss the point though that these are inevitably

---

4   We should note also how these different moments of the accumulation process are internally related to one another: divisions of labor have to have a geography as do institutions; power relations are implicated in divisions of labor; and so on.

capitalist or *working class* strategies informed by more globally experienced contradictions and possibilities. What is possible today, what would be required today, would not have been the case fifty years ago.

The division of labor is a case in point. It is indeed a simple category. It always means what it says: a division of labor into specialized roles. But beyond that it has clearly become much more and cannot be understood outside of the new relations it has acquired. It is a division that is simultaneously a spatial division: an allocation of particular parts of the labor necessary for social reproduction to particular geographic scales or regions. As a technical division it is one in which to an increasing degree people can move from one position to another with relative ease. And it is a division in which the specialized equipment used and the raw-materials that are worked on by different positions are owned by another. It has become, in short, a *capitalist* division of labor.

The critical realist approach to explaining, say, changing forms of industrial organization would be to bring together what it regards as two contingently-related structures: capital and the division of labor. The adoption of different spatial divisions of labor à la Massey then depends not just on capital's drive to accumulate but also on the possibilities and limitations defined by the division of labor and the concrete labor processes which compose it. So, and for example: a) whether or not particular parts of the labor process are sufficiently deskilled to be relocated to areas of cheaper labor; and b) recalling that transport is part of the division of labor, whether or not the parts manufactured at outlying branch plants can then be brought together cheaply at the point of final assembly. What this brushes over, though, is how capital creates the conditions for these changes in the division of labor: how it deskills, how it revolutionizes transportation so as to lower its costs of production and speed up the rotation of capital; how, in other words, these changes are internal to and not external to capital.[5]

To return to the question of abstraction: Spatial arrangement does indeed have a trans-historic applicability. But this is only in a limited sense and always depends on the prevailing relations of production. Spatial arrangement as a historical as opposed to empiricist abstraction acquires new relations under different relations of production. Capitalism utterly transforms it. Space is now produced through the insertion of massive items of physical infrastructure. The division of land into a privately owned mosaic of holdings facilitates the assembly of land allowing developers to plan on a large scale and so take advantage of spatial arrangements that they themselves have created. A new substitutability is achieved suggesting, so long as one abstracts from the social relations of production, that location is indeed a contingent matter.

Through the dialectic, Marx saw the understanding of the universal as something that developed over time. So in the case of money, "This very simple category...makes a historic appearance *in its full intensity* only in the most developed conditions of society" (*Grundrisse*: 103; my emphasis); and "...

---

5   On capital and the division of labor, see also Gough and Eisenschnitz (1997).

although the simpler category may have existed historically before the more concrete, it can achieve its full (intensive and extensive) development precisely in a combined form of society..." (ibid.). Universals are understood relationally and those relations change over time: so too is it the case with the division of labor or space.

With this is as background, it is useful to examine Noel Castree's recent attempts to split the difference between the contrasting views of space held by Sayer and Harvey. In his own words, "...*both* thinkers are saying something right about space: that is, the difference that space makes can be necessary *and/ or* conditional since there is nothing contradictory about holding to either or both positions simultaneously" (p. 189). Rather, he argues, a proper appreciation of the difference that space makes requires work at a variety of levels of abstraction (p. 209). According to this view Harvey works at a higher level of abstraction, demonstrating how the dynamics of the accumulation process work themselves out over space in the abstract rather than in particular places with all their contextual variety. Sayer, on the other hand, believes that concrete research into particular cases is necessary since the sort of abstract claims of people like Harvey are so general as to shed little light on how things work out in practice. Castree is not about to accept Sayer's limited view of how historical geographical materialism has incorporated space into its claims; but nor is he willing to accept Harvey's refusal to work at lower levels of abstraction. As a result, for him "It is, *contra* Sayer possible to make theoretical claims about space. But *contra* Harvey, we have to recognize that, in practice, the necessary properties of space are realized in and through contingent conditions" (p. 209).

Yet it seems to me that this approach is too critically realist for comfort. The particular notion of levels of abstraction drawn on is the critical realist one of empirical abstraction that entails a pluralist understanding of the world. Accordingly, Castree refers to how "...only concrete research will be able to account for how capital, patriarchy, racism, the division of labor, etc., *articulate* in and through particular geographical landscapes" (p. 209); and how "the contingent question of how real spaces are necessarily co-determined by and co-determining of a plethora of relatively autonomous relations and structures."

Likewise the notion of contingency drawn on in Castree's account is, as it has to be, given this pluralist approach, the flat, un-dynamic one of critical realism; not something that is acted on, transformed, and incorporated into the ongoing social process as a necessary aspect of it as it is manifest in particular places; not something therefore consistent with the way in which, as Harvey has urged, "processes of capital circulation bring the unique qualities...of given places... into a framework of universal generality" (1985b, 45). Sayer has claimed that capitalism has a high degree of context independence. This is because it seems to be able to exist in a vast range of situations. As a result the settings cannot be considered necessary aspects of capital. Yet this is to ignore the way in which capital works on those contingent conditions to, as Harvey puts it above, 'bring the unique qualities ...of given places...into a framework of universal generality.' It does not take things as it finds them but transforms them so that they can be effective in the valorization of capital.

Accordingly, concrete research of a historical geographical materialist sort should focus on how various configurations of agents and conditions are selected in, how they are articulated one with another, become the object of struggle and transformed into a structure of relations that can function as a necessary aspect of the circulation of capital as it seeks to suspend the barriers inherent in its own nature. The locally specific is not accepted by capital as such, and nor could it be. Capital, *pace* Sayer, is not indifferent to context. It has to work to transform it in accord with its totalizing impulse so that it becomes something quite different and internal to capital. Structures get constructed and draw on the conditions encountered in particular localities or regions and they get constructed to respond to the geohistorically specific forms in which capital's contradictions are being experienced at a particular time. To research a history of structures is therefore to situate them with respect to those specific forms and how they came into being. At the same time, it is to explore the ways in which the institutional fixes arrived at will themselves get challenged, defended, reworked, as capital's contradictions assume new forms: new configurations of the fixed and the mobile, for example, as Harvey outlined them in discussing the geopolitics of capitalism.

The Accumulation Process and Structures

Given these serious incompatibilities, does this mean that historical geographical materialism as a method has nothing to gain from an awareness of at least some of the claims and research strategies of critical realism? I think such a conclusion would be unwarranted. It is this possibility of a limited – a very limited – rapprochement that I now want to examine. The critical realist concept that I believe to be relevant to historical geographical materialist research is that of structure. Structures entail causal properties. People are enabled or limited in various ways because of their substantive connections with others. Those in a division of labor are enabled in terms of developing their skills and understandings of particular physical processes and under capitalism that can be converted into monetary gain. They are also limited, however, by the efficiency with which others perform their roles. This can be countered by the creation of relations of trust or governance institutions as an essential aspect of the division of labor. Structures can be emergent or they can be constructed in order to achieve a particular purpose. The school classroom can be regarded as a highly purposive set of relations involving blackboards, the physical arrangements of the students relative to the teacher, the placing of windows, all with a view to facilitating the teaching process. In any case, it is clear that new structures emerge and old ones dissolve or get transformed in some way, which sounds promising from the standpoint of conducting concrete historical geographical materialist research.

As we have seen, critical realism imposes a particular view of the world: one which precludes situating structures with respect to a developing, contradictory totality. Evidently that does not have to be. Rather, they can be regarded as coming into being to serve some purpose in the struggles around accumulation, whether those of the capitalist and working class; or those between factions that are spun off by the inevitable tensions generated by the accumulation process. There is, in other words, a history of structures waiting investigation. This is a history which would focus on their necessary conditions in the shifting dynamics of the accumulation process, conditions possibly entailed by previous 'solutions' to its contradictions, but always to be understood in terms of their own contradictory nature and eventual supersession or transformation.

The work that I did with Andy Wood (1997) on what we called the local economic development network provides a useful case in point. What we were interested in were the institutional arrangements through which the inward investment favored by urban growth coalitions actually came about; in other words, its institutional mediation. What we discovered was a division of labor between three different sorts of agents: the gas and electric utilities which had the data banks on potential sites and which therefore served as gatekeepers; the chambers of commerce which provided more locality-specific information, particularly on labor relations; and local governments which provided the incentive packages and permits. We were interested in why these particular agents were involved: the nature of their material interests, in other words; and the governance mechanisms that had come into being to make sure that everyone performed the role assigned to them. It was, in short, a defensibly critical realist piece of research.

However, what we *weren't* interested in and arguably should have been, was the local economic development network as something historical, something that had come into being to negotiate a problem in the accumulation process; an obstacle to its smooth functioning and to the circulation of capital, therefore. To explain it in terms of the interests of the different agents in seeing inward investment come about was clearly not enough. This is because such an explanation would presuppose that there was inward investment to begin with and that it could not occur without their mediation.

A conclusive answer to this question is not clear at present, though one can make some plausible suggestions. Inward investment in the growth coalition sense assumes a particular stage in the development of the capitalist labor process: one where, in virtue of emancipation from dependence on locality-specific availabilities of raw-materials or labor skills there can be some locational discretion. The idea of locational choice becomes plausible: something that would have been less the case in the age of the steam engine. Second, it assumes that firms actually want to expand somewhere else or move their operations, or at least part of them, elsewhere. We know that firms moved around within particular urban areas in response to the need for a physical expansion that current sites did not allow (Gordon 1977). Locating these sites would not have been problematic given the presumed insertion of the business in local networks of communication.

Expansion in a distant location would have been more challenging, though, unless it was a matter of taking over another firm and its physical facilities. Then the problem of information on potential sites looms much larger. Location consultants would have been part of the answer but they would have lacked the specificity of the information that the local economic development network could provide. At the very least, therefore, it is clear that a lot had to happen before the functions performed by the local economic development network could become meaningful.

On the other hand, the local economic development network as it occurs in the United States is only one possible response to this contradiction. With a degree of emancipation from raw-material and skill constraints, firms could expand elsewhere, whether that was in search of new markets or as part of an attempt to recast a firm's (parts-process)[6] division of labor. But this would mean a site search problem. This is obviously a contradiction not unique to American capitalism. Given contextual variability, though, one can well imagine that the structures coming into being to respond to it would be quite variable. Institutions and institutional resources vary. Accordingly, in Great Britain, as Alan Townsend and I (2005) were able to show, there is something very similar to the local economic development network, but the different functions are performed by different agents. The utilities are not part of it, which is reasonable given their long history as nationalized industries with limited interest in locality-specific markets. Rather it is the county and metropolitan borough councils that have the data banks.

This seems to me to be important, not least from the standpoint of doing concrete historical geographical materialist research. Structures need to be situated with respect to the ongoing contradictions of the accumulation process but the same functions can be performed with very different geographic configurations and agent identities. Migratory labor is a common means of securing access to low wage labor reserves but the way it connected Californian firms with Mexican villages was empirically different from the structure relating South African mines and the former native reserves (Burawoy 1976). The function was the same: from the American standpoint Mexico functioned like a Bantustan; but the institutional configurations were quite different. The US could rely on a historic inter-state boundary and the regulatory functions that went along with it; the apartheid governments of South Africa had to try to construct those boundaries internally in the form of the homeland project.[7]

---

6   A division of labor in which, as Massey (1984) makes clear, different facilities owned by the same firm relate to one another through the transfer of materials and components in various stages of transformation or assembly.

7   And incidentally, given the pervasiveness of state fetishism, that meant that the ethical implications were constructed differently.

The Urban Question

I now want to take this idea of structure, suitably reworked for historical geographical materialism to shed light on the urban question. This re-entered academic debate with a vengeance round about the same time as the different arguments about society and space were being rehearsed by, in particular, Sayer and Harvey. Harvey was once again involved but this time the antagonist was the sociologist Peter Saunders. The urban question, it will be recalled, revolved around whether or not one could defensibly talk about urban processes. For Saunders (1981; 1985) the idea that one could was the foundational myth of the various 'urbans' in the social sciences: urban sociology, urban economics and so on. Rather for him cities were simply, in the language of critical realism, contingent conditions affecting the form and intensity of expression of more general social processes. For Harvey (1985c), it was otherwise. There were indeed specifically urban processes. These depended in the first place on the productive advantages of cities: notably the various economies of agglomeration that they generated. And in the second place, on the development of interests in the preservation of those advantages *in particular cases*. It was this, he argued, that generated a relatively autonomous urban politics. Those with interests in the reproduction of that particular structured coherence – as he called it – which facilitated their accumulation projects, would come together in a coalition to defend it and to ensure its viability in the face of a development process that was inevitably spatially uneven.

What I am going to suggest is that neither position is entirely satisfactory, though Harvey comes closest to a defensible resolution of the issue. This is because he sees the urban as a crucial structure of social relations from the standpoint of the accumulation process. The issue of fixity, though, is beside the point. Even without fixity the urban will generate its own distinctive politics, though whether that will be at the level of the individual city or not will vary.

To address first the urban as a crucial structure of social relations: Like other structures of social relations under capital, it is there because of its significance for the accumulation process. Capitalism develops through the development of the productive forces and the primary way it does that is through the socialization of production. This means two related things. The first is the division of labor. As Allen Scott (1982; 1985) has been at pains to point out the fact of size and the achievement of market thresholds allows the vertical disintegration of production and the advantages of specialization, including more specialized means of production. This division of labor between firms can then lay the basis for the development of new products, either through collaboration or through the entry of new businesses drawing upon the skills and knowledges already available in a particular urban area.

The second and related way in which the city socializes production is through the provision of means of production in common. These include shared physical infrastructures: water provision and distribution, sewage systems, highway systems, airports, commuter rail and so on. It also means shared social infrastructures: urban universities channeling students towards white collar jobs, technical schools catering to the needs of engineering firms, fire services with the equipment to service tall buildings and the like.

The fact is, capitals cannot do without cities. Firms relocating their headquarters will do so to a city with similar facilities. To the extent that those facilities, like airline hubs, are lost, then relocation may follow. The same applies to the location of branch plants or research and development facilities. Note, though, that this is different from a dependence on the *particularized* social relations of cities that generate the sort of territorialized agenda that Harvey places at the center of his relatively autonomous urban politics. Rather, the mechanisms through which cities get reproduced, and upgraded in their physical and social infrastructures vary. Harvey identified one but it is not the only one.

How, therefore, might we understand the politics of maintaining those urban fabrics clearly necessary to the functioning of national as well as of particular urban economies? As Harvey outlined, in the US it does indeed work through the creation of a market in urban locations. Cities compete for new investment, both from firms already there and for those coming in from elsewhere. They compete for the reasons that Harvey outlined. There are firms, particularly in the real estate development sector, the utilities, some banks, some major employers who are dependent on a particular, relatively skilled, labor force, which exhibit high levels of local dependence. Facilitating the growth of the local economy through the continual refurbishment of shared infrastructures is of major interest to them. The same applies to urban governments which are heavily dependent through local property, income and sales taxes on the vibrancy of the urban economy. As the geography of uneven development shifts, so what is being offered has to change as well. Having an airline hub wasn't always critical to a city's competitive success. Sectoral change can reap whirlwinds of devaluation to which local growth coalitions seek to respond.

In the United Kingdom and Western Europe more generally it has been different. The local structures of social relations connecting all those who seek salvation through a local growth coalition tend to be much less in evidence, though not entirely absent. On the other hand, those radically decentralized state structures which allow the urban growth coalitions of the US to be effective *are* absent. But the city as a force of production remains important. No matter the degree to which the revenue needs of local governments are externalized to central branches of the state, or firms develop multi-locational forms which reduce their dependence on particular urban economies, the city remains a major means through which firms seek to develop their productivity and so their capacity to accumulate. For a very large part, national economies and therefore central government fortunes depend on what happens in cities.

There *has* to be an urban policy somewhere, therefore. Instead of through a competitive relation between cities, though, it works top down through the planning of urban locations and with a view to the achievement of *national* urban goals. This has been true ever since the immediate postwar period and despite the emergence of some degree of urban competition in the last twenty or thirty years. Accordingly the countries of Western Europe have their national airport policies, national dock policies and railroad policies. Debates about the addition of a third runway at Heathrow or the extension of the TGV network in France are national ones. Major urban initiatives like Canary Wharf, Thames Gateway, 'Le Grand Paris', the redevelopment activities of the Urban Development Corporations of the Thatcher era or the earlier French 'métropoles d'équilibre' are national, orchestrated and largely financed from the center. Urban planning, unlike the American case, has a central coordinating arm that can override local decisions where there is some national interest. National urban planning departments issue advisories to their local branches. Local government plans are vetted by the center. In France local governments *have* to make provision for social housing. In Great Britain national housing targets have been divided up regionally and then locally within regions in order to ensure that new housing will be where it is most needed.

Just how significant this is, is apparent in the recent twists and turns of the British Coalition government's (2011) planning policy. The imposition of housing targets on localities by the previous Labour government had been a sore point among residents in some areas, particularly in what had been the booming Southeast, and one which the Conservative Party had sought to exploit in its election campaign. Accordingly the announcement on the accession of a new coalition government led by the Conservative Party was that local housing targets, imposed top-down, would be scrapped. Henceforth it would be up to local councils to decide how much new housing they wanted to allow. This, of course, is impossible if cities are to function as productive forces. Local electorates have limited incentive to ensure that any housing supply constraints on local accumulation be mitigated. It should come as no surprise, therefore, that the coalition government has now backtracked on this. The jubilation of local residents has given way to dismay as the government has rolled out a new planning framework which decidedly tilts the balance in favor of developers. Local authorities will still be responsible for housing targets as per the original post-election announcement, but now they have to plan for a 20 percent increase in the land available for housing. Planning permission can still be withheld, but if developers appeal to the central government then permission will be granted on grounds of the national interest. The new framework has been attacked by conservation and environmentalist groups on the grounds that it was heavily lobbied for by the construction industry. But the fact remains, if cities are to be allowed to function as productive forces, then there has to be a mechanism for assuring a supply of housing adequate to demand. If nationally enforced housing targets are dispensed with then the alternative is to consign the decisions to market forces.

***

The debates of the early 1980s around society, space and the city were crucial ones in the history of human geography. Yet in many ways the issues raised then continue unresolved. Harvey's claims about accumulation and the capitalist nature of space have been only imperfectly internalized. The status of the urban as a concept typically goes unremarked. They have, however, been ones that have been central to my own work. Yet it is only recently that I have been able to recognize the serious incompatibilities between historical materialism and critical realism and recognize the greater fertility of the former. One of my aims in this paper has been to explore and explain those incompatibilities.

Even so, the critical realist concept of structure is something that can usefully be mobilized by Marxists in their empirical studies. It is through the development and transformation of structures of relations that capital seeks to suspend its contradictions, opening up new space for accumulation where it seemed to have been blocked or diminished in some way. The urban seems to me to be one such structure – a major force of production – and it helps shed critical light on the respective claims of Saunders and Harvey regarding the urban question.

The contradiction between fixity and mobility has been central to Harvey's attempt to spatialize Marx. He has explored its significance in his writings on the geopolitics of capitalism in general and how it is manifest in the emergence of a relatively autonomous urban politics in particular. Yet where and how that contradiction is expressed, the degree to which it is more urban, more regional or more national, for example, can vary. In the US it happens to be experienced much more keenly at the local level than in, say, Great Britain or France. But it won't go away. Cities are of crucial significance to central states. This is because of the role they perform in the socialization of production: a major force of production, therefore.

Capitalist states vary. The United States has a much more decentralized form than most capitalist states. But they remain capitalist and their structures have been reworked, mobilized, in accord with facilitating the accumulation process. This has resulted in different practices in the United States for the reproduction and transformation of the urban in accordance with the changing challenges of the accumulation process than in Western Europe; which is why urban politics is expressed in such sharply different ways, even while it remains an urban politics.

References

Burawoy, M. (1976), 'The functions and reproduction of migrant labor: comparative material from Southern Africa and the United States', *American Journal of Sociology* 81, 1050-87.

Castree, N. (2002), 'From spaces of antagonism to spaces of engagement', in A. Brown, S. Fleetwood and J. M. Roberts (eds), *Critical Realism and Marxism* (London, Routledge), 187-214.

Cox, K. R. and Mair, A. (1988), 'Locality and community in the politics of local economic development', *Annals of the Association of American Geographers* 78, 307-25.

Cox, K. R. and Townsend, A. R. (2005), 'Institutions and mediating investment in England and the United States', *Regional Studies* 39, 541-53.

Cox, K. R. and Wood, A. (1997), 'Competition and cooperation in mediating the global: the case of local economic development', *Competition and Change* 2, 65-94.

Gordon, D. (1977), 'Class struggle and the stages of American urban development', in D. C. Perry and A. J. Watkins (eds), *The Rise of the Sunbelt Cities* (Beverly Hills, Sage Publications), 55-82.

Gough, J. and Eisenschnitz, A, (1997), 'The division of labor, capitalism and socialism: an alternative to Sayer', *International Journal of Urban and Regional Research* 21, 23-37.

Gunn, R. (1989), 'Marxism and philosophy', *Capital and Class* 37, 87-116.

Harvey, D. (1975), 'The geography of accumulation', *Antipode* 7, 9-21.

Harvey, D. (1985a), 'The geopolitics of capitalism', in D. Gregory and J. Urry (eds), *Social Relations and Spatial Structures* (London, Macmillan), 128-63.

Harvey, D. (1985b), 'The urbanization of capital', Chapter 8 in *The Urbanization of Capital* (Baltimore, Johns Hopkins University Press), 185-226.

Harvey, D. (1985c), 'The place of urban politics in the geography of uneven capitalist development', Chapter 6 in *The Urbanization of Capital* (Baltimore, Johns Hopkins University Press), 125-64.

Harvey, D. (1987). 'Three myths in search of a reality in urban studies', *Environment and Planning D: Society and Space* 5, 367-76.

Harvey, D. (1996), *Justice, Nature and the Geography of Difference* (Oxford, Blackwell).

Harvey, D. (2010), *The Enigma of Capital* (London, Profile Books).

Harvey, D. and Scott, A. (1989), 'The practice of human geography: theory and empirical specificity in the transition from Fordism to flexible accumulation', in B. Macmillan (ed.), *Remodelling Geography* (Oxford, Blackwell), 217-29.

Johnson, R. (1982), 'Reading for the best Marx: history-writing and historical abstraction', in R. Johnson, G. McLennan, B. Schwartz and D. Sutton (eds), *Making Histories: Studies in History-Writing and Politics* (London, Hutchinson).

Logan, J. and Molotch, H. (1987), *Urban Fortunes: The Political Economy of Place* (Berkeley and Los Angeles, University of California Press).

Marx, K. and Engels, F. (1845-46. Re-published 1978), *The German Ideology* (New York, International Publishers).

Marx, K. (1857-58. Re-published 1973) *Grundrisse* (Harmondsworth, Penguin).

Marx, K. (1867. Re-published 1976). *Capital Volume 1* (Harmondsworth, Penguin).

Massey, D. (1984), *Spatial Divisions of Labor* (London, Macmillan).

Massey, D. (1985), 'New directions in space', in D. Gregory and J. Urry (eds), *Social Relations and Spatial Structures* (London, Macmillan), 9-19.

Saunders, P. (1981), *Social Theory and the Urban Question* (London, Hutchinson).

Saunders, P. (1985), 'Space, the city and urban sociology,' in D. Gregory and J. Urry (eds), *Social Relations and Spatial Structures* (London, Macmillan), 67-89.

Sayer, A. (1984), *Method in Social Science* (London, Hutchison).

Sayer, A. (1985), 'The difference that space makes', in D. Gregory and J. Urry (eds), *Social Relations and Spatial Structures* (London, Macmillan), 49-66.

Sayer, A. (1987), 'Hard work and its alternatives', *Environment and Planning D: Society and Space* 5, 395-9.

Scott, A. J. (1982), 'Production system dynamics and metropolitan development', *Annals of the Association of American Geographers* 72, 185-200.

Scott, A. J. (1985), 'Location processes, urbanization, and territorial development: an exploratory essay', *Environment and Planning A* 17, 479-501.

Walker, R. (1978), 'Two sources of uneven development under advanced capitalism: spatial differentiation and capital mobility', *Review of Radical Political Economics* 10, 28-38.

PART II
URBAN POLITICS AND LOCAL ECONOMIC DEVELOPMENT IN TERRITORIAL CONTEXT

Chapter 5
Re-Imagining Local Politics: Territorialisation, Economic Development and Locality

Allan Cochrane

Introduction

Why should anyone be interested in local politics?

After all, it's only concerned with the most mundane of activities and is generally tightly constrained by rules, regulations and even directives from on high. And if that is a widespread popular perception (reflected, for example, in persistently low voter turn outs in local elections), how much more is it true of an academic world in which what tends to interest serious students of politics focuses on the national or (increasingly) international relations (or global governance). Even from a critical position outside the mainstream academy, the issue cannot be avoided: why be interested in the local, when it's all really global, or (as Ralph Miliband suggested) all just the capitalist state (Miliband 1969)?

The best that is possible seems to be the promise that easier access at local level allows for the exploration of political processes that illuminate wider processes of governance – not only is it all a bit more manageable, but it is easier to persuade the various political actors to talk to you (see, for example, John 2009).

And yet, the local and local politics (sometimes labelled urban politics) stubbornly keep reappearing as issues in their own right, with a degree of autonomy that is sometimes capable of upsetting the apparent certainties of national politics, and sometimes even the apparently inexorable 'rolling out' of neo-liberalism.

It is with attempts to resolve this apparent paradox that this chapter is concerned. Although it begins with a personal detour into the British experience, the issue is not one that is restricted to British debates – on the contrary (as will be clear) there is a long and impressive history of authors seeking to rescue local politics from the dead hand of the local government experts, developing political geographies which point to the wider possibilities (and challenges) of place-based politics. Rather than identifying local politics as some sort of backwater the 'local' or 'urban' are understood as dynamic political spaces within which and across which a range of class and other interests play, space itself becomes an actor – from his earliest writings Kevin Cox identified the difference that locality made to voting behaviour (Cox 1969) before going on to develop a wider concern with the ways in which x defined and were defined by y practices, etc.

But this is to jump ahead of the story. What follows is a tale of one person's attempt to grasp some of the complexities and significance of local politics, to understand how the political geographies of the local are made up, not by institutional structures (however important) but by the practices of social relations...And it starts with a particular set of problems.

Trying to Make Sense of It All

In the mid-1980s, I was trying to make sense of what was going on in the British local state in the context of wider sets of political and economic changes (Thatcherism on the one hand and the new urban left on the other).

In Britain in the early 1980s it was the 'new urban left', associated with a range of city councils (including the Greater London Council, Lambeth, Sheffield, Manchester and Liverpool) which set out directly to challenge the logic of what Stuart Hall so memorably described as the 'authoritarian populist' ideological hegemony of Thatcherism and the Thatcher government (see, for example, Boddy and Fudge 1984; Cochrane 1986; Gyford 1985; Lansley et al. 1989). They were duly cut down to size, as some were abolished and others brought to heel through draconian financial controls and privatisation. But, at the end of the decade, it was local politics that came back to haunt the Thatcher regime, and directly to question its neo-liberal certainties. Who would have thought that political mobilisation around changes to the local tax system (the replacement of the old property based rates system with what was called a community charge levied on individuals, even if it was soon universally labelled the 'poll tax') would have generated riots – the 'poll tax' rebellion (Burns 1992) – which resulted in a statue of Winston Churchill being given a Mohican haircut? The more global message of this particular political moment was confirmed when the image was used as a cover illustration to underline the message implied by the title of Paul Gilroy's book *After Empire* (Gilroy 2004).

The basic frames that were available for thinking about these issues somehow did not seem very helpful or did not seem quite to work, although each pointed to something important. As Patrick Dunleavy noted at the time the dominant tradition in local government studies tended to take the structures of local government for granted, seeking to provide insider stories of local professionals in practice to a captive audience (Dunleavy 1980). The pluralist alternative, at least as represented by Robert Dahl, helpfully identified the existence of a complex political process of 'polyarchy', but it has been justifiably criticised because of the way in which it underestimates the role of structural factors and the extent to which particular groups are excluded from the pluralist game (Dahl 1961; Dahl 1971). One response to this in the British context was to develop rich and carefully modulated studies that drew on the US community power tradition (see, for example, Newton 1976; Saunders 1980), but despite their ambitions to deliver wider lessons, such studies were too easily trapped in the detail of the cases with which they were concerned.

More radical perspectives also raised all sorts of possibilities. Although not strictly concerned with local politics (and in some respects taking an explicitly aspatial position) Manuel Castells famously focused his attention on collective consumption, as a means of defining the urban and identifying an urban politics based around social movements – urban social movements (see Castells 1977; 1978); Cynthia Cockburn more directly set out a framework for local politics in identifying the local state as focus of collective reproduction, allowing her to explore the politics of managing that process, both from the perspective of the local managers and the community activists (mainly women) who made their own claims as part of it (Cockburn 1977); meanwhile Peter Saunders, Simon Duncan and Mark Goodwin worked along related lines in developing the dual state thesis, and exploring its implications. In an unintended echo of Jim Bulpitt's distinction between 'high' and 'low' politics (Bulpitt 1983), they associated the big economic (corporatist) decision-making with the national state and the more specific welfare politics (or social consumption) with the local state, where a more pluralist set of political practices dominated (Saunders 1984; 1986; Duncan and Goodwin 1988).

These interventions helped to open up ways of thinking about local – or what some preferred to label urban – governance in ways that highlighted its political nature. They made it impossible to reduce it to a series of administrative or technical arrangements. They also (explicitly as well as implicitly) began to explore some of the more radical possibilities associated with local politics in its re-imagined form – so, for example, the formation of cross-class urban social movements around issues of collective consumption might directly challenge capitalist logics as they played themselves out in place; the emergence of community politics might offer a means of challenging systems aimed at managing processes of social reproduction; and maybe a relatively pluralist local politics focused on issues of social consumption was possible, potentially also allowing marginal or excluded groups to find some voice.

However, despite these undoubted strengths, some important issues remained underdeveloped: the first relates to the nature of the 'local' or 'urban' which was the subject and object of political processes (for some the 'local' was seen as a level of government or geographical scale; for others the urban was resolutely unplaced, defined in terms of particular forms of 'consumption' or 'social reproduction'); the second relates to the extent to which defining local politics in this way (in a sense as the politics of the welfare aspects of the welfare state) also somehow seems to miss the significance of some aspects of local or urban politics in practice, relating to the local economy or economic development, particularly as what was understood as 'welfare' was being actively redefined (through the prism of competitiveness), globally as well as locally (Buck et al. 2005).

Defining the Local

One way of moving beyond these approaches was more explicitly to focus on geographical difference – on the existence of discrete 'localities'. This was at the centre of some not always very fruitful or conclusive debates in the 1980s and into the early 1990s, particularly framed around a major UK based research programme (on the Changing Urban and Regional System) under the aegis of the ESRC (Economic and Social Research Council). Doreen Massey nicely set out the issues that framed the debates: 'particular places are embedded in wider social structures, are part of broader spatial divisions of labour – a fact they share with other places...each locality brings to that situation its own specific history and its own character...the challenge is to hold on to both the general movement and the particularity of circumstance' (Massey 1984, 8).

For some, like Massey, the task of understanding localities and how they are made up was part of a wider commitment to understanding the political economy of contemporary capitalism, while for others it seemed to offer a means of identifying political processes only loosely related to the pressures of capitalist development, and within which different political identities might be forged. So, for example, Phil Cooke looks for social processes 'that have their source in the local sphere, most notably local or urban social movement' (Cooke 1989b, 268), to the extent that 'locality as one of the bases around which people may mobilise' (Cooke 1989b, 269). Reworking Marx's famous phrase, he sought to identify ways in which localities might become "spaces for themselves' as well as 'spaces in themselves" (Cooke 1987b, 412). In an almost poetic turn of phrase, it was claimed that: 'Localities are not simply places or even communities: they are the sum of social energy and agency resulting from the clustering of diverse interests, individuals, groups and social interests in space. They are not passive or residual but, in varying ways and degrees, centres of collective consciousness' (Cooke 1989a, 296).

More prosaically, Cooke suggested that

> the existence of a local political culture which involves close political and administrative interaction with industry, and policy-making that is disposed to meet industry's needs, may under appropriate circumstances, cause restructuring to happen with more positive effect in A than B (1987a, 74).

Indeed those associated with the ESRC programme effectively seemed to see the existence of local economic policy-making as a surrogate for the existence of locality (Cooke 1989a; Harloe et al. 1990).

The value of this work lies in the extent to which it highlights the possibility of the local as a political space, but its weaknesses are also apparent. The focus is on local results of uneven development rather than seeing it as a continuing process shaping and reshaping what is possible. David Harvey and Neil Smith were particularly scathing about the whole enterprise, with the former describing it as 'mere empiricism directed at purely parochial targets of enquiry' (Harvey 1987, 368) while the latter stressed that the task was 'to construct sustainable generalizations and to judge when these generalizations are no longer sustainable', which was impossible for those resolutely focused on local experiences (Smith 1987, 67). The danger was said to be that such a focus would do little more than deliver a series of discrete case studies, as well as implying a retreat into wider political passivity.

Simon Duncan and Mark Goodwin sought to find a way out of this apparent dead end, noting that 'The uneven development of societies also means that class structures and other social relations are constituted spatially, sometimes in rather specific ways' (Duncan and Goodwin 1988, 73). Because, they said, systems 'are spatially constituted and differentiated, it is necessary for state systems to respond with the development of local states' (Duncan and Goodwin 1988, 69). Since 'social mechanisms are not necessarily universal but can be derived locally' (Duncan and Goodwin 1988, 60), the task was to identify 'causal local processes' (Duncan and Goodwin 1988, 58).

So, where did that leave us? Well, the localities debate pointed towards the significance of the local, of locality, as a focus of political formation and political action, even if it tended to take spatial variation for granted and rather too readily slipped into the construction of 'localities' as social actors in their own right. Duncan and Goodwin began to follow through the logic of uneven development in terms of state systems and, in seeking to move away from the merely empirical and contingent, sought to identify local social and economic logics, too. But quite what this might mean and quite how it was possible to escape from the tyranny of the local as a series of unique cases remained uncertain. In other words the choice seemed to be between some sort of recognition of the importance of the local politics of welfare (connected into a national local government system and sets of professionally based policy networks) or an emphasis on particularity, in which each locality had the potential to develop its own distinctive politics and particular political settlement.

Theorising the Local

It was in this context Kevin Cox's writing of the late 1980s and early 1990s with Andy Mair (and building on Cox's longer history of work focused on understanding the significance of the 'local' in urban politics) (see, e.g., Cox 1973; 1978) was so stimulating and helpful, in opening up a means of understanding and exploring the politics of local economic development. Here, instead of seeing 'locality' just as something to be taken for granted was a serious attempt to theorise it, to provide for agency and to distinguish between necessary and contingent and the relationship between them. And here, too, was a way into understanding economic development as a local political issue as much as a national one. If the European debate had tended to define local politics through collective consumption, by contrast from this perspective it became possible to imagine a local politics of production.

In these papers (1988; 1989a and b; 1991) Cox and Mair construct a way of exploring and understanding locality and local politics in ways that builds on Harvey's notion of 'structured coherence'. Harvey's criticism of localities research emphasised what he saw as the danger of a drift into empiricism, a focus on the unique and a celebration of the parochial as politically significant. By drawing on Harvey's own theorisation, however, Cox and Mair were able to reposition locality not only in terms of the consequences of uneven development but also as part of the process of reproducing it.

As they put it:

> Socio-spatial structures of immobility, in combination with geographical delimitations that effectively maintain social relations, are the material bases for the production of actual territories (at various scales). It is through these socio-spatial structures that capitalists obtain profits, landlords gain rents, and workers earn wages. While certain generalized technological and social conditions may obtain, there will be particular socio-spatial structures, located around particular sites, necessary to their maintenance. If socio-spatial structures are limited to a particular scale, such as the local, various economic agents acquire interests that are defined at that scale (Cox and Mair 1989a, 126-7).

In other words, 'locations that are initially contingent to each other may come to assume a degree of necessity in their relations...We have tried to capture this idea at the local scale through the concept of 'local dependence' of firms, governments and people' (Cox and Mair 1989a, 126).

Through this process, localities are produced which may only be 'semi-coherent, but [are] nonetheless recognisable' (Cox and Mair 1991, 201). The territory of the 'local' becomes the site of significant political interaction, particularly because it is the locally dependent who are forced to confront, negotiate, form coalitions and possibly even achieve consensus. Although this approach includes the possibility that localities may be 'active in their own right' it is an 'irreducibly political' process – 'it is not just produced, it is struggled over' (Cox and Mair 1989a, 129).

Urban growth coalitions will be organised between groups and organisations which are, in some sense, locally dependent, more or less immobile. This implies not only that people and organisations cannot move very easily, but also that they define themselves (and reproduce themselves in specific ways because of) their particular location. There may be conflicts between different groups at this level (with the possibility of anti-growth coalitions developing over industrial restructuring, or over environmental issues) and it is because of these that business coalitions develop. They are made up of local firms which 'attempt to ward off opposition to their plans for local economic development by forging a consensus based on the co-optation of their potential opponents, a consensus in which the politics of restructuring is conceived of as a competition among localities rather than a struggle within them' (Cox and Mair 1988, 307-8). In places of a politics based on class or other social divisions, this is a process that generates a territorial politics, at local rather than national level.

This (in contrast to some of the other localities work discussed above) usefully highlights how the appearance that localities are active in their own right may be constructed, because of the ways in which locally based alliances are developed and seek to position themselves as the 'voices' of their localities. For Cox and Mair what matters is not simply that localities are produced (or, to use a rather different theoretical language, assembled) but also that they and their meanings are actively struggled over and contested. They highlight the ways in which coalitions may be constructed so that competition (and conflict) is re-imagined to emphasise divisions between rather than within localities. This is a process of consensus building in which the growth coalitions move to remove the possibility of any other way of thinking about the politics of development.

The understanding being developed by Kevin Cox and his colleagues had some similarities with two parallel attempts to characterise the changing world of local or urban politics, but the differences were equally significant. Urban regime theory, for example, was more concerned with the process of alliance construction among urban elites as well as assuming that the 'local' could simply be assumed as a starting point for that process (Stone 1989; 1993) – for Cox what mattered was how the 'local' itself was constructed out of conflict and contestation and how it was located within a wider set of (globalised) social processes. The 'urban growth machine' model (Molotch 1976; Logan and Molotch 1987) also pointed, to structural factors underpinning the working of local politics, but the 'growth coalitions' identified by Cox, always involved wider sets of interests and implied a more contested political space than seemed possible within the 'growth machine' with its overriding emphasis on the importance of property development and land ownership.

Cox's interpretation of the notion of 'locality' begins to make it clear how different places are able to develop their own distinct political arrangements, so that their 'uniqueness' can be acknowledged, while still making it possible to relate that 'uniqueness' directly to wider theoretical understandings, balancing the two sides of the dichotomy identified by Massey and referred to above. It is very helpful in identifying some of the potential bases for local politics in different places. What is interesting here is the way that detailed local knowledge is combined with theoretical approaches, in a model of the way in which empirical research and theoretical analysis can be combined – who would have thought that Columbus, Ohio could deliver quite so much to the world of urban studies and geographical theory? Instead of the local being a backwater, from this perspective it became part of a wider system, no less important than the 'global' which it helped to constitute, just as it in turn was shaped by global processes (see, for example, Cox 1997; 2004).

Conclusions: Just How Local is Local?

Despite the strength of these arguments, however, concerns remain. So, for example, there is a danger that the causal direction assumed in the notion of local dependence may be inverted. Those who are actively involved in growth politics may simply become defined as locally dependent through the research process, rather than being identified because they are locally dependent. The process of looking for locally dependent interests may, in other words, mean we 'find' them, if only because they are our research objects. In this context the notion of 'immobility' as a defining characteristic can be seen to be problematic, since it is likely to vary over time (Massey 2005) and degrees of 'immobility' may be influenced by political success as much as any other factor – some firms, for example, may be 'immobile' because they have the local state in their pocket rather than being interested in influencing the local state because of their inherent 'immobility'. In other words, instead of identifying some necessary relationship of dependence, immobility may be a (contingent) outcome of political processes.

A related critique of this approach (and others which emphasise the necessity of urban growth as a local political driver, see Jonas and Wilson 1999) highlights the problems of its translation to cultures and countries outside the US (see, e.g., Harding 1991). In the countries of Western Europe local governments are less dependent on taxes raised from local businesses (in the case of England, for example, all business tax is collected centrally before being redistributed to local authorities) and it is much more difficult to find the locally based interests (including financial institutions and development companies) which play such an important role in the analysis. This is something that has been recognised by Kevin Cox as he has developed his work in different contexts, becoming a means of developing comparison without remaining trapped in a specific national paradigm, while retaining a commitment to the significance of territorial politics (see, e.g., Cox 1999; 2004b; Cox and Townsend 2005).

More important, perhaps, like the other writers on locality, there is a real danger that by defining the scope for local (and, by implication, local autonomy) in this way there is a risk of downplaying non-local agents and agencies who may be more important for the local state than any specifically local players. It might, of course, be argued that some branches of non-local corporations are, nonetheless, locally dependent, but the ambiguity of their position highlights the difficulty of conclusively identifying interests in those terms, since the threat of movement is also actively mobilised in negotiations with local governments. The underlying issue is further highlighted in the politics associated with attempts by local governments to encourage corporations to relocate to, or invest in, their areas, since that (of course) assumes that business is not locally dependent.

The recognition that local politics and the local state are not solely concerned with issues of reproduction or welfare is an important one, particularly in a world in which the competitive success of cities is held to underpin the well-being of their citizens (see, e.g., Cochrane 2007, Ch. 6). The identification of a local politics of economic development is persuasive and necessary. However, an overemphasis on this aspect may also be misleading. The networks of public policy that link professionals and politicians across geographical scales and levels of government are vital to any understanding of local politics. In other words, issues of reproduction and forms of welfare (or collective consumption) are significant even if the 'local state' or urban politics cannot be reduced to them, and it is through them that a national system of local government may be constructed (see Cochrane 1993). Cox has from time to time (see Cox and Jonas 1993) considered the possible impact of welfare based (often neighbourhood level) concerns on the local economic development agenda, but it is that agenda, its construction and realisation, with which he is primarily concerned.

Focusing on these concerns and lacunae, however, should not allow us to miss the significance of the insights associated with the approach developed by Cox and Mair in the 1980s and which continues to underpin much of Kevin Cox's work as it has been taken further, taking the notion of uneven development seriously and exploring its implications for political geography (see, Cox 1998; 2001; 2002; 2004a and b). In this chapter the emphasis has been on the local, but Cox's focus on the possibility of territorial politics remains an important insight in a world of flows, networks and stretched relationships. It not only reminds us of the importance of territory in a supposedly increasingly non-territorial world, but actually shows how the making of territories combines the necessary and contingent to deliver the meaning of such a world – the meaning of globalisation as a placed phenomenon, for example in identifying the significance of mediating organisations (see, e.g., Cox and Townsend 2005; Cox and Wood 1997). His work provides a basis on which to explore the increasingly complex interrelationships of negotiation that produce institutional governance arrangements in which the national, regional and local, public, private and third sector are often difficult to disentangle (see Allen and Cochrane 2007; 2010). Above all, it makes it possible to explore the workings of local (and regional) politics without risking the accusation of parochialism, because of the way in which it unapologetically positions them in a wider structural and scalar context.

References

Allen, J. and Cochrane, A. (2007), 'Beyond the territorial fix: regional assemblages, politics and power', *Regional Studies* 41, 1161-75.

Allen, J. and Cochrane, A. (2010), 'Assemblages of state power: topological shifts in the organization of government and politics', *Antipode* 42, 1071-89.

Boddy, M. and Fudge, C. (eds) (1984), *Local Socialism? Labour Councils and New Left Alternatives* (London, Macmillan).

Buck, N., Gordon, I., Harding, A. and Turok, I. (2005), *Changing Cities: Re-thinking Urban Competitiveness, Cohesion and Governance* (Basingstoke, Palgrave Macmillan).

Bulpitt, J. (1983), *Territory and Power in the United Kingdom* (Manchester, Manchester University Press).

Burns, D. (1992), *Poll Tax Rebellion* (London, Attack International/AK Press).

Castells, M. (1977), *The Urban Question* (London, Edward Arnold).

Castells, M. (1978), *City, Class and Power* (London, Macmillan).

Cochrane, A. (1986), 'Local employment initiatives: towards a new municipal socialism', in P. Lawless, P. and C. Raban (eds), *The Contemporary British City* (London, Harper and Row), 144-62.

Cochrane, A. (1993), *Whatever Happened to Local Government?* Buckingham, Open University Press.

Cochrane, A. (2007), *Understanding Urban Policy: A Critical Approach* (Oxford, Blackwell).

Cockburn, C. (1977), *The Local State: Management of Cities and People* (London, Pluto).

Cooke, P. (1987a), 'Clinical inference and geographical theory', *Antipode* 19, 191-9.

Cooke, P. (1987b), 'Individuals, localities and postmodernism', *Environment and Planning D, Society and Space* 5, 408-12.

Cooke, P. (1989a), 'The local question – revival or survival', in P. Cooke (ed.), *Localities. The Changing Face of Urban Britain* (London, Allen and Unwin), 296-306.

Cooke, P. (1989b), 'Locality theory and the poverty of spatial variation', *Antipode* 21, 261-73.

Cox, K. (1969), 'The voting decision in a spatial context', *Progress in Human Geography* 1, 81-117.

Cox, K. (1973), *Conflict, Power and Politics in the City. A Geographic View* (New York, McGraw Hill).

Cox, K. (1978), 'Local interests and urban political processes in market societies', in K. Cox (ed.), *Urbanization and Conflict in Market Societies* (London, Methuen), 94-108.

Cox, K. (ed.), (1997), *Spaces of Globalization: Reasserting the Power of the Local* (New York, Guilford).

Cox, K. (1998), 'Spaces of dependence, spaces of engagement and the politics of scale, or: looking for local politics', *Political Geography* 17, 1-24.

Cox, K. (2001), 'Territoriality, politics and the urban', *Political Geography* 20, 745-62.

Cox, K. (2002), *Political Geography: Territory, State and Society* (Oxford, Blackwell).

Cox, K. (2004a), 'Globalization and the politics of local and regional development: the question of convergence', *Transactions of the Institute of British Geographers* 29, 179-94.

Cox, K. (2004b), 'The scalar politics of local and regional development in the U.S.: How and why it is peculiar', in D. Valler and A. Wood (eds), *Governing Local* and *Regional Economies: Institutions, Politics and Economic Development* (Aldershot, Ashgate), 247-76.

Cox, K. and Jonas, A. (1993), 'Urban development, collective consumption and the politics of metropolitan fragmentation', *Political Geography* 12, 8-37.

Cox, K. and Mair, A. (1988), 'Locality and community in the politics of local economic development', *Annals of the Association of American Geographers*, 72, 307-25.

Cox, K and Mair, A. (1989a), 'Levels of abstraction in locality studies', *Antipode*, 21, 121-32.

Cox, K. and Mair, A. (1989b), 'Urban growth machines and the politics of local economic development', *International Journal of Urban and Regional Research* 13, 137-46.

Cox, K. and Mair, A. (1991), 'From localised social structures to localities as agents', *Environment and Planning A* 23, 197-213.

Cox, K. and Townsend, A. (2005), 'Institutions and mediating inward investment in England and the USA', *Regional Studies* 39, 541-53.

Cox, K. and Wood, A. (1997), 'Competition and cooperation in mediating the global: the case of local economic development', *Competition and Change* 2, 65-94.

Dahl. R. (1961), *Who Governs? Democracy and Power in an American City* (New Haven, Yale University Press).

Dahl, R. (1971), *Polyarchy. Participation and Opposition* (New Haven, Yale University Press).

Duncan, S. and Goodwin, M. (1988), *The Local State and Uneven Development* (Cambridge, Polity).

Dunleavy, P. (1980), *Urban Political Analysis* (London, Macmillan).

Gilroy, P. (2004), *After Empire: Melancholia or Convivial Culture?* (London, Routledge).

Gyford, J. (1985), *The Politics of Local Socialism* (London, Allen and Unwin).

Harding, A. (1991), 'The rise of urban growth coalitions, U.K. style', *Environment and Planning C. Government and Policy* 9, 295-317.

Harloe, M., Pickvance, C. and Urry, J. (eds), (1990), *Place, Policy and Politics. Do Localities Matter?* (London, Unwin Hyman).

Harvey, D. (1987), 'Three myths in search of a reality in urban studies', *Environment and Planning D. Society and Space* 5, 367-376.

John, P. (2009), 'Why study urban politics', in J. Davies and D. Imbroscio (eds), *Theories of Urban Politics* (London, Sage), 17-23.

Jonas, A. and Wilson, D. (eds), (1999), *The Urban Growth Machine: Critical Perspectives Two Decades Later* (Albany NY, State University of New York Press).

Lansley, S., Goss, S. and Wolmar, C. (1989), *Councils in Conflict. The Rise and Fall of the Municipal Left* (Basingstoke, Palgrave Macmillan).

Logan, J. and Molotch, H. (1987), *Urban Fortunes: The Political Economy of Place* (Berkeley, University of California Press).

Massey, D. (1984), *Spatial Divisions of Labour: Social Structures and the Geography of Production* (London, Macmillan).

Massey, D. (2005), *For Space* (London, Sage).

Miliband, R. (1969), *The State in Capitalist Society* (London, Weidenfeld and Nicholson).

Molotch, H. (1976), 'The city as growth machine', *American Journal of Sociology* 82, 309-30.

Newton, K. (1976), Second City Politics: Democratic Processes and Decision-making in Birmingham (Oxford, Clarendon Press).

Saunders, P. (1980), *Urban Politics: A Sociological Interpretation* (Harmondsworth, Penguin).

Saunders, P. (1984), 'Rethinking local politics', in M. Boddy and C. Fudge (eds), *Local Socialism? Labour Councils and New Left Alternatives* (London, Macmillan), 22-48.

Saunders, P. (1986), 'Reflections on the dual state thesis', in M. Goldsmith (ed.), *Urban Political Theory and the Management of Fiscal Stress* (Farnborough, Gower), 1-40.

Smith, N. (1987), 'Dangers of the empirical turn: some comments on the CURS initiative', *Antipode* 19, 59-68.

Stone, C. (1989), *Regime Politics: the Governing of Atlanta 1946-1988* (Lawrence, University Press of Kansas).

Stone, C. (1993), 'Urban regimes and the capacity to govern: a political economy approach', *Journal of Urban Affairs* 15, 1-28.

Chapter 6

Capital Accumulation in Space, Capital-Labour Relations, and Political Strategy

Jamie Gough

Introduction

In this chapter, I give an appreciation of two central aspects of Kevin Cox's work, and link them to parallel and contrasting ideas in my own work. Firstly, I discuss his views on method, which he has developed in critiquing other authors, but also exemplified in his own subtle analyses. Cox insists that concrete studies must be based on – and feed into – an elaboration of abstract concepts if they are not to fall into mere description. In particular, he emphasises the importance of the abstractions of Marxist political-economy, and the need to elaborate medium-level concepts such as 'spaces of dependence'. But Cox's concern with abstraction does not lead him to neglect empirical detail and difference: precisely the opposite. Cox has also shown the importance of necessary relations in social analysis, and how one can relate them to contingencies dialectically, avoiding a simple dualism of the two. His work is always concerned to find the internal relations of social-spatial processes which are often analysed separately.

This method leads to my second focus: Cox's emphasis on the importance of capital accumulation in production, particularly as analysed by Marx in *Capital,* to all aspects of spatial economics and politics. He argues, with Marx, that one needs to go beneath the appearance of capitalism as markets and prices into the realm of *production* and its social relations and technologies. Economic competitiveness, then, appears not only as reduction of input costs but as achievement of increasing productivity and value added. He therefore emphasises the importance of accumulation through mechanisation, innovation and skill, rather than through wage restraint and intensification of work. On this basis, he criticises much radical geographical and economic literature for focusing on prices, costs and the distribution of income between the classes rather than the materiality of production. He critiques accounts of the contemporary space economy which privilege capital mobility, cost cutting and so-called 'low road' strategies, and which picture local economies and economic actors as simply subordinate to these 'global' pressures. He argues that many local economies use 'high road' strategies which shelter them from price competition, and which also make their economic resources relatively immobile. This produces contradictions for the neoliberal project and gives possibilities for (local) democracy. Cox extends this argument by arguing that labour's share of output is mainly dependent on the strength and type of capital accumulation rather than a political balance of forces between labour and capital.

While I agree with the general thrust of Cox's arguments concerning capital accumulation, I have reservations. While 'high road' strategies are very important in the contemporary world economy, with the effects Cox cites, I argue that he downplays capital's discipline of labour – wage restraint and intensification of work, especially in a long wave of stagnation. This results in accentuated uneven development, and instability even in 'strong competition' local economies. Cox therefore does not sufficiently explore the limits and failures of 'high road' strategies. I argue that this lacuna in Cox's work is associated with a limitation of his methodology: that he does not sufficiently analyse variety and change in terms of *systemic contradictions*. I draw out some ways in which failures of 'high road' local economies arise from fundamental contradictions of capitalism. This has implications for political strategy. Cox's analysis can be read as supporting a left-Keynesian strategy of strengthening territorially-embedded 'high road' accumulation. In contrast, my argument implies that the organisation of working class struggle against capital remains essential everywhere, a specifically socialist strategy.

The Relations Between Abstract and Concrete in Social-spatial Analysis

In various works, most of which were written in the late 1980s and early 1990s (e.g. Cox and Mair 1989a; 1989b; Cox 1991a; 1991b), Cox and his collaborators undertook critiques of the methods of many academic urbanists, centring on criticism of their use – or lack of use – of abstraction and of necessary relations. In doing so he developed a method of analysis which he has since fruitfully applied in his own writing. Cox's approach has three key elements. First, he argued that the observable forms of urban politics cannot be understood without the deployment of abstract concepts and processes, themselves grounded in long traditions of academic study. Abstract/concrete is not, however, a dualism: the task of social analysis is to develop a continuous spectrum of abstraction from highly abstract concepts through medium-level ones to concrete analysis, and back again (see also Cox 2001, 748-55).

Secondly, relations between some social entities are necessary ones: for example, industrial capital and wage workers *exist* only in relation to the other, so that their relation is necessary or internal (Ollman 1993). The latter example is of a necessary relation at the highest level of abstraction; but they occur also at lower levels of abstraction. Thus the relation between the state and capital is internal at the highest level of abstraction; the institutional separation between them poses them as external to each other; but at a more concrete level, the state and sections of capital develop forms of dependence on each other which make them necessary to each other's form of existence (Cox 1991b). Similarly, relations between economic actors within a locality may historically be contingent and external; but as their interaction deepens they become conditions of each other's way of functioning (Cox and Mair 1989a). Analysis of any social phenomenon thus requires a careful *teasing out* of what is necessary and what is contingent; there are no short cuts to this end.

Thirdly, through this methodology Cox seeks to both develop and disrupt and many of the dualisms common in social science and geography: use value/ exchange value, economics/ politics, economics/ social life, fixity/mobility, local/ global, and so on. On the one hand he shows the necessary relations between these poles, their mutual construction, as against their empiricist use as separately-given entities; the poles of the dualisms are then no longer pristine, separate entities. On the other hand, he traces their development from abstract to more concrete forms, introducing elements of contingency and well as new necessary relations. Cox does not refer to his overall method as 'dialectics' (possibly as a tactic to avoid scaring Anglo-American academics); but to me his method is splendidly dialectical.

Cox's criticism of much of the New Urban Politics writing of the 1980s accurately portrayed it as positivist and undialectical. This work was not the 'simple empiricism' of pure description; rather, it proceeded through the specification of *medium level abstractions* such as 'urban regime', 'growth coalition', and so on, or Saunders' (1981) division of welfare and accumulation governance respectively between the local and regional-national scales. Following Wright Mills (1959), we may call this method 'abstract empiricism'. The analyst proposes a *model* or ideal type, and then squeezes all empirical examples to fit the model (cf. Gough 1976). But these medium-abstraction models are not constructed from more fundamental social processes (for example the capital-labour relation or local inter-dependence) *developed* in and through particular historical and spatial contingencies (for example US cities in the 1980s). If this were done, then the underlying *dynamics, tensions and limitations* of the 'model' could be understood. Moreover, one could then see the potential contestation of the model, rather than portraying it as in some way structurally determined. And one could see the great variety of possible ways in which the fundamental relations and interests could be expressed in the given historical and geographical circumstances, for example, that a growth coalition may or may not be present in a particular city at a particular time.

Note that Cox is here emphatically not reducing everything to abstractions, as his critics maintained; to the contrary, part of his argument was precisely that the urban theorists he criticised could not account for concrete differences. This, of course, was very different from a postmodern accusation of 'grand narrative'. Indeed, Cox (2005) has criticised postmodernism's take on difference and its rejection of abstraction. He argues that there can be common processes underlying different concrete forms, and that these common processes are essential in theorising, rather than merely describing, difference. A corollary is that there may be *limits* to difference. For example, in a certain sense, there are undoubtedly 'different capitalisms' – different periods of capitalism (Cox 1991a), national or urban regimes, or forms of capitalist enterprise – and these make a significant difference to employment and other outcomes. But no capitalism can escape the processes which are necessary to capitalism as such: the drive to accumulate, competition, exploitation of workers, uneven development, and so on.

More recently, Cox has made a similar critique of the use of Regulation Theory to analyse contemporary spatial political-economy (Cox 2002; 2009). He argues that Regulation Theory posits structures and processes at medium levels of abstraction, but without showing how these arise from more fundamental potentials of capital and the state, weakening their explanatory power (cf. Gough 1996). In addition, the internal relations of economics and politics are not acknowledged and developed. Again, Cox argues that Regulation Theory's lack of attention to fundamentals *also* leads to lack of sensitivity to difference, for instance in conflating structures and changes which have taken place in Western Europe with those in the US. Cox has also made this latter criticism of some of my and Eisenschitz's early writing on local economic policy (Gough and Eisenschitz 1996), in which we wrongly claimed that this scale and focus of state action has emerged in all developed countries during the present neoliberal epoch. He pointed out (private communication) that local economic policy was present in the US many decades before. The class tensions we analysed need to be more strongly differentiated by nation, and more strongly related to different scalar-state structures (cf. Cox 2004b).

Cox's methodological approach has been most fertilely deployed in his concepts of 'local dependence' and 'local coalitions' (Cox and Mair 1991b; Cox 1993), later developed in the ideas of 'spaces of dependence' and 'spaces of engagement' (Cox 1998; 2001). Cox has deployed these concepts with great sensitivity to difference. Thus in examining residents' dependencies in their social lives, he carefully differentiates by people's class, gender and age; in analysing workers' dependencies and their spatiality he emphasises the variety created by, amongst other things, skill, income and age. In discussing firms' dependencies, he does not merely distinguish locally- and non-locally-dependent firms à *la* New Urban Politics, but distinguishes between very different forms of dependence arising from labour processes, customer base, form of the firm, and so on; within *each one* of these basic processes there are, then, major differences which lead to varied spatial dependencies. The important point here is *how* Cox introduces difference. He *melds* the medium-level abstraction of 'space of dependence' (say) with high level abstractions such as class, gender or the labour process, or with medium level abstractions such as sector or form of the firm. The variation of spaces of dependence is then not simply described but theoretically constructed. Once again, it is through dialectic interconnections between apparently separate social entities that Cox produces difference.

Cox's discussion of spaces of dependence and territorial coalitions is not only sensitive to social and economic difference but, connectedly, to different spatial scales. For instance he stresses that territorially-based dependence through different types of social interaction, and engagement of different social actors, may take place at many different scales, not simply the urban (Cox 2001, 755-

60). Again, these scalar distinctions are constructed by internally relating spatial dependence with varied social-spatial relations at different levels of abstraction. One consequence of this approach is that Cox is able to show the *importance* of space (territory, scale, distance) without *reifying* space, that is, without attributing causal powers to space as such.[1] Another consequence is that locality is shown to be constructed by abstract and necessary relations and to *not* be synonymous with the concrete and the contingent.

Cox (2001, 748-53) has used his approach to examine a key debate within meta-geography: at what level of abstraction/concreteness does space enter? He examines Andrew Sayer's (1985) argument which uses a (particular) critical-realist methodology. Sayer notes that space only exists through the objects within it. But 'objects' here are understood as concrete. Space is therefore constituted by the concrete spatial arrangements of objects; space has effects, sometimes major effects, on those objects, but these are contingent. Thus Sayer makes a sharp distinction: some social relations exist at abstract levels, but the effects of space are concrete. Cox counterposes to this a more relational approach (see also Cox 1991a; 1991b). He argues that some abstract processes of capitalist society integrally involve space, use space, and thereby constitute space. For example, the capital-labour relation presupposes both the spatial separation of home and work (the independence of the wage labourer) and certain links between them (the journey to work, reproduction with the wage) (cf. Gough 1991). Harvey's 'structured coherence' of territorial economies integrally involves space, in that relations between economic actors may depend on their proximity and (sometimes) a common culture of the territory. Thus space is involved at high and medium levels of abstraction. Cox attributes Sayer's failure to see this as due to his treating abstract/concrete and necessary/contingent as dualisms rather than developing out of each other (cf. Roberts 2001). Critical realism in this mode has not travelled a sufficient distance from positivism.

In this context, Cox also clarifies his understanding of 'abstraction'. Following Gunn's (1989) exposition of Marx's method, we can distinguish between 'empiricist abstraction' – to leave out *in thought* more or less essential qualities of the objects concerned – and 'determinate abstraction' – in which real social processes themselves disregard these qualities. For example, value in the Marxist sense abstracts from the particular use values of commodities, rendering them as a pure quantity (socially-necessary labour time). This is not an arbitrary abstraction by the theorist, but is *effected by* the exchange of commodities, which in turn is a social practice. Similarly, the market in labour power *creates* 'abstract labour'. Extending this argument to space, Cox argues that in capitalism there are real processes which give space *characteristic* forms at high and medium levels of abstraction. The wage relation, for example, constitutes the home and

---

1 Cox has, however, sometimes used short-hand formulations which can too easily be understood to attribute powers to space as such: 'localities as agents' (Cox and Mair 1991), 'the power of the local' (Cox 1997c).

the workplace as distinct spaces, and constitutes the distance between them as significant. Such 'shapes' of space are therefore not simply empirical regularities (empirical abstractions) but rather are determinate abstractions (cf. Gough 1991). Similarly, the capitalist land market – land as an asset with value – abstracts from the particular qualities of a piece of land by rendering them as a number; this is created by the social practice of monetarised exchange of land, and is thus a determinate abstraction. Though Cox does not refer to his work in this context, this is implicit in Lefebvre's (1991) category of 'abstract space' – the homogenising of space precisely *by* capitalism. Thus Cox criticises Sayer's view of space as being limited both by a failure to develop abstractions towards the concrete, and by an implicit method of empirical abstraction; this is congruent with Cox's criticism, already noted, of the New Urban Politics as abstract empiricism.

Notice that Cox's method of introducing space at abstract levels of analysis is radically different from the abstract treatment of space in the 'scientific geography' of the 1950s and 1960s. In propounding a 'law of distance decay', for example, scientific geography ignored the *real substance* of social processes and, in particular, their historical specificity. This kind of empiricist abstraction has unfortunately continued in many subsequent urban studies, for example in reified notions of 'neighbourhood effects' (for an egregious example, see Partridge and Rickman 2007) or in generic, ahistorical notions of 'community' and 'social capital' (see the critique of Das 2004). In contrast, Cox insists that space can only be considered in relation to substantial social processes; the latter therefore often differ, for example, between capitalism and its antecedents (cf. Lefebvre 1991).

Cox's work shows, then, contrary to what empiricists and postmodernists maintain, that a dialectical method which integrally involves abstract processes and necessary relations can address social and spatial difference. Better, it can *theorise* these differences and their limits, and can map out tensions within, and dynamics of, concrete cases. Moreover, Cox shows how social relations are spatial at all levels of abstraction, thus showing the possibility of genuinely social-spatial *theory*. He demonstrates that 'geography matters' *both* because fundamental social processes are geographical *and* because abstract social–spatial processes can be developed to understand people's concrete experiences and consciousness (Cox 1991b, 303-4).

High Roads, Low Roads, and Class Relations Within Territories

A major body of work in which Cox has deployed necessary and internal relations considers varied social structures in relation to *the accumulation of capital*. In work in the last 15 years, Cox has emphasised the crucial role of capital accumulation in production, in both its quantitative and qualitative aspects, for our understanding of both class relations and spatial economies. In this field Cox is, again, attempting to show the internal relation between processes which are too often analysed as externally related, or indeed analysed quite separately. Here and in the next two sections I will discuss two connected arguments which Cox has made in this vein.

Since the early 1990s, Cox has constructed a powerful argument concerning trajectories of the capitalist economy within territories and the class-political strategies that they imply (Cox 1993; 1995; 1997a; 1997b; 2001; 2004a). The argument may be summarised in three linked points:

1. The Capitalist Labour Process: The Importance of Productivity

Cox follows Marx in arguing that the most profitable and sustainable form of capital accumulation centres on the use of new technologies to create substantial rises in labour productivity *rather than* lowering wages and intensifying the pace of work. In *Capital*, Volume 1, Marx distinguishes between two different paths by which capital can increase the extraction of surplus value from its workforce. The first is 'absolute surplus value' (ASV): the real wage is forced down, particularly by using the availability of unemployed workers; the length of the working day is increased, using fixed capital for longer periods and sometimes lowering the wage per hour; and/or the intensity of work is increased by speed-up and elimination of 'slack time'. These methods are sometimes facilitated by redesigning the work process and the division of labour in order to deskill jobs; this enables less skilled labour to be employed, and the simpler tasks make speed-up easier to impose and to measure. ASV, then, increases the production of surplus value at the direct expense of the worker, in both the reduced wage and in strain on the workers' body and mind within the workplace. Marx's second, broad method of exploiting workers is 'relative surplus value' (RSV). The worker uses machinery rather than tools, and this machinery is subject to constant improvement, enabling large rises in labour productivity (volume of output per worker-hour). The latter lower the value of consumer commodities, and thus allow the value of labour power to be lowered while maintaining a given consumption basket. Thus more surplus value is extracted, but without cutting the living standard of workers and without (necessarily) increasing the intensity of their labour.

Cox uses the ASV/RSV distinction, though without using those terms: he presents ASV as a strategy of cost cutting, and thus in the realm of prices and market exchange, while RSV is a strategy rooted in intensive investment in production. (I shall continue here to use the ASV/RSV nomenclature for conciseness.) Cox also updates the RSV category, by arguing for the importance within it of workers' skill and of knowledge applied to production. The capitalist application of ever-changing machinery to production is often thought to lead inevitably to deskilling, and indeed to have this as aim. But much deskilling is done without change in technologies; and more complex machinery often requires higher skills from the operator as well as from the setter and repairer (Gough 2004a, 156-8). Moreover, in many production processes where machinery is relatively unimportant, worker skill can greatly increase productivity (Rowthorn 1980). In addition, technical knowledge is applied not only to processes but also to product innovation, which can give an edge over competitors and enable prices above value to be charged, reaping technical or design rents (Gough 2004a). Thus if one accompanies Marx in

defining RSV (and its contrast with ASV) as the pursuit of increased productivity
and high value added, then we may, with Cox, say that this production often
requires high skilled labour power and a dynamic development of products as well
as processes.

Marx argued that RSV *rather than* ASV is characteristic of industrial capitalism
in its fullest, most complete and internally-sustainable form. RSV constitutes a
qualitative step forward in the domination of labour by capital – 'real subsumption'
rather than 'formal subsumption'. The use of machinery – and more generally
technical knowledge – enables capital to design the labour process, substantially
taking it out of the control of the worker. ASV, on the other hand, is limited by the
constraints of the physical survival of the worker: the basket of commodities the
worker can afford cannot fall so low that workers (and their dependents) starve
or die of privation, unless there is a supply of new labour power from *outside* the
capitalist system. The intensity and hours of work cannot be increased beyond
what is physiologically and mentally possible, and the level at which the worker
becomes incapable of further work. ASV therefore cannot be deepened and
widened *indefinitely* in a closed capitalist society (though its barbaric limits have
been achieved many times in the history of capitalism). Yet the logic of capital,
according to Marx, is precisely to expand its value indefinitely; and this *can* be
achieved through RSV.

Marx argued that the ASV/RSV contrast is therefore also an historical
trajectory. In Britain, the putting-out system and some early factory production
operated through ASV; but the invention of the large factory using partly
automated machinery signalled a transition to RSV. ASV was possible while there
was a reserve army of labour being created through the eviction of workers from
the land and by rises in productivity in agriculture. But as an industrial and urban
system, ASV production could not sustain its own population. Thus from the mid-
19th century, as RSV rose in importance, real living standards for the working
class could rise in parallel to increases in productivity, and this could enable the
'internal' reproduction of the working class without recourse to immigration from
outside (urban) capitalism. This was the basis for a class alliance between the
organised working class and 'progressive' sections of capital. The urban politics
of Britain from the mid-19th to mid-20th century, in both the workplace and the
residential sphere, was thus profoundly bound up with the contrast between ASV
and RSV and a tendential shift between these forms, powered in part by working
class struggle.

Drawing both of Marx's treatment and – I would guess – this social-economic
history, Cox has argued that RSV is the dominant means of surplus value extraction
in the present day. It is dominant in the sense that the highest rates of profit, and
the most sustainable profits in the medium and long term, are to be made through
this path. It is also numerically dominant within the MDCs. To be sure, there are
also firms and sectors within the MDCs and, *a fortiori*, in the LDCs where ASV
predominates. In this sense, within the MDCs at least, there is a choice of path,
which is a political choice; Cox emphasises the possibilities for RSV paths. He

therefore polemicises against those who see in the contemporary neoliberal world only wage cutting and the degradation of conditions of labour. He criticises those academics who picture wage labour as a simple *market-exchange* relation, the buying and selling of 'labour', while neglecting its essential nature as *production*. This is the theoretical mistake of neo-classical economics, within which 'labour' is a simple cost of production rather than the creator of variable value; neoliberal political ideology rests on precisely this view. It is also the mistake of Ricardians. Ricardo pictured the relation of capital and labour as lying within the labour market rather than production; output per worker is exogenous to this relation; labour and capital therefore compete in a zero-sum game for the distribution of the given product; it is always in capital's interest to drive down the wage. Marx criticised this view for occluding the crucial relation of exploitation within production. Again, Cox follows Marx closely in focusing on production, and emphasising capital's drive to raise productivity.

2. Fixity and Mobility: The Importance of Territorial Embeddedness

Cox's view of contemporary economic geography follows, in a large part, from this emphasis on RSV. The most dynamic capital does not make a priority of seeking out cheaper or more malleable supplies of labour power by relocating to lower-wage regions or countries. It is concerned, rather, to use an experienced, often skilled, labour force, which is more productive, cooperative and innovative than green labour, requiring continuity of production in place. The use of skilled labour on a long-term basis implies good welfare services and housing, reinforcing the logic of remaining in high-income locations. This kind of capital also seeks to benefit from dense exchanges of commodities and knowledge with other firms, and there are often advantages of these being proximate. Spatial agglomeration of production at varied scales thus increases the productivity, quality and innovativeness of production; spatial arrangement is a productive force (cf. with the earlier discussion above) and *intrinsic* to the RSV strategy.

Cox therefore concurs with the theorists of the New Regionalism concerning the possibility and desirability of 'strong competition' rather than cost cutting strategies in the MDCs and even in the LDCs, based on spatial agglomeration (Storper and Scott 1992; Storper 1998; Scott 1998). For the most part, the New Regionalist theorists use institutionalist or socio-economics, focusing on 'untraded dependencies', social habits and rules; they reject Marxist theory, most sharply the Marxist thesis of antagonism between employers and workers (Storper 1999). Cox nonetheless reaches a similar conclusion based on his reading of Marx.

Accordingly, Cox criticises authors who focus solely on the flight of US production to low wage, low unionisation States or abroad (Bluestone and Harrison 1980; Peet 1987). He similarly criticises the World System approach of Wallerstein and others, much of the (connected) World City literature, and the New International Division of Labour (NIDL) literature for over-emphasising or over-generalising capital's search for cheaper and more malleable labour power –

the 'race to the bottom'. Cox criticises these views as Ricardian or neo-classical, in that they assume that location of production is governed above all by minimisation of the costs of factors of production. He argues that, especially in the MDCs, a RSV strategy of continuous technological innovation and application is possible; capital to this extent does not seek mobility but rather to root itself durably in the rich productive interdependences of the MDCs. Moreover, the resultant rises in productivity mean that wages can be raised without cutting profitability, so that capital has no *need* to seek out cheaper sources of labour power. Cox refers back here to the debate in the 1980s, in which a number of Marxists argued that the NIDL School, using Ricardian assumptions, had neglected the attractions for capital of RSV strategies in the MDCs (Jenkin 1984; Gordon 1988). A corollary is that Cox pictures the public discourse of 'globally-mobile production' as being essentially ideological, a cover for capital to drive down wages and conditions.

With his usual attention to difference, Cox has nuanced this analysis. First, he acknowledges the actually-existing persistence of low skill, casualised employment within MDCs. But he points out that many of the latter jobs are in consumer service sectors, the majority of which are necessarily located in the same locality as their consumers, and therefore have no possibility of international mobility. The final market ties of these jobs therefore make it possible for unions to press for better wages and conditions without employers being able to use the threat of relocation (one could cite the Los Angeles janitors, the Las Vegas hotel workers, or many targets of the current London living wage campaign). Secondly, he acknowledges ways in which economic fixities can be eroded or destroyed by mobilities. Following Harvey (1982), he argues that developments in communications, aimed at reducing circulation time of capital, can weaken local ties and facilitate more distant ones. Technical change in production methods or products can also change the forms of production interdependency within territory, at the extreme making them obsolete. Fixity and mobility are, then, in tension. But this complicates, rather than invalidates, an RSV spatial strategy.

3. Strategies for 'Economic Development' and Class-Political Relations

On the basis of this spatial-economic analysis, Cox and collaborators (e.g. Cox and Mair 1989b; Cox 1993; 1995) have argued forcibly for a particular approach to local (city, region) economic development (LED): to pursue a 'strong competition' strategy. Cox does not see this as a panacea. The variety of local economies and political traditions in, say, the US, mean that the possibilities for pursuing an RSV strategy are varied. The positive impacts of such a strategy can be undermined by property capital siphoning ground rents from the technical rents being earned (Cox 1995; 1997a). And the employment benefits of a high-road strategy tend to flow to better-off sections of the workforce rather than the disadvantaged (cf. Gough 1986). But the high road strategy is nevertheless possible.

On this theoretical basis, Cox made his famous criticism of the New Urban Politics, both as the practice of US city and State governments and as academic argument (Cox and Mair 1989b; Cox 1991a; 1991b). This politics as based on an assumption that capital is overwhelmingly set on an ASV path: interested above all in lowering costs, and for this reason highly mobile.[2] Moreover, on this basis local states have focused their economic development policies on attracting inward investment rather than developing indigenous resources, and have done so by offering to cut their costs: the promise of a 'ready' workforce, low wages, state subsidies for land and fixed investment, and, in the case of 'Right to Work' States, the promise of non-unionised labour. The dominant strategy has thus appealed to the supposed 'low road' requirements of potential inward investors. Cox sees this strategy as misleading: it fails actively to provide for and foster high-road development; it wastes state funding on subsidies to cost-cutting firms; and it positions the local state as patron of low wages and poor conditions. In this way, the essentially neoliberal ideas of the New Urban Politics actually undermine better forms of capital accumulation.

Cox is famously reticent about arguing positively for a political strategy. But it is clear that he thinks the 'strong competition', territorially-embedded strategy *should* be pursued, whether at local or national scale, and that this would lead to benefits for wage earners. At the local scale this is clear in his conclusions in Cox (1993), and his support for Stone's (1987) 'progressive' local strategy in Cox (1995). At the national scale, in Cox (1997a, 126) he quotes approvingly Hirst and Thompson (1992) when they argue for national industrial policy with a large role for the state; and he clearly prefers national-developmental industrial models such as those of Germany and Japan beside the liberal Anglo-American model. He describes the RSV strategy in general as 'progressive' (1997a, 131).[3] Although Cox does not express the matter in these terms, he is in effect proposing a class alliance of labour with productivist capital. In Meszaros's (1995) terms, this accumulation strategy expresses the 'universal' side of capital – its ability to develop the productive forces and thus raise living standards for the working class, rather than its 'partial' side – capital's discipline over the working class and their opposed interests.

2　This is not to say that the low road strategy is supported only by mobile capital. On the contrary, academic commentators have pointed to the crucial role in US local politics of certain locally-dependent sectors of capital which have propelled the growth coalitions: utility companies, infrastructure providers, medium scale property companies, local media, and sometimes regionally-limited banks (e.g. Logan and Molotch 1987). We thus have the paradox of capital which is relatively *immobile* seeking to attract *mobile* capital. But notice the *type* of local tie of the sectors leading the growth coalition: they are dependent on local *market demand*; and some of them are inhibited from moving because of their large *fixed capital*. These local ties, then, are very different to the productive linkages highlighted in Cox's RSV strategy and by the New Regionalists. One may suppose, then, that capital supporting the growth coalitions is not, from its own experience, *aware* of the RSV strategy.

3　The editors of this volume have suggested to me that Cox does not *urge* an RSV strategy but rather points out the *possibilities* for it. But this interpretation seems at odds with these texts, and with Cox's argument discussed in subsequent sections below.

Cox (2004a) links the fatalism of ASV strategies to a belief in the inevitable decline of *democracy* in the present period. He has discussed this link at both local and national scales. The New Urban Politics offers, at best, low wage, insecure jobs to local workers, while to local residents it offers reduced welfare services 'to pay for' subsidies to business. This militates against involvement in local politics by the majority of the population, and in some cases business interests directing the growth coalition seek to exclude the general population. At the national level, the argument that 'globalization' is a cost-cutting race to the bottom leads directly to the view that austerity within production and the welfare state is the only way for MDCs to maintain employment. 'Reacting to globalized production', states try to hold down or reduce wages, and offer subsidies to capital to locate within their territory. Reacting to 'globalized finance', governments implement a deflationary policy in order to maintain the value of their currency against attacks by hyper-mobile money capital. This tends to erode democracy: a fatalistic discourse is propagated that impersonal, unstoppable market forces require austerity – 'there is no alternative' – so that democratic debate is ruled out; popular pressure to maintain good jobs and welfare services has to be suppressed through blocking channels of popular representation, and *in extremis* through repression of 'the enemy within' (Cox 1997b; 2004a). Cox retorts that the RSV strategy can – potentially – allow consensual class relations. Wages and spending on public services can rise over time. The state therefore does not need to be authoritarian its actions and undemocratic in its methods.

A Critique of Cox's View of the Relations Between High and Low Roads

Cox's arguments are a powerful corrective to those politicians and academics who accept neoliberal work relations and state policies as inevitable, in particular on grounds of 'globalization'. I agree with his argument on the importance of RSV strategies for capital, and the substantial *im*mobility and territorial enclosure this implies. I agree also that for workers RSV strategy tends to offer better wages and conditions and more-skilled and autonomous jobs than does ASV.

But Cox's argument suffers from an important theoretical, and thus political, problem. He pictures RSV and ASV strategies as essentially *externally-related alternatives*: some capitals (and workers) in some sectors in certain times and places take one path, others take the other, and yet others proceed through hybrids. They therefore present an economic-political-cultural *choice* for both capital and labour. To be sure, firms, sectors and territorial economies may shift between RSV and ASV; but this is due essentially to changes external to them, such as technological change or (spatial-) political regulation. In my view, however, RSV and ASV should be seen as a *contradictory unity*: they are contrary aspects of *all* capital accumulation. As a political strategy, then, labour (and indeed capital) cannot simply *choose* the RSV path. RSV production, especially in its territorially-agglomerated form, faces ubiquitous and permanent contradictions, which tend to push it in ASV directions; this is particularly, though not only, true in (territorial) economic crises. Workers in RSV therefore have to be prepared to organise themselves to oppose capital, rather than rely on their productiveness. To use Meszaros's (1995) terms, capitalism can never escape its partiality. At the methodological level, then, my criticism is that Cox does not take his dialectical approach quite far enough, to focus not merely on complexity and contingency arising *out of* abstract structures, but on *contradictions within them*. I develop this extension of Cox's work by examining his three fields of theorisation above:-

1. The Capitalist Labour Process

Marxist analysis of the capitalist labour process since the 1970s has argued that the relation between capital and labour in production is not merely conflictual but contradictory (Friedman 1977; Edwards 1986; Jonas 1996). This is so in both the labour process and the employment contract. Within the labour process, capital has to elicit some degree of conscious purposive action (initiative, effort) from the worker for to be performed, and especially to be performed rapidly and well; this implies a minimum level of cooperation of the worker with her employer (Manwaring and Wood 1985). On the other hand, the employer must monitor, supervise and discipline the worker to ensure that the quantity and quality of work are sufficient to create surplus value. Control of workers has no point without their cooperation, and their cooperation no point without their control – they are a unity. But they are also opposed: voluntary cooperation is undermined by workers' perception of excessive managerial control, and imposition of discipline is made more difficult the more autonomy the worker has achieved. In every capitalist labour process, then, there is a strictly contradictory (unity of opposites) relation between cooperation and discipline, autonomy and authority (Hyman and Elger 1981). This contradiction is intimately bound up with another lying in the wage contract. The more initiative the worker has, the higher the acquired skill, the scarcer this skill is likely to be, and therefore the better wage and contractual conditions tend to be. Since all capitalist production has to reap surplus value, these cost pressures are never irrelevant.

These tensions mean that capital often seeks to introduce ASV measures. This is most obvious in sectors with combinations of: long production runs of a standardised product; the use of simple, automated machinery which can dictate work pace and quality; jobs which can be designed with fragmented, low skill tasks; slow change and low variety in product and production technologies; and/or labour intensive production. This accounts for the large amount of ASV production in the MDCs, and its dominance in the LDCs. But pressures towards aspects of ASV are present even within RSV-type production (Gough 2004a, 49-63). When RSV sectors introduce new production technologies, the employer has to be able to guarantee a certain pace of work in order to amortise the cost of the production equipment; closer supervision of work and speed-up thus often accompany the introduction of the new production techniques crucial to RSV. In knowledge-intensive labour processes, too much worker autonomy not only gives workers wage-bargaining power but renders them able to work according to their own interests, and potentially move to another firm or set up on their own account. Capital therefore often attempts to deskill tasks, or to split off parts of jobs that can be performed with lower-skilled labour; examples are the software industry in recent decades (Morris-Susuki 1997) or school teaching in Britain (see also Gough 2004a, 156-8).

Such ASV measures in RSV production are particularly common at times when profitability of the (territorial) sector declines: employers often seek to restore profitability by cutting costs, including wages, or by intensifying work through greater discipline. Much of the industrial studies and economic geography literature on high-road production neglects the latter processes: RSV sectors (if not individual firms and workplaces) are seen as operating securely through innovation and technical rents. But erosion of profits in dynamic sectors is inherent in the accumulation of value. High-profit sectors attract more investment, which is uncoordinated between firms, and therefore eventually results in overcapacity, leading to intensified competition and cost cutting (Gough 2004a, 247-51). It is logically impossible for all or most firms to avoid this overcapacity through further technical innovation within the sector (though radical diversification is sometimes possible). Moreover, dynamic accumulation in the economy as a whole leads to downturns, and these impinge negatively even on RSV sectors through cuts in final demand. Thus profit squeezes in RSV sectors are inevitable, and these often result in ASV-type attacks on the workforce (ibid., 159-78, 251-9). These then tend to undermine the cooperation of workers required by the RSV model. This has been only too evident in RSV production in the last 25 years or so, under impulsion of insufficient sustained rates of profit across the world economy. In the more routine jobs in RSV production, especially in capital-intensive manufacturing, 'lean production' has become the norm; while this is often presented by management as job enrichment, it typically involves intensification of work rate and imposed hours of work (Smith 1994). But in higher-skilled RSV jobs, too, the dominant trend has been what Thompson (2010) calls the 'qualitative intensification of labour' through management's better appropriation of workers' tacit knowledge, initiative and emotional labour, and commitment to working 'whatever hours are necessary', requiring much greater effort and with negative impacts on workers' free time (see also Green 2006; Boltanski and Chiapello 2005). Thus RSV class relations, especially in production with strong worker autonomy, are always vulnerable to employer attacks, especially in times of sectoral, local or national crisis.

2. Localities, Fixity and Mobility

Cox argues that for labour RSV is a better local strategy than ASV. But RSV localities have necessary relations to others, and these can be damaging (Gough 1996b). Firstly, if the strategy seeks to capture a larger slice of a national or global

RSV sector, rather than upgrading a local sector from ASV to RSV, this is at the expense of other localities. Secondly, RSV industrial sectors drain value from ASV ones: the technical and design rents realised by RSV sectors are paid by capital and/or labour in other sectors (Gough 1986); and RSV (sub)sectors which are command functions – headquarters, medium and high level finance and business services, property management companies – directly appropriate surplus value from other sectors of the economy (Harvey 1982, chapters 10 and 11). Thus the prosperity of localities which concentrate on RSV is partly at the expense of ASV sectors and the places where they are located (Forbes and Rimmer 1984). The wages of workers in ASV sectors are reduced by their relation to RSV sectors. The point here is that one cannot pursue a high road strategy without considering its impacts on other areas and their workers.

Cox discusses some ways in which the fixity of production within a territory (including RSV production) can be undermined by mobility (1995, 218-20; 2001, 750-1). But the processes he discusses are rather narrowly drawn: changes in technology within a sector, changes in communications which affect the sector (inputs, outputs), changes in the political regulation of trade, and, in a rather different register, better opportunities elsewhere for the sector's capital. What this omits are the ways in which RSV-dominated territories undermine themselves from within, and do so most strongly precisely when they are at their most successful. One way this can happen is through imbalances between economic/social sectors, broadly defined, transmitted through land and labour markets. Insufficient investment in physical or social infrastructures lead to congestion and inflation; high wages in RSV bid up the price of housing and consumer services; lower wage workers, including those working in sectors tied to the locality, find it increasingly difficult to afford to live locally; and capital in sectors which are not RSV or which cannot earn high technical rents is squeezed out (Peck and Tickell 1995; Abdallah, Jackson and Marks 2008). Moreover, the very strength of accumulation tends to generate particularly strong cycles, in the RSV sectors themselves, in commercial property (Lizieri 2009) and in housing. Thus periodic layoffs are to be expected by workers in these localities. In short, there is combined and uneven development between different sectors and their workforces, and uneven development over time, which damage overall accumulation and employment. Again, from the point of view of political strategy, RSV production needs to be assessed in its relations to other production.

Another important way in which RSV regions may undermine themselves is that labour becomes too strong from the point of view of capital (Massey and Meegan 1978; Gough 1996b; Eisenschitz and Gough 1996). This takes us back to the points I made above about the contradictory nature of the labour process. Workers in RSV sectors, particularly those that are locally agglomerated, often develop a sense of their own power to bargain against management. This can take the form of strong union organisation, not only in skilled manual work but in business services and creative industries; or it can take the form of aggressive individual bargaining, or of individual slacking. Moreover, the spatial agglomeration of the sector makes is easier for workers to leave for another firm or to set up on their own account. The labour process thus becomes difficult for the employer to manage. The inflationary pressures of these localities just referred to tend to exacerbate wage-cost pressures. Under these conditions, RSV employers may attempt disciplinary measures against their workforce: job cuts, greater supervision of work, speed-up, partial deskilling, or wage cuts; the offensive against print workers in London in the 1980s is a classic case (for the case of London see also Gough 2004a, 159-64, 197-203, 234-8). Alternatively, employers will be tempted to consider relocation to places where skilled workers are available but where they are less socially concentrated, or where living costs are lower (ibid., 169-78); the relocation of much software production from Silicon Valley is an example. Workers in locally-agglomerated RSV sectors cannot, therefore, assume that they will be immune from the kind of disciplinary measures experienced by ASV workers.[4]

Two conclusions may be drawn from Cox's overall argument. Firstly, mobility and dispersal of production may take place not only because of changes external to that production such as in communications, trade or technologies, but also because of *internal* disruptions, that is, strictly *contradictory* economic-territorial processes. Pressures towards mobility are thus stronger than Cox allows. Secondly, and consequently, Cox does not sufficiently consider the difficulties for localities in carrying out an RSV strategy; these are problems for both capital and, especially, labour.

3. Neoliberalism, Austerity and Democracy

Cox rightly argues (1993; 1995) that neoliberalism is not a reaction to prior 'globalisation', rather that increased international mobility of productive, money and commodity capital is to a large degree a product of capital's neoliberal strategy. He draws the conclusion that a Keynesian strategy which embeds high road production within a territory is feasible, since it is not contradicted by any 'economic fact' of globalisation; accordingly, democracy, as an aspect of Keynesianism, is possible. This second argument appears to me to be questionable. First, as we saw in (2) above, territorially-concentrated RSV production is subject to erosion not merely from neoliberal politics but from its own internal contradictions, which are deeply rooted in capitalist class relations. Secondly, Cox's argument for a high road strategy implicitly regards neoliberalism as a free political choice, so that we can and should make a different choice. But – as Cox is aware – neoliberalism has a profound *logic* for capital in a long wave of economic crisis, such as we have experienced since the late 1960s. Freeing of markets from social-political impediments, including state regulation, promotion of greater capital mobility, fragmentation of economic decision making and individualisation of social life, cutting of state expenditure and privatisation of state employment have been

---

4   I have argued (Gough 2004b) that Harvey, like Cox, downplays the role of inter-class struggle in disrupting the structured coherence of local economies.

aimed at raising the average rate of profit, opening up new profitable accumulation paths, weakening working class organisation, and deflating the politicisation at both national and local levels which was such a notable feature of the early years of the crisis. Thirty-five years after its inception, one has to say that, in these aims, neoliberalism has had very substantial success. By 2008 the average rate of profit in the MDCs had risen from its nadir in the mid-1970s to mid-1960s levels. Capital has flowed into production in new, relatively profitable places and sectors. Working class collective organisations everywhere have been weakened numerically and politically. Neoliberalism, then, is not a narrowly-political choice to which one can counterpose Keynesian democracy; rather, it is the major way in which capital has sought to restore accumulation and re-constitute the class relations which are the essence of the capitalist mode of production.

It may be objected that neoliberalism has been replete with contradictions for capital itself; and that the global credit crunch and recession since 2008 show that it has not succeeded in installing a new, epochal, stable regime of accumulation. I accept these points (on the first see Gough and Eisenschitz 1996; Gough 1996c; 2002). But they do not demonstrate that capital made a *mistake* from the 1970s in going down the neoliberal path. The fundamental contradictions of the capitalist mode of production mean that *any* capitalist strategy has its contradictions and failures; but that strategy may still be the best one available in the circumstances. Neoliberalism appeared to capital as the most promising strategy because it acted *with the grain* of the most fundamental capitalist social relations, namely private property, the law of value, and the discipline of capital over labour.

The logic of neoliberalism can be seen in the effects of economic crisis on RSV production. An average low rate of profit and particularly low rates of profit in specific industries and places have led to attacks on workers' jobs and conditions even in RSV sectors. These have been most dramatic during the deep recessions, including the present one, which have marked the period. These attacks reflect the *value* relations of the long crisis and of the business cycle, that is, basic value relations of capitalism. When profitability is low and competition intense, most capitals will seek to use ASV techniques to increase profitability; and states will attempt to cut spending and reduce taxation, which is ultimately a routing of surplus value away from private appropriation. In this sense, the attacks on (even) RSV workers and the erosion of welfare services have not been a political choice but rather the unfolding logic of capitalism in crisis. The same is true of the erosion of democratic procedures and state repression of labour.

If neoliberalism is a logical path for capital in the present epoch, then there are implications for labour's politics. Labour cannot rely on the beneficial logics of RSV production to improve its economic and political situation. Much ASV production remains; and even RSV employers turn to ASV strategies at various times and places. Labour therefore has to have the collective organisation and political preparedness to confront capital. This is needed not simply to pursue an ultimate goal of socialism, free from the contradictions of capitalism discussed above; it is also needed for the 'reformist' – or more precisely, shorter term –

aims of defending RSV-type conditions of work against capital's attacks, pushing capital towards high roads of accumulation, and achieving a less repressive state. The productive logic of RSV itself is not enough to do this.

I suspect that Cox would agree with most of the individual points I have made in these three arguments. But he seems to put a different theoretical and political interpretation on them, at two levels. First, on the level of methodology, while Cox's writing painstakingly analyses different and contrary processes, and relates these to abstract and necessary relation, he has not carried this through to analysing necessary *contradictions* of the capitalist space-economy, particularly those involving the capital-labour relation. This may owe something to Cox's espousal, at some stages of his work, of a certain reading of critical realism: some critical realists, such as Sayer, have rejected the notion of contradiction as metaphysics. Or it may be that Cox has followed the structuralist tradition inherited from Althusser which deploys 'over-determination' in preference to contradiction.

A second conclusion concerns working class political strategy. The deep contradictions of high road strategies, and their necessary patchy nature within capitalism, mean that labour needs to develop its own power through collective organisation, and needs to have a long term target of socialism. It is certainly feasible and desirable for labour to make local and temporary alliances with sections of capital in order to pursue RSV production and progressive state policies (Eisenschitz 2008). But the working class movement needs to be aware of the limits of such tactics, and in particular that even the most 'progressive' capital may turn against labour (ibid.; Gough and Eisenschitz 2010).

In the final section of this chapter, I will briefly take up an argument of Cox's which is congruent with, and reinforces, his argument on high/low roads.

Labour's Share of Output: How Autonomous is Wage Bargaining from Accumulation?

In his 2004 paper 'Globalization, the class relation and democracy', Cox argues that 'the balance of class forces' – the relative power of capital and labour – is strongly dependent on accumulation within production. Quantitatively, Cox argues that the share out of value created in production between capital and labour respectively (in Marxist terminology S/V, the 'rate of exploitation') is principally dependent on quantity and quality of capital investment. In particular, Cox argues that militancy of (collective) workers cannot reduce S/V substantially except 'in the very, very short term' (ibid., 31). This is because capitalist investment is capable of raising S/V and the rate of profit on capital, through various mediations:

i.   RSV investment which involves new production or product technologies, can increase productivity and thus –
     – reduce the value of consumer commodities, lowering the value of labour power; and

– lay off labour, replenishing the reserve army of labour, thus exerting downward pressure on wages.

ii A decrease in the quantity of new investment and scrapping of capacity –
– can increase unemployment, and thus again exert downward pressure on wages; and
– the scrapping of capacity reduces the quantity of capital with a claim on profit, thus tending to raise the *rate* of profit on capital.

These arguments are derived from Marx's *Capital*: (i) is a part of Marx's discussion of the 'real subsumption of labour' by capital, while (ii) includes two processes which Marx discussed as countering the tendency of the rate of profit to fall in the long term. The processes in (i) are high road accumulation, those in (ii) low road or neoliberal paths; Cox again puts a particular emphasis on the former. Capital is thus able to raise the rate of exploitation not only through using the discipline of unemployment but also through productive investment to lower commodity values and thus reproduce labour power at lower cost. Moreover, through this productive investment and/or through devalorisation of capital assets, the rate of profit can be raised, encouraging stronger capital accumulation.

The implication for labour's politics appears to be that militancy is not the best way to raise the real wage, at least in the MDCs where RSV is central. Rather, the real wage is most effectively raised by labour supporting and promoting RSV strategies for capital accumulation (cf. section 3 above, (1) and (2)). There are important antecedents for this political perspective in the history of Marxist politics: in the Second International before the First World War, Bernstein argued that labour would be economically and politically strengthened by supporting strong capitalist accumulation; and the official Communist Parties from the Popular Front in the 1930s through to the 1970s argued that the workers' movement should ally itself with nationally-rooted capital, particularly industrial capital.

Cox uses this value analysis to criticise what he sees as dominant arguments in economic geography since the 1980s:

a. A Ricardian view of the conflict between capital and labour. In this view, class struggle is about the distribution of value created; the latter is taken as given, exogenous to the class struggle. But Marx showed that, through RSV, *both* the value created *and* its distribution between the classes can be changed. The Marxist approach thus emphasises the process of *production*, whereas the Ricardian approach sees only the process of *exchange*, in this case the sale of labour power. Marx's critique of Ricardo centred on this distinction, arguing that the essence and specificity of industrial capitalism does not lie in market exchange but rather in the relations within production.

b. A focus on trade union organisation and militancy, and a belief that this can substantially raise labour's share of value created. The leftwing of economic geography in the last twenty years has given much attention to workers' organisation. This 'labour geography' has argued that workers are not passive within capitalism, as some left economic geography had implicitly portrayed them (Herod 1997). In particular, workers are sometimes able to make gains at the expense of capital (Castree et al. 2004).

Cox argues against this view: labour's gains, at least in terms of the share-out of value, are undermined by capital's patterns of investment. The mistake of labour geographers is to have ignored the fundamental value processes. This error is implicitly based either on treating industrial relations as a 'factor' which can be studied in itself, separate from capital accumulation; or on a Ricardian view that the distribution of the product is determined within the labour market, studied separately from production. Cox might here have referred back to a major debate among radical economists in the 1970s concerning the role of militant workers' organisation in lowering the rate of profit. Glynn and Sutcliffe (1972) argued that the declining rate of profit in the major countries during the 1960s had been mainly due to the balance of class forces shifting to the benefit of labour, leading to a falling rate of exploitation. This view was extensively criticised by other Marxists as Ricardian, in particular in downplaying the role of rising capital intensity (Mandel 1978).

Cox's arguments here are important, analytically and politically. They caution against reducing left economic geography to a sociology or 'pure politics' of labour organisation. Value relations have effects 'behind the back' of economic agents, particularly workers. But some caveats are needed. Firstly, there is a tension between Cox's arguments (i) and (ii). These are not just different ways of raising S/V, they are *contrary* ways. The low road of deflation is not compatible, *as a strategy*, with the high road of RSV investment and consensual class relations. In particular, while scrapping of capacity, at the level of value, tendentially raises the rate of profit, it also, at the level of the use values of production, disrupts productive interdependencies within the economy, thus decreasing efficiency and productivity and inhibiting the recovery of profits.

Secondly, rising, or even high, unemployment does not *automatically* lead to workers reining in their wage demands. For example, in Britain between the late 1960s and 1985, trade union militancy continued despite high unemployment. The reaction of workers to rising unemployment depends on their long-embedded expectations; under some circumstances it may be a provocation to organise. Moreover, in a parliamentary democracy, workers may put effective pressure on the state to counter unemployment by reflationary measures, and indeed these may be supported by sections of capital. For this reason and the previous one, scrapping and unemployment are not necessarily effective in increasing S/V in the medium term.

Thirdly, an RSV strategy to increase S/V may not occur if the workers' offensive has reduced the rate of profit so low that capital's expectations of future profitability are depressed, and if capital perceives workers as too obstructive within the labour process. For instance, the rate of intensive investment was very low in Britain in the 1970s and first half of the 1980s (Glyn 1989).

Taking these points together, we may conclude that the processes cited by Cox which tend to raise the share of output appropriated by capital are real and important processes. But their unfolding needs to be considered in its historical and geographical specificity, including the consciousness and expectations of both workers and capitals. In their bald form, the logic of Cox's arguments is, as in section 3, towards collaboration of labour with capital pursuing an RSV strategy. As a strategy rather than a local and temporary tactic, this, again, diverts attention from building labour's collective strength *against* capital. The labour geographers are, then, right to see strong workers' organisation as always and everywhere important.

References

Abdallah, S., Jackson, T. and Marks, N. (2008), *The 2008 Regional Index of Sustainable Economic Well-Being* (London, New Economics Foundation).

Boltanski, L. and Chiapello, E. (2005), *The New Spirit of Capitalism* (London, Verso).

Bluestone, B. and Harrison, B. (1980), *Capital and Communities* (Washington D.C., The Progressive Alliance).

Castree, N., Coe, N., Ward, K. and Samers, M. (2004), *Spaces of Work* (London, Sage).

Cox, K. (1991a), 'Questions of abstraction in studies of the New Urban Politics', *Journal of Urban Affairs* 13, 267-80.

Cox, K. (1991b), 'The abstract, the concrete, and the argument in the New Urban Politics', *Journal of Urban Affairs* 13, 299-306.

Cox, K. (1993), 'The local and the global in the New Urban Politics: a critical view', *Environment and Planning D: Society and Space* 11, 433-48.

Cox, K. (1995), 'Globalisation, competition and the politics of local economic development', *Urban Studies* 32, 213-24.

Cox, K. (1997a), 'Globalization and the politics of distribution', in K. Cox (ed.), *Spaces of Globalization: Reasserting the Power of the Local* (New York, Guilford Press), 115-36.

Cox, K. (1997b), 'Globalisation and geographies of workers' struggles in the late twentieth century', in R. Lee and J. Wills (eds), *Geographies of Economies* (London, Arnold), 177-85.

Cox, K. (ed.) (1997c), *Spaces of Globalization: Reasserting the Power of the Local* (New York, Guilford Press).

Cox, K. (1998), 'Spaces of dependence, spaces of engagement and the politics of scale; or, looking for local politics', *Political Geography* 17, 1-24.

Cox, K. (2001), 'Territoriality, politics and the 'urban'', *Political Geography* 20, 745-62.

Cox, K. (2002), '"Globalization", the "Regulation Approach," and the politics of scale: an alternative view', in A. Herod and M. Wright (eds), *Geographies of Power* (Oxford, Blackwell), 85-114.

Cox, K. (2004a), 'Globalization, the class relation and democracy', *GeoJournal* 60, 31-41.

Cox, K. (2004b), 'Globalisation and the politics of local and regional development', *Transactions, Institute of British Geographers* 29, 179-94.

Cox, K. (2005), 'From Marxist geography to critical geography and back again', Presentation to the Critical Geography Conference, Miami University, Ohio, USA, October (mimeo).

Cox, K. (2009), Review of Neil Brenner, *New State Spaces*. *American Journal of Sociology* 115, 931-3.

Cox, K. and Mair, A. (1989a), 'Levels of abstraction in locality studies', *Antipode* 21, 121-32.

Cox, K. and Mair, A. (1989b), 'Urban growth machines and the politics of local economic development', *International Journal of Urban and Regional Research* 13, 137-46.

Cox, K. and Mair, A. (1991), 'From localised social structures to localities as agents', *Environment and Planning A* 23, 197-213.

Das, R. (2004), 'Social capital and poverty of the wage-labour class: problems with the social capital theory', *Transactions, Institute of British Geography* 29, 27-45.

Edwards, P. (1986), *Conflict at Work* (Oxford, Blackwell).

Eisenschitz, A. (2008), 'Town planning, planning theory and social reform', *International Planning Studies* 13, 133-50.

Eisenschitz, A. and Gough, J. (1996), 'The contradictions of neo-Keynesian local economic strategy', *Review of International Political Economics* 3, 434-58.

Forbes, D. and Rimmer, R. (eds), (1984), *Uneven Development and the Geographical Transfer of Value* (Canberra, Australian National University).

Friedman, A. (1977), *Industry and Labour* (Basingstoke, Macmillan).

Glyn, A. (1989), 'The macro-anatomy of the Thatcher years', in F. Green (ed.), *The Restructuring of the UK Economy* (London, Harvester Wheatsheaf), 65-79.

Glyn, A. and Sutcliffe, B. (1972), *British Capitalism, Workers and the Profit Squeeze* (Harmondsworth, Penguin).

Gordon, D. (1988), 'The global economy: new edifice or crumbling foundations?' *New Left Review* 168, 24-64.

Gough, J. (1976), 'Social physics and local authority planning', in M. Edwards, F. Gray, S. Merrett and J. Swann (eds), *Housing and Class in Britain* (London, Conference of Socialist Economists), 87-104.

Gough, J. (1986), 'Industrial policy and socialist strategy: restructuring and the unity of the working class', *Capital and Class* 29, 58-82.

Gough, J. (1991), 'Structure, system and contradiction in the capitalist space economy', *Environment and Planning D: Society and Space* 9, 433-49.

Gough, J. (1996a), 'Not flexible accumulation: contradictions of value in contemporary economic geography, Part 1: Workplace and inter-firm relations', *Environment and Planning A* 28, 2063-2079.

Gough, J. (1996b), 'Not flexible accumulation: contradictions of value in contemporary economic geography, Part 2: Regional regimes, national regulation and political strategy', *Environment and Planning A* 28, 2179-2200.

Gough, J. (1996c), 'Neoliberalism and localism: comments on Peck and Tickell', *Area* 28, 392-8.

Gough, J. (2002), 'Neoliberalism and socialisation in the contemporary city: opposites, complements and instabilities', *Antipode* 34, 405-26.

Gough, J. (2004a), *Work, Locality and the Rhythms of Capital* (London, Routledge).

Gough, J. (2004b), 'The relevance of *The Limits to Capital* to contemporary spatial economics: for an anti-capitalist geography', *Antipode* 36, 512-26.

Gough, J. and Eisenschitz, A. (1996), 'The construction of mainstream local economic initiatives: mobility, socialisation and class relations', *Economic Geography* 76, 178-95.

Gough, J. and Eisenschitz, A. (2010), 'Local left strategy now', in A. Pike, A. Rodríguez-Pose and J. Tomaney (eds), *A Handbook of Local and Regional Development* (Abingdon, Routledge).

Green, F. (2006), *Demanding Work: The Paradox of Job Quality in the Affluent Economy* (New Jersey, Princeton University Press).

Gunn, R. (1989), 'Marxism and philosophy', *Capital and Class* 37, 87-116.

Harvey, D. (1982), *The Limits to Capital* (Oxford, Blackwell).

Herod, A. (1997), 'From a geography of labor to labor geography: labor's spatial fix and the geography of capitalism', *Antipode* 29, 1-31.

Hyman, R. and Elger, T. (1981), 'Job controls, the employers' offensive and alternative strategies', *Capital and Class* 15, 115-49.

Jenkin, R. (1984), 'Divisions over the international division of labour', *Capital and Class* 22, 28-58.

Jonas, A. (1996), 'Local labour control regimes: uneven development and the social regulation of production', *Regional Studies* 30, 323-38.

Lefebvre, H. (1991), *The Production of Space* (Oxford, Blackwell).

Lizieri, C. (2009), *Towers of Capital* (Chichester, Wiley-Blackwell).

Logan, J. and Molotch, H. (1987), *Urban Fortunes* (Berkeley, University of California Press).

Mandel, E. (1978), *The Second Slump* (London, New Left Books).

Manwaring, T. and Wood, S. (1985), 'The ghost in the labour process', in D. Knights, H. Willmott and D. Collinson (eds), *Job Redesign* (Aldershot, Gower).

Massey, D. and Meegan, R. (1978), 'Industrial restructuring versus the cities', *Urban Studies* 15, 273-88.

Meszaros, I. (1995), *Beyond Capital* (London, Merlin).

Morris-Susuki, T. (1997), 'Robots and capitalism', in J. Davis, T. Hirschl and M. Stack (eds), *Cutting Edge: Technology, Information, Capitalism and Social Revolution* (London, Verso), 13-28.

Ollman, B. (1993), *Dialectical Investigations* (New York, Routledge).

Partridge, M. and Rickman, D. (2007), 'Persistent pockets of extreme American poverty and job growth: is there a place-based policy role?' *Journal of Agricultural and Resource Economics* 32, 201-24.

Peck, J. and Tickell, A. (1995), 'The social regulation of uneven development: 'regulatory deficit', England's South East and the collapse of Thatcherism', *Environment and Planning A* 27, 15-40.

Peet, R. (1987), 'The geography of class struggle and the relocation of US manufacturing industry', in R. Peet (ed.), *International Capitalism and Industrial* Restructuring (Winchester MA, Allen and Unwin).

Roberts, J. M. (2001), 'Realistic spatial abstraction? Marxist observations on a claim within critical realist geography', *Progress in Human Geography* 25, 545-67.

Rowthorn, B. (1980), *Capitalism, Conflict and Inflation* (London, Lawrence and Wishart).

Saunders, P. (1981), *Social Theory and the Urban Question* (Hutchison, London).

Sayer, A. (1985), 'The difference that space makes', in D. Gregory and J. Urry (eds), *Social Relations and Spatial Structures* (Basingstoke, Macmillan).

Scott, A. (1998), *Regions in the World Economy* (Oxford, Oxford University Press).

Smith, T. (1994), *Lean Production: A Capitalist Utopia?* (Amsterdam, International Institute for Research and Education).

Storper, M. (1998), *The Regional World* (New York, Guilford Press).

Storper, M. (1999), 'The poverty of paleo-leftism: a response to Curry and Kenney', *Antipode* 31, 37-44.

Storper, M. and Scott. A. (eds) (1992), *Pathways to Industrialization and Regional Development* (New York, Routledge).

Thompson, P. (2010), 'The capitalist labour process: concepts and connections', *Capital and Class* 34, 7-14.

Wright Mills, C. (1959), *The Sociological Imagination* (New York, Oxford University Press).

Chapter 7

The Urban Politics of Global Cities

Delphine Ancien

Introduction

Across the broad theoretical spectrum in the social sciences, and in particular in political and economic geography, scholars have argued that urban (Harvey 1973; 1989; 1996), regional (Florida 1995; Storper 1997; Agnew 2000), city-regional (Scott 2001; Rodríguez-Pose 2008; Harrison 2011), or metropolitan (Veltz 2005; Florida 2008) economies are to be understood as the main loci of contemporary capitalist development in an increasingly globalizing world, and one further characterized by accelerated urbanization. Therefore, understanding urban and regional politics is crucial to our knowledge of the production and (social) reproduction of capitalist economies and their uneven geographies. That is something that has been recognized, investigated and consistently emphasized and developed in Kevin Cox's work from the 1970s onward, through his engagement with a variety of theoretical frameworks, literatures, concepts, empirical foci and places ranging from the workplace to the living place. What has emerged as increasingly pivotal in Cox's thought is the power of historical geographical materialism in addressing urban politics, the significance of issues of scale in understanding these politics and in conceptualizing the role of space in capitalist development, and the importance of understanding cities and urban regions as 'spaces of globalization' (Cox 1993; 1995; 1997; 2004a), as well as 'spaces of dependence' and 'spaces of engagement' (Cox 1998).

The politics of urban and regional development is something that Cox has explored quite extensively in the context of the United States (US) and in particular in the context of the Midwest where he has spent most of his academic career (see, for example: Cox and Nartowicz 1980; Cox and Mair 1988; 1991; Cox and Jonas 1993; Cox and Wood 1994; Cox 1995; Cox 2004b; Cox 2010). Whilst this empirical context may be what people associate most immediately him with, he has had, nevertheless, a profound, although perhaps less known, interest in other places. These include South Africa, as discussed by other contributors to this edited volume. But there is also the United Kingdom (UK), often in a comparison with the US (Cox 2004a; 2009; Cox and Townsend 2005) or with particular attention devoted to London and the Southeast of England – in his graduate seminars for instance – and, especially in the past decade, France (Cox 2008). Their peculiar geographies of uneven development, (territorial) state forms, and national and urban politics, have consistently provided him with food for thought. This is where our respective interests met, both empirically and theoretically: we were both interested in the highly uneven geography of development in France and Britain, including the overwhelming significance of their capital cities, Paris and London, in their respective national space economies.

Those who are personally acquainted with Kevin Cox and/or have worked with him know that he sees the research process as fundamentally iterative. Crucially, for him, students – past and present – contribute to his intellectual stimulation as much as he does to theirs. What I brought to that iterative process and to his historical geographical materialist approach to urban politics was my interest in global city theory in understanding the politics of local economic development in London and Paris, a scholarship that Cox has always been 'intrigued by' whilst remaining 'cautious about'. This is what this chapter is about: the urban politics of global cities.

The chapter itself is divided into two main sections followed by some concluding remarks on the research process. In the first section I provide a brief overview of the development of the world and global city literatures and of some of the major criticisms attached to them, before drawing the contours of a 'Coxian' skepticism vis-à-vis the very concepts of world or global city. I argue that whilst we should remain critical of the world/global city approach, so-called global cities can nevertheless be explored as particular 'spaces of globalization' that are produced and reproduced through a particular logic of accumulation as it unfolds in particular geohistorical contexts, including a pattern of geographically uneven development. In a second section, I ground these theoretical concerns by examining how global cities' urban politics might be investigated, with respect to issues of both production and social reproduction. In this section I draw from elements of my work on London, with particular reference to the politics of mitigating the problem of London's shortages of affordable housing. In the concluding remarks, I return to Cox's contribution to the shaping of my own thinking and the development of my research on the politics of global cities, highlighting the importance and fruitfulness of the 'iterative process' in doing research and the significant potential of comparison for this iterative process.

Revisiting World and Global City Theory and its Critiques: A 'Coxian' Perspective

Whilst New York, Paris, London and Tokyo have a long history of urbanization and have long been at the heart of an abundant literature on the urban, since the mid-1980s they have been redefined and understood by a number of scholars as a new 'type' of cities called 'world' or 'global cities', which are characterized by their very high concentration of the world's advanced producer services, in particular financial and related industries. These are the new drivers of late capitalism under conditions of rapidly increasing globalization, financialization and deregulation of the world economy. Particularly seminal to the development of a vibrant scholarship around this new 'type' of city were the contributions of Friedmann and Wolff (1982; see also Friedmann 1986), who emphasized the functions of command and control of the global economy located in certain cities – defined in particular in terms of the number of transnational corporate headquarters that these cities are home to – which give them a privileged position in the new international division of labor. These world cities are viewed as the key urban nodes through which an increasingly global rather than international economy articulates itself, replacing an old, less integrated and interconnected system organized around national economies. Many scholars operating within the rich world city literature have worked toward shedding light on what exactly are the conditions and factors that lead to the location and concentration of corporate headquarters in these particular cities rather than elsewhere (see, for example, Taylor et al. 2002, on inter-city connectivity and Derruder et al. 2008, on airline networks, or Beaverstock and Smith 1996, on migration patterns of highly-skilled workers). Another key element that has emerged through this scholarship is the role of advanced producer services and, very importantly, financial and related services (Cohen 1981) and their very strong clustering pattern (Thrift 1987; Daniels 1991; Moulaert 1991; Taylor and Walkers 2001) in determining how places rank in the urban hierarchy of world cities (Lyons and Salmon 1995; Beaverstock et al. 1999), potentially lending them the status of what Sassen named 'global cities' (1991). In her seminal book, *The Global City*, Sassen argues that in a world characterized by the increasingly global reach of markets, the need for centralizing corporate functions of coordination and control – including, crucially, financial activities – in a few powerhouses, is also increasingly pressing.

The contribution of the world and global city scholarships to our understanding of late capitalism is as extensively acknowledged as its criticisms. From a political geographer's standpoint the very limited attention paid to the relationship between these cities, their national space economies and their central states constitutes a major lacuna. The assumption often is that such cities operate in a de-territorialized global economy organized through urban networks, rather than within particular national and regional space economies regulated by a state apparatus or supranational authorities (as in the case of the European Union). With some noteworthy exceptions such as Brenner's endeavor (1998) to integrate state theory and global city analysis to understand global city formation as an element of the spatial rescaling of the state (see also Hill and Kim 2000), issues of institutional contexts, state regulation and more generally politics are still often left out of the global city scholarship. This leads to the production of a partial and limited analysis that does not allow for an understanding of what conditions drive, enable or constrain the transformation, development and reproduction of particular cities *as* so-called global cities, i.e. a specific type of urbanization. Part of the issue could have to do with the fact that world/global city theory may not be considered as a theory of the urban. After all, Sassen (1991; 2006), for example, was more interested in the organization of globalization rather than in cities *per se*. Another ontological issue that has been raised by a number of critics is that of what makes a city 'global' or not. Focusing on specific global functions and connections, economic and financial in particular, means that most cities, especially in the 'global South' are left out of the analysis and off the global map of urban studies (Amin and Thrift 2002; Robinson 2002). This also means that an understanding of those cities that are deemed 'global' in the mainstream literature ends up being extremely partial because of the overwhelming focus on global connections of an economic and financial nature, to the detriment of a wide range of other aspects of what we might call 'global*ness*' (Smith 2001; Massey 2007). Even if one holds on to an economic and financial understanding of global cities, 'globalness' should be understood as a dynamic and ongoing process, because many cities are in the process of becoming global cities, at least in certain aspects: they are 'globalizing cities' (Marcuse and van Kempen 1998; González 2009), or 'cities in globalization' (Taylor, 2004). Moreover, one could argue that 'globalness' may not be understood in an absolute way: the 'global' does not necessarily mean the scale of the whole world; it may relate to another geographical or scalar imaginary. For example, some cities do perform 'global city functions' but only with respect to certain parts of the world: Miami, for instance, can be seen as a global city for Latin America. Ultimately, it may prove quite difficult to distinguish clearly what separates world and global cities from those that are not.

The absence of clear cutoffs in determining whether a city is 'global or not' is something that has always made Cox quite skeptical of the very concepts of world city and global city. However, his critical stance would be rooted in a more theoretical concern which has to do with the particular understanding of capital that underpins world and global city theory, which he provides a critique of in his reassessment of the New Urban Politics literature (Cox, 1993): capital as an exchange relation rather than a production relation. The emphasis that this literature puts on the sphere of circulation and on a refashioned version of Massey's *Spatial Division of Labor* (1984) – with a focus on cities this time, and their particular specializations in the international technical division of labor but also the social division of labor between cities that are the loci of global corporate power and 'other' cities – leads to a neglect of a crucial axis of investigation from a 'Coxian' perspective: the accumulation process, of which the class relation and exploitation are fundamental elements. A reassessment of world/global city theory from a 'Coxian' perspective takes issue with its focus on territorial competition and the spatial distribution of market power rather than class exploitation: the dominance of corporate power (in world cities) and representatives of financial capital (in global cities) in particular cities create variations in economic power in the exchange process. Broadly speaking, a consideration of space and the meaning of space for understanding urban development under late capitalism is often limited to the space of competition, with the underlying assumption that competition between places for attracting capital has intensified as a result of the so-called hyper-mobility or footlooseness of capital – financial capital in particular – under late capitalism. In this sense, the mainstream literatures on world and global cities tend to consider space more as a container of social processes rather than a constitutive element of the development of capital.

The critical perspective on world/global city theory inspired and informed by Cox's theorization of capitalism and space that I have just outlined is what initially triggered my interest in and my critical engagement with global city theory. Although I adhere to the critique of an overwhelming focus on exchange relations, I argue that it is worth distinguishing between, on the one hand, the concept of world cities characterized almost solely by their specialization in the technical international division of labor as the hosts of large numbers of corporate headquarters – where capitalism is purely understood in terms of exchange processes – and, on the other hand, the idea of global cities, as originally conceptualized by Sassen (1991), which does relate to an understanding of capital as a production relation to a certain extent. Although Sassen's global city resembles the world city, her understanding of the power embedded in these cities is different: what puts a global city at the top of the urban hierarchy is not the location of the headquarters of the multinational firms that control the global economy; rather, it is its capacity to produce commercial and financial services, to innovate, to come up with new financial products, and to create new ways to make money with money. These commercial and financial services, she claims, are the new drivers of the global economy. The 1980s are a milestone in Sassen's analysis because that was when the financialization of the world economy, long in gestation, really developed, in particular through neoliberal policies such as the deregulation of financial markets in the UK in 1986, nicknamed the 'Big Bang'. So, in Sassen's work, the emergence of these global cities is situated in time and is conditioned by a particular geohistorical material context: that of a financialization of the world economy, made possible through the development of information and communication technologies in particular. Although the sphere of exchange, circulation and flows remains a key to Sassen's global city theory, production relations understood in particular time-space contexts, albeit not central, are not completely absent from it. In this sense, they can be conceived as particular 'spaces of globalization' – something in which Cox has had an interest (Cox 1997) – but also particular 'spaces of dependence' (Cox, 1998) from the standpoint of the embeddedness of financial capital in these cities. This has led me to examine how their specific politics might be investigated, which I discuss in the next section.

Addressing the 'Urban' Politics of 'Global' Cities: a Conceptual Framework

Notwithstanding Cox's critical stance on the understanding of capital that underlies global city theory (i.e., primarily as an exchange relation), I contend that the historical geographical materialist theoretical framework through which he has developed much of his scholarship in the past couple of decades is precisely what helps understand global cities as particular 'spaces of globalization' and how their specific politics might be addressed. As repeatedly illustrated through Cox's work on the politics of local economic development, historical geographical materialism is a particularly compelling interpretive framework for addressing contemporary urban politics because it offers the possibility to situate parts within the context of wholes and to understand at the same time how these parts also produce the wholes. This includes the possibility to make sense of the politics of scale involved in the production and reproduction of so-called global cities by exploring, for example, what exactly is 'urban' and what is 'global' in the urban politics of global cities. I would add that another powerful feature of historical geographical materialism as a framework to understand the urban politics of global cities is that it allows for combining different conceptualizations of capital and for bringing back an understanding of capital as a production relation at the fore of the analysis, in addition to the analysis of exchange relations – including the strong focus on the links that cities have with the global arena through different networks and flows – which typically characterizes the global city literature. Whilst I acknowledge that we need to hang on to the useful link to wider circuits of capital when addressing the urban politics of global cities, an analysis limited to exchange processes, resulting in an overemphasis on flows of money and investment seen as embodiments of capital's increasing mobility, is problematic for understanding the nature of contemporary capitalism and its implications for cities and their particular politics. This is because of its failure to assimilate the centrality of accumulation (Cox 1993) conceived as a complex and situated social process: processes of production, exploitation and competition must be understood in relation to processes of social reproduction and (state) regulation in particular, and within particular time-space contexts. With respect to global cities, this implies that attention must be paid to the particular histories and geographies of specific global cities, characterized by particular spatialities of power and their legacies, beyond and within the city (Allen 1999; 2010).

Bringing together the above theoretical considerations and material from my research on London has led me to develop a conceptual framework to explore the urban politics of global cities that relies on three major axes of investigation. These are discussed in detail in Ancien (2011) and in a summarized form here. First, global cities' urban politics must be examined in the light of the broader historical geographies of capitalism and related patterns of uneven development within which they are embedded. On the one hand, it is crucial to situate an analysis of global cities and their politics within a broader context of the historical development of late capitalism as increasingly globalized, financialized, deregulated, and, arguably, more mobile, although not completely footloose, if we want to understand the very emergence and development of the so-called global cities. But our analysis must also be very sensitive to variegated geographical contexts, including particular national and regional contexts. The mainstream literature on global cities tends to assume that global cities are to a great extent disconnected from the historical development trajectories of their national and regional space economies. There have been some noteworthy exceptions, including, for example, in Abu-Lughod's comparison of global cities in the US (1999), Machimura's work on Tokyo (1992), and one of Massey's latest books on London (2007). In the case of London, one cannot make sense of the development of the city as one of the most important financial centers in the world without taking into account the progressive ascendance of financial capital over industrial capital in the UK since the late nineteenth century (see, for example: Ingham 1984; Leys 1986; Anderson 1987; Cain and Hopkins 1993; Rubinstein 1993). A key element here is the international bias of financial capital 'City-style' and its neglect of domestic industries, which is to be understood against the background of the industrialization of other countries in the nineteenth century, in particular through the overseas investments that the City mediated – largely through the purchases of the bond issues of foreign governments that went into physical infrastructures like railroads in Canada, Argentina, Australia or the US. Whilst this gave the City an early start as a major 'banker of the world', it benefitted from other historical events and trends such as the defeat of the Tariff Reform in 1906, the 'stop-go' economic policies of the 1960s to maintain a strong pound sterling, the development of the Eurodollar and Eurobond markets at the same time (as a result of the heavy constraints imposed by the US federal government to US firms on overseas investment), the 1986 'Big Bang', or more recently the 2002 Sarbanes-Oxley legislation in the US that increased the regulation of listings on the American stock exchanges compared to the more relaxed British ones.

Over time, London has become increasingly attractive to financial and related firms by benefiting from an agglomeration effect. The concept of economies of agglomeration provides insights that are essential to an understanding of historical geographies of accumulation, how they emerge, develop and change over time, and produce new forms of urbanization. London, for instance, is unlikely to lose its position in the international division of labor as a world financial center in the near future, in spite of major shocks such as the 2008 global credit crunch. This is because of the strongly immobilizing effects, creating strong local dependencies (Cox and Mair 1988; Cox 1998), of agglomeration economies for most service industries (Scott 1988), and even more so for advanced producer services (Moulaert 1991), including finance-related activities. This helps understand capital's strong tendencies to fixity in addition to, and in contradiction with, its fundamental tendency to mobility (Harvey 1982; 1985). Therefore, maintaining the agglomeration effect has become a fundamental aspect of the politics of global cities, one that can be highly contentious.

Second, as hinted in the previous point, the lens that we use to understand the urban politics of global cities must be positioned at the intersection of multiple scales, including the urban and the global, but also the regional, the national and the sub-urban understood as the scale of the neighborhood or district for example. One of the interesting developments of global city research in the 2000s has been its 'rescaling' through the idea of global city-regions (Scott et al. 2001; Harrison 2011). Unlike the global city literature that emphasizes solely cities' external linkages, this literature focuses on the cities' internal linkages or functional connections to other towns in their region in addition to their external linkages. Whilst this is a promising development in terms of making global city analysis more 'multiscalar', much more remains to be done to make our understanding of the politics of global cities truly scale-sensitive. The production and reproduction of global cities are indeed embedded in particular national and regional (uneven) geographies of development that cannot be ignored and must be central to our analysis. Going back to the case of London, and its surrounding region – the Southeast of England – is quite illustrative, in particular with respect to the housing problem that the city is experiencing. In the past couple of decades, London has experienced an escalation of its housing prices parallel to no other British city, aggravated by the influx of 'new high-income urban elites' (Sassen 1995: 66) or 'high-income managers and professionals' as well as 'wealthy overseas buyers' (Hamnett 2009: 302), which has driven London housing prices upwards (see also Hamnett 2003), making housing in the city less affordable for those with lower earnings.[1] The increase in single-person households since the 1980s has also created additional pressure on housing demand there (Hall and Ogden 2003; Ermisch and Murphy 2006). Between 1995 and 2007, house prices increased by 233 percent on average (Hamnett 2009). As a result, London has experienced difficulty accommodating more people and ensuring the social reproduction of its labor force, potentially jeopardizing future growth. A major problem for London in dealing with its housing problem has been its limited ability to rely on localities in the broader region to provide affordable housing for London's workers. This is because the Southeast has its own affordable housing shortage problems. These shortages are the product of its own growth since the 1980s – based on high-tech industries and other growth industries like pharmaceutical and health industries, as well as aircraft and aerospace industries, i.e. parallel to, but to a great extent disconnected from, the growth of financial services in London – and of its own politics of the living place that favors low-density housing and the preservation of a semi-rural and small-town landscape. This situation illustrates how an understanding of the politics of global cities necessitates an examination of what is global and what is local or urban, but also regional, national, sub-national, or metropolitan in global city politics. Therefore, not only is the concept of scale crucial to our analysis of the politics of global cities, so is the concept of the 'politics of scale' (Swyngedouw 1997; Delaney and Leitner 1997; Cox 1998), which allows for an understanding of how global cities are always embedded in broader sets of socio-spatial relations that need to be managed if they are to be reproduced.

The politics of scale that has emerged around the necessity to solve London's housing problem is more complex than the difficulty for the city to offload part of it on near-by localities across the Southeast. Stakeholders at the sub-urban scale – i.e. at the scale of the thirty-two boroughs that form the city of London, at the

---

1   Shortages of affordable housing have affected two groups in particular: first, people who have started a family and, as a result, need more living space; second, the armies of low-wage unskilled workers who service, for example, the hotel, catering, office cleaning needs of the financial and related industries (Sassen 1991; 2006), as well as the public sector workers (Massey 2007) such as nurses, firefighters, police officers, or bus drivers, often collectively referred to as 'key workers'.

metropolitan scale – but also at the metropolitan and national scale have different and sometimes divergent interests in the potential solutions to London's housing issue. As a result, this politics of scale is characterized by both conflict and cooperation. For example, most boroughs, which are responsible for delivering planning permissions, have had a tendency to indulge in some sort of exclusionism characterized by a reluctance to promote affordable housing and to put pressure on developers to include affordable housing units in their projects as a condition to be granted permission to build. This may be viewed as NIMBY-ism, but it can also be understood in terms of the lack of incentives for the boroughs to promote residential development: municipal finance in England is ultimately controlled by the central state and any increase in the local tax base is compensated by a reduction in the central government contribution. The attitude of some borough councils (in particular the ones with less developable land) has frustrated the Greater London Authority (GLA) – London's metropolitan government – especially under the leftist mayorship of Ken Livingstone (2000-2008). As a result, the GLA turned to the national government in order to be granted enhanced powers in 2007. The Mayor of London is now able to overcome planning decisions made by the boroughs. The national government – dominated by New Labour at that time – was quite keen to reinforce the GLA's powers because it also has an interest in resolving London's housing problem: mitigating the housing problem to support the reproduction of London's global-city economy is seen as crucial to the preservation of the country's alleged 'golden goose'. The influences, therefore, have moved both up the scalar hierarchy of the state, from the boroughs and the GLA – albeit on their own terms – and down from the national government and, eventually, from the GLA downwards to the boroughs (Ancien 2011). Therefore, the politics of London's housing question is one in which the standard categories of national, local and regional politics make little sense on their own.

Finally, the case of London's housing problem and the politics of scale that has developed around the necessity to mitigate it leads me to the third and last axis of my framework for exploring global cities' politics: the role of the state in shaping the urban politics of global cities must be restored and must feature as a pivot of our investigation. Local states are clearly a key element of our analysis of the politics of global cities as illustrated by the role played by London's boroughs in conditioning potential solutions to the city's housing problem. So is the development of new forms of government, in particular metropolitan or regional governments, such as the establishment of the GLA in London in 2000 and the ongoing development of a metropolitan-wide governing authority of the so-called 'Grand Paris' by the French government. Particular attention must be paid to the politics underpinning the development of such strategic new government agencies: how they are created and for what purposes are important questions to ask when one tries to make sense of the urban politics of these global cities. National states and national governments must also be at the heart of our investigation. Global cities are considered as key drivers of national economies and important pieces of national legislation are produced with a view to protect the continuous development of financial and related industries. This has been the case of monetary policy in Britain, for instance: maintaining the value of the pound sterling as an international reserve currency so as to preserve the City's status as a dealer in pound-sterling-denominated securities and as an international banker is what explains the British government's reluctance to devalue the pound in order to stimulate the export performances of its struggling manufacturing sector from the 1960s on. The same sort of interests motivated the deregulation of capital controls and the liberalization of financial markets in the 1980s or the rezoning of large portions of land for office development like Canary Wharf.

In addition to shedding light on the role played by the state, at different scales, in shaping the material production and reproduction of global cities (and particular geographies of uneven development), we must also explore the range of ways in which hegemonic 'global city discourses' promoted at various scales of the state play a role in framing the urban politics of global cities (Ancien 2011). In the case of London, the 'scalar narrative' (González 2006) or the 'global city rhetoric' that underlies the 2002 London Plan (Gordon 2004) is part of a broader economic geographical imaginary in which London is represented as the 'golden goose that lays eggs for the rest of the country' (Massey 2007). Such a representation is then used to rationalize and to legitimate particular national policies that continue to favor London's financial and related industries often at the expense of other parts of the country, even when the actual contribution of these industries to the national economy is questionable: for the 2006-2007 fiscal year, for example, the estimated total tax receipts for the financial services sector as a whole in the UK was £67.8bn or 13.9 percent of total government tax receipts (PWC 2008). In the aftermaths of the 2008 financial crisis, this fell to £53.4bn or 11.2 percent for 2009-2010 (PWC 2010).

Starting to reexamine global cities from the standpoint of the three major axes of investigation – a list that is by no means exhaustive – aims at producing an analysis of their politics that is particularly sensitive to space, scale and time, and how they impact and shape a broad set of causal processes, rather than being mere 'containers' of social processes. Global cities such as London, Paris or New York represent particular spaces of globalization where global financial capital is embedded – or more embedded than in other places – and this has particular implications for different space economies including the global economy and their own urban economies, but also their regional and national space economies. But London, Paris and New York are also different global cities, and their development paths into so-called global cities have significantly differed. A lot of the global city research so far has tended to reify the concept of global city and thereby detached it from its geographical context(s). This is why unpacking the geohistorical social processes and forces that have conditioned, enabled, constrained the production and reproduction of these particular spaces of globalization must be a priority of future research on global cities. We must ask why and how they have become what they are, and what that means for understanding their specific politics, in particular with respect to social reproduction.

Concluding Remarks: on the 'Iterative Process' of Understanding Global Cities' Politics

Earlier in this chapter I discussed Cox's skepticism vis-à-vis the concepts of world city and global city and the theories that have developed around these concepts. That was very clear from the very first time I talked to him about my interest in using this literature for exploring the very uneven geographies of Britain and France for my doctoral research. His skepticism was a good thing because it triggered an intellectual conversation that carried on throughout my PhD and beyond, one that is quite exemplary of the way Cox conceives the research process: the back-and-forth nature of working with students in particular, which he often refers to as an 'iterative element' of the research process, is, in his eyes, a crucial element of the production of knowledge. Cox's interest in revisiting theories, concepts, empirical material, etc. back and forth is motivated by his desire to build on what happened earlier in Geography and in cognate disciplines, to revisit his own work and the work of other scholars, to improve it and to move forward with newer and better ideas. This is what stimulated, for instance, his interest in Harvey's and Massey's different conceptions of space (see his chapter in this book). His back-and-forth between different theories, ontologies, epistemologies, methodologies and empirical foci highlighted in the different contributions to this edited volume is what allowed for the emergence of new abstractions and new ways of conceptualizing the politics of local economic development and urban politics in particular, always with a view to refining our knowledge of the world around us. This quiet and humble enterprise has produced some ground-breaking contributions to contemporary urban political geography, from the understanding of local dependence in the politics of local economic development in the US that he developed with Mair (Cox and Mair 1988), to his reassessment of the New Urban Politics (Cox 1993), to his theorization of the politics of scale through the concepts of spaces of dependence and spaces of engagement (Cox 1998).

My research on global cities has benefited from Cox's iterative approach in many ways, from the development of research questions and research plans to the revision of ideas as the research progresses, and to the development of the conceptual framework discussed in this chapter. This framework is empirically informed by the work on London, and its relations both to the surrounding region, to the British state and to forces of a more global nature, which I started with my doctoral research. But what led me to revisit and sharpen my ideas to develop a refined conceptual framework for exploring the politics of global cities from a historical geographical materialist standpoint was more of a chance event. It was a call for papers for a series of sessions organized by Martin Jones and Gordon MacLeod on 'The New Urban Politics (NUP) twenty years on' at the 2009 meeting of the Association of American Geographers (AAG), which got me to start thinking about how the NUP literature and its emphasis of the political in its understanding urbanization under late capitalism could contribute to a better understanding of global cities. The initiation of a dialogue, a back-and-forth between the two bodies of work, played an important role in the refining of my thoughts on global cities as particular spaces of globalization and elements of particular geographies of uneven development.

Another increasingly key aspect of this 'iterative process' is the development of a comparative approach to global cities and their politics. This is also inspired by Cox's view on the production of geographical knowledge. Although Cox has not engaged explicitly in comparative studies throughout his career, comparison – whether explicit or implicit – has continuously informed his thought and his work, and its importance has been noted by other scholars in the discipline (Ward 2008; 2010). In the case of the urban politics of global cities, comparing different cities is potentially quite powerful in terms of understanding what is 'global' about them – which aspects of a global city's politics are largely shaped by global forces and/or shape globalization – and what is 'urban', or 'more local' (including national, regional, metropolitan, sub-urban), what is more place-specific about them, what is conditioned by their embeddedness in more local geographical contexts and the history of these places. This is what makes them different global cities with different politics. For example, earlier in the chapter I mentioned the role of the British state in creating the conditions for the increasing dominance of financial capital over (and often at the expense of) industrial capital, notably through monetary policy. The spatial implication of this was to provide the City of London with a clear competitive advantage which allowed for the further growth of expertise in financial services there, leading to its development as a modern-day global city. This has also meant that financial and related services have taken an increasing importance in London's economic fabric, whilst the share of industry has considerably shrunk. This contrasts with neighboring France where governments in the past have regularly engaged in strategic devaluations of the franc in order to stimulate the export performances of its industries, at least until the switch to the euro. Financial capital has developed in France, but not to the extent that it has in Britain, and not in a way that has contributed to the decline of industrial capital as it has in the UK. Unlike London, Paris has remained a major center of industrial production while becoming a world-class center of high-order services including finance. And this has implications for the respective politics of economic development of the two cities.

A lot of work has been done outside of the Anglo-Saxon world on global or globalizing cities across the world. This constitutes an important stock of material that we could build on, use, revisit in a comparative perspective to continue to refine our understanding of global cities and their politics. This would contribute to an internationalization of Geography as a discipline and as a community of scholars. This last point gives the opportunity to conclude the chapter by returning to Cox's contribution to urban political geography and highlighting his own increasing effort in this direction in recent years, reaching beyond the Anglo-American world of geography through engagements with continental European geography and geographers – francophone in particular – echoing a call for internationalization made by other scholars (see, for example: Garcia-Ramon

2003; Minca 2005; Paasi 2005; Samers 2005; Aalbers and Rossi 2006; Fall and Rosière 2008). As Fall and Rosière (2008) note, Anglo-American geography makes great reference to French sociologists and philosophers who have added to spatial thinking including Foucault's theories on governmentality and biopolitics, Latour's actor-network theory, Lefebvre's call for *The Right to the City* (1968), but also Bourdieu, Derrida, Deleuze, Certeau, and Sartre, to name a few. But it is still rare that French and francophone geographers in general see their work used and built upon in Anglo-American geography. By the same token, some key concepts developed in Anglo-American literatures have been notably absent from French geographical scholarship, in particular from urban political geography. This is the case of the politics of scale for instance, which is only starting to be picked up by francophone political geographers. There might be some language barrier here for works that are not translated, but the possibilities are there and the scope for dialogue and cross-fertilization is broad.

References

Aalbers, M. B. and Rossi, R. (2006), 'Beyond the Anglo-American hegemony in human geography: a European perspective', *Geojournal* 67, 137-47.

Abu-Lughod, J. (1999), *New York, Chicago, Los Angeles: America's Global Cities* (Minneapolis, University of Minnesota Press).

Agnew, J. (2000), 'From the political economy of regions to regional political economy', *Progress in Human Geography* 24, 101-10.

Allen, J. (1999), 'Cities of power and influence: settled formations', in J. Allen, D. B. Massey and M. Pryke (eds), *Unsettling Cities: Movement/Settlement* (New York, Routledge), 181-228.

Allen, J. (2010), 'The City and finance: changing landscapes of power', in N. M. Coe and A. Jones (eds), *The Economic Geography of the UK* (London, Sage).

Amin, A. and Thrift, N. J. (2002) *Cities: Reimagining the Urban* (Cambridge, Polity Press).

Ancien, D. (2011), 'Global city theory and the New Urban Politics twenty years on: the case for a geohistorical materialist approach to the (new) urban politics of global cities', *Urban Studies* 48, 2473-93.

Anderson, P. (1987), 'The figures of descent', *New Left Review* 161, 20-77.

Beaverstock, J. V. and Smith, J. (1996), 'Lending jobs to global cities: skilled international labour migration, investment banking and the City of London', *Urban Studies* 33, 1377-94.

Beaverstock, J. V., Smith, R. G. and Taylor, P. J. (1999), 'A roster of world cities', *Cities* 16, 445-58.

Brenner, N. (1998), 'Global cities, glocal states: global city formation and state territorial restructuring in contemporary Europe', *Review of International Political Economy* 5, 1-37.

Cain, P. J and Hopkins, A. G. (1993), *British Imperialism: Innovation and Expansion, 1688-1914* (London, Longman).

Cohen, R. (1981), 'The new international division of labour: multinational corporations and the urban hierarchy', in M. Dear and A. J. Scott (eds), *Urbanization and Urban Planning in Capitalist Society* (London, Methuen), 287-315.

Cox, K. R. (1993), 'The local and the global in the New Urban Politics: a critical view', *Environment and Planning D: Society and Space* 11, 433-48.

Cox, K. R. (1995), 'Globalisation, competition and the politics of local economic development', *Urban Studies* 32, 213-25.

Cox, K. R. (ed.), (1997), *Spaces of Globalization: Reasserting the Power of the Local* (New York, The Guilford Press).

Cox K. R. (1998), 'Spaces of dependence, spaces of engagement and the politics of scale, or: looking for local politics', *Political Geography* 17, 1-24.

Cox, K. R. (2004a), 'Globalization and the politics of local and regional development: the question of convergence', *Transactions of the Institute of British Geographers NS* 29, 179-94.

Cox, K. R. (2004b), 'The scalar politics of local and regional development in the U.S.: how and why it is peculiar', in D. Valler and A. Wood (eds), *Governing Local and Regional Economies: Institutions, Politics and Economic Development* (Farnham, Ashgate), 247-76.

Cox, K. R. (2008), 'The territorialization of politics and what happened in Western Europe', Paper presented at the International Political Geography Colloquium, Reims, France, April 2, 2008.

Cox, K. R. (2009), 'The politics of local economic development', in R. Kitchin and N. Thrift (eds), *The International Encyclopaedia of Human Geography* (London, Elsevier).

Cox, K. R. (2010), 'The problem of metropolitan governance and the politics of scale', *Regional Studies* 44, 215-27.

Cox, K. R. and Jonas, A. E. G. (1993), 'Urban development, collective consumption and the politics of metropolitan fragmentation', *Political Geography* 12, 8-37.

Cox, K. R. and Mair, A. (1988), 'Locality and community in the politics of local economic development', *Annals of the Association of American Geographers* 78, 307-25.

Cox, K. R. and Mair, A. (1991), 'From localised social structures to localities as agents', *Environment and Planning A* 23, 197-213.

Cox, K. R. and Nartowicz, F. Z. (1980), 'Jurisdictional fragmentation in the American metropolis: alternative perspectives', *International Journal of Urban and Regional Research* 4, 196-211.

Cox, K. R. and Townsend, A. R. (2005), 'The English politics of local economic development and the American model', *Regional Studies* 39, 541-53.

Cox, K. R. and Wood, A. (1994), 'Local government and local economic development in the United States', *Regional Studies* 28, 640-45.

Daniels, P. W. (1991) *Services and Metropolitan Development: International Perspectives* (London, Routledge).

Delaney, D. and Leitner, H. (1997), 'The political construction of scale', *Political Geography* 16, 93–7.

Derudder, B., Witlox, F., Faulconbridge, J. and Beaverstock, J. (2008), 'Airline data for global city network research: reviewing and refining existing approaches', *Geojournal* 71, 5-18.

Ermisch, J. and Murphy, M. (2006), 'Changing household and family structures and complex living arrangements', ESRC Seminar Series Mapping the public policy landscape. Available on line at http://www.esrc.ac.uk/ESRCInfoCentre/Images/ESRC_household_tcm6-15384.pdf (First accessed on 17 May 2010).

Fall, J. and Rosière, S. (2008), 'On the limits of dialogue between Francophone and Anglophone political geography', *Political Geography* 27, 713-16.

Florida, R. (1995), 'Towards the learning region', *Futures* 27, 527-36.

Florida, R. (2008), 'The rise of the mega-region', *Wall Street Journal*, 12-13 April 2008, A8.

Friedmann, J. (1986), 'The world city hypothesis', *Development and Change* 17, 69-83.

Friedmann, J. and Wolff, G. (1982), 'World city formation: an agenda for research and action', *International Journal of Urban and Regional Research* 6, 309-44.

Garcia-Ramon, M-D. (2003), 'Globalization and international geography: the questions of languages and scholarly traditions', *Progress in Human Geography* 27, 1-5.

González, S. (2006), 'Scalar narratives in Bilbao – A cultural politics of scales approach to the study of urban policy', *International Journal of Urban and Regional Research* 30, 836-57.

González, S. (2009), '(Dis)connecting Milan(ese): deterritorialised urbanism and disempowering politics in globalizing cities', *Environment and Planning A* 41, 31-47.

Gordon, I. R. (2004), 'Capital needs, capital growth and global city rhetoric in Mayor Livingstone's London Plan', GaWC Research Bulletin #145. Available online at: http://www.lboro.ac.uk/gawc/rb/rb145.html (First accessed on 1 February, 2011).

Hall, R. and Ogden, P. E. (2003), 'The rise of living alone in Inner London: trends among the population of working age', *Environment and Planning A* 35, 871-88.

Hamnett, C. (2003), *Unequal City – London in the Global Arena* (New York, Routledge).

Hamnett, C. (2009), 'Spatially displaced demand and the changing geography of house prices in London, 1995-2006', *Housing Studies* 24, 301-20.

Harrison, J. (2011), 'Global city-region governance, ten years on', in P. J. Taylor, M. Hoyler, B. Derudder and F. Witlox (eds), *International Handbook of Globalization and World Cities* (London, Edward Elgar Publishing).

Harvey, D. (1973), *Social Justice and the City* (Baltimore, John Hopkins University Press).

Harvey, D. (1982), *The Limits to Capital* (Oxford, Blackwell).

Harvey, D. (1989), 'From managerialism to entrepreneurialism: the transformation of urban governance in late capitalism', *Geografiska Annaler, Series B*, 71, 3-18.

Harvey, D. (1996), *Justice, Nature and the Geography of Difference* (Oxford, Blackwell).

Hill, R. C. and Kim, J. W. (2000), 'Global cities and developmental states: New York, Tokyo and Seoul', *Urban Studies* 37, 2167-95.

Ingham, G. (1984), *Capitalism Divided? The City and Industry in British Social Development* (London, Macmillan).

Leys, C. (1986), 'The formation of British capital', *New Left Review* 160, 114-20.

Lyons, M. and Salmon, S. (1995), 'World cities, multi-national corporations, and urban hierarchy: the case of the United States', in P. Knox and P. Taylor (eds) *World Cities in a World System* (Cambridge, Cambridge University Press), 98-114.

Machimura, T. (1992), 'The urban restructuring process in Tokyo in the 1980s: transforming Tokyo into a world city', *International Journal of Urban and Regional Research* 16, 114-28.

Marcuse, P. and van Kempen, R. (2000), *Globalising Cities* (Oxford, Blackwell).

Massey, D. B. (1984), *Spatial Division of Labour: Social Structures and the Geography of Production* (London, Macmillan).

Massey, D. B. (2007), *World City* (Cambridge, Polity Press).

Minca, C. (2005), 'Review essay on key thinkers on space and place', *Environment and Planning A* 37, 168-70.

Moulaert, F. (1991), *The Changing Geography of Advanced Producer Services* (London, Belhaven Press).

Paasi, A. (2005), 'Globalisation, academic capitalism, and the uneven geographies of international journal publishing spaces', *Environment and Planning A* 37, 769-89.

PriceWaterhouseCoopers (2008), 'Total tax contribution: PriceWaterhouseCoopers LLP study of the UK financial services sector for the City of London Corporation', available online at: http://www.cityoflondon.gov.uk/NR/rdonlyres/EA028832-F883-4305-9E4CB4AE7FC9A6C/0/BC_RS_TotalTaxContributionfortheCityofLondonCorp11Feb.pdf (First accessed on 20 January, 2011).

PriceWaterhouseCoopers (2010), 'Total tax contribution: PriceWaterhouseCoopers LLP study of the UK financial services sector for the City of London Corporation', available online at: http://217.154.230.218/NR/rdonlyres/68F49A7E-8255-415B-99A8-1A8273D568D9/0/TotalTax3_FinalForWeb.pdf (First accessed on 20 January, 2011).

Robinson, J. (2002), 'Global and world cities: a view from off the map', *International Journal of Urban and Regional Research* 26, 531-54.

Rodríguez-Pose, A. (2008), 'The rise of the "city-region" concept and its development policy implications', *European Planning Studies* 16, 1025-46.

Rubinstein, W. D. (1993), *Capitalism, Culture, and Decline in Britain, 1750-1990* (London, Routledge).

Samers, M. (2005), 'Dancing on the asymptote, and conveying it: review essay on key thinkers on space and place', *Environment and Planning A* 37, 171-3.

Sassen, S. (1995), 'On concentration and centrality in the global city', in P. L. Knox and P. J. Taylor (eds), *World Cities in a World-System* (Cambridge, Cambridge University Press), 63-75.

Sassen, S. (2001[1991]), *The Global City: New York, London, Tokyo* (Princeton, Princeton University Press), 2nd edition.

Sassen, S. (2006), *Cities in a World Economy* (Thousand Oaks CA, Pine Forge Press).

Scott, A. J. (1988), *New Industrial Spaces* (Los Angeles, University of California Press).

Scott, A. J. (2001), 'Globalization and the rise of city-regions', *European Planning Studies* 9, 813-26.

Scott, A. J., Agnew J., Soja, E. W. and Storper, M. (2001), 'Global city-regions', in A. J. Scott (ed.), *Global City-Regions: Trends, Theory, Policy* (Oxford, Oxford University Press), 11-30.

Smith, M. P. (2001), *Transnational Urbanism* (Malden MA, Blackwell).

Storper, M. (1997), *The Regional World: Territorial Development in a Global Economy* (New York, The Guilford Press).

Swyngedouw, E. (1997), 'Neither global nor local: 'glocalisation' and the politics of scale', in K. R. Cox (ed.), *Spaces of Globalization: Reasserting the Power of the Local* (New York, The Guilford Press), 137-66.

Taylor, P. J. (2004), *World City Network: A Global Urban Analysis* (London, Routledge).

Taylor, P. J., Catalano, G. and Walker, D. R. F. (2002), 'Measurement of the world city network', *Urban Studies* 39, 2367-76.

Taylor, P. J. and Walker, D. R. F. (2001), 'World cities: a first multivariate analysis of their service complexes', *Urban Studies* 38, 23-48.

Thrift, N. (1987), 'The fixers: the urban geography of international commercial capital', in M. Castells and J. Henderson (eds), *Global Restructuring and Territorial Development* (London, Sage), 203-33.

Veltz, P. (2005), *Mondialisation, Villes et Territoires* (Paris, Quadrige, Presses Universitaires de France).

Ward, K. (2008), 'Editorial: Towards a comparative (re)turn in urban studies? Some reflections', *Urban Geography* 29, 405-10.

Ward, K. (2010), 'Towards a relational comparative approach to the study of cities', *Progress in Human Geography* 34, 471-87.

Chapter 8

Policy Transfer in Space: Entrepreneurial Urbanism and the Making Up of 'Urban' Politics

Kevin Ward

Quite clearly any geographic research...needs to be critical of its categories (Cox 2001, 746).

Introduction

It is hard to over-estimate the impact of Kevin Cox's (1991; 1993; 1995) foundational insights into what he labeled 'the New Urban Politics' (NUP). Building on earlier work from outside human geography (see for example Stone and Sanders 1987; Cummings 1988; Stone 1989), he applied his critical realism and historical-materialist Marxist approach to the literature on local economic development, often to the chagrin of his intellectual contemporaries (Fainstein 1991; Stone 1991). This chapter draws on his NUP work, and in particular, his more general concern to unpack taken-for-granted understandings of 'the urban'. It builds on this work by arguing for an approach to urban politics that pays attention to inter-locality politics and the movement of policy across localities, using the example of the Business Improvement District model. The chapter is thus both a critical review of one aspect of Cox's work and an attempt to take it in a direction that he probably did not envisage when writing the key contributions more than twenty years ago.

Business Improvement Districts are territorial alliances, in which property and business owners in a defined geographic area vote to make a collective financial contribution to the area's maintenance, development and marketing/promotion. The impetus for the formation of a Business Improvement District is often the defending of existing, and the capturing of new, flows of value. Individual businesses vote 'yes' (or 'no'). If businesses vote 'yes' they do so as a result of 'some place-based stake in the expansion of the local market, such as arises from the fixity of capital invested in the built environment, ...the non-transferability of markets or of local knowledge and contacts...or the in-situ reproduction of inter-firm and industry-wide linkages (Cox and Jonas 1993, 11). So, differently placed dependent fractions of capital exercise their place-based dependency by voting to collect a levy from each other that can be used to increase revenues (see Harvey 1985; Cox and Mair 1988).

The first Business Improvement District (BID) was established in the Bloor Jane-Runnymede Improvement Area in Toronto, Canada, in 1970. Since then this model of downtown revitalization has spread around the globe. New Orleans was the first US city to establish a Business Improvement District in 1975. Since the early 1990s variations on the US BID model have subsequently been introduced into Australia, Canada, Japan, New Zealand, Serbia, and South Africa (Hoyt 2006; Ward 2007a). At the beginning of the 2000s the UK state announced it would establish a national framework for the introduction of BIDs. By the middle of 2010 over ninety had been established in a range of culturally, economically, politically and socially diverse localities (although another twenty localities had voted against the creation of a BID). At the beginning of 2010 the Dutch government announced it was piloting its own version of the BID, the Business Improvement Zone, with the intention that as of 2012 they will be established in localities around the country. More recently various agents with a stake in the economic fortunes of Sweden's city centers – the Swedish Road Administration, Swedish Property Federation and the Swedish Town Centre Management agency – have been considering whether or not to lobby the Swedish government for BIDs to be introduced into the country, building on its existing network of town centre management schemes (Tunström 2007). These examples of the BID model of downtown governance continuing to appear in geographically discrete locations suggest it has not yet reached its geographical limits.

A number of important questions are raised by the introduction of BIDs in so many different localities around the world over the last fifteen years or so. Some of these questions are about territory. Others are not, however. They are questions about relations *in* localities and *beyond and between* localities. These include: why is it that so many geographically discrete localities have 'chosen' to introduce BIDs, often along remarkably similar lines? In what ways do localities with BIDs learn from each other? What sort of techno-political infrastructure exists to make the international movement of the BID model more likely? What agents are involved in the transference and reproduction of BIDs from one city to another? What are the necessary and the contingent conditions for the creation of BIDs in different localities?

In answering these questions, this chapter takes as its intellectual point of departure the work by Cox (1993; 1995; 1998a; 2001) on the location of the New Urban Politics (NUP) and that on entrepreneurial urbanism (Harvey 1989; Hall and Hubbard 1996; 1998; Ward 2003a; 2003b; 2010). It is organized into three sections. The first, discusses the basics of what Cox (1993) terms the NUP. It focuses on its constitution, on who is involved in it and why, and the sorts of policies that are pursued. The section reviews the entrepreneurial urbanism literature as a means of highlighting this work's contributions and also its silences. The second section addresses Cox's (2001) concern to locate urban politics, taking a slightly different approach from that in much of the literature. It highlights the verticality in the relations behind the formation of territorial alliances and economic development strategies (Cox 2010). The section uses the examples of

Business Improvement Districts and focuses on the means by which strategies around economic development are put together through various evidence-assembling strategies, such as the expansion in number and size of inter-city urban policy networks on the one hand, and, on the other, the growth of policy tourism as a normalized way of learning for city politicians and practitioners. In the third and final section the chapter makes two concluding points. First, it acknowledges that work on the NUP and on local dependence, together with other contributions on territory and the state, has been spectacularly illuminating and insightful. It has set the groundwork for more recent theoretical advances in a number of areas, including that on environmental sustainability (Jonas and While 2007; While et al. 2007; Jonas et al. 2010) and state spatiality (Jones 1997; 1998; Brenner 2004). Second, the chapter argues that work in this vein has tended to under-estimate the inter-urban, cross-scale circuits and webs of policy and program transfer in locating local politics. In conclusion this chapter points to this aspect of the NUP as one worthy of future research.

Assembling the 'New Urban Politics' I: Entrepreneurial Urbanism, Territoriality and Local Dependence

Over the last four decades a large and heterogeneous body of work has been produced on the changing political economies of North American, Western European and, more recently, Asian cities. While building on earlier work from across the social sciences in the Marxist tradition, this more recent scholarship has differed from past work on collective consumption and welfare, what is considered as that on the so called 'old urban politics' (Cochrane 1999; and see his chapter in this volume). According to Cox (1995, 455):

> The NUP has two points. The first is that urban politics is about local economic development...The second point refers to the framework for understanding this politics. Major significance is assigned to relations with more global events.

More specifically, this 'new' variation has had four important defining features. It has paid specific attention to *what* constitutes 'urban politics', *who* – the agents – that participate in it, *why* they are involved, and *what* policies are pursued. Cox (1993, 433) puts it thus: '[q]uite clearly, urban development, for many scholars, is now what the study of urban politics is about.' According to Cox (1995, 214) the substance of the NUP is:

> ...the competition of local governments in metropolitan areas for major shopping malls; the resuscitation of downtowns through public investment in convention centres and enclosed shopping malls and through the promotion of gentrification; the competition of cities for airline hubs as a stimulus to attracting corporate headquarters; and conflicts over the funding of these projects.

In terms of who is involved in the NUP, much has been made of ways in which the state, capital and other agents have worked in unison to oversee a transformation in the ways in which cities are governed, to the point that 'where the local state ends and private firms begin is often very obscure' (Cox and Mair 1988, 311). Terms such as 'alliance', 'coalition' and 'regime' have been used to invoke the structured participation of differently situated agents (Harvey 1985; Logan and Molotch 1987; Stone 1989). These seminal contributions have revealed both the structures that shape the involvement of different agents and the agency each one is afforded in coming to territorial decisions over economic development strategies. The third component to this renewal of intellectual interest concerns different agents' material rationales for participation. Cox (1991, 273; see also Cox and Mair 1988; 1991) developed the notion of 'local dependence', which argues that 'all firms, branches of the state, are locally dependent, that is dependent on a localized set of social relations.' He questioned the assumption that capital is always mobile, which characterized some of the NUP work. Rather, the term 'local dependence' sought to capture the 'fixity' or 'embeddedness' of different interests and how this condition translates – or not – into a particular form of politics. As Cox (1995, 216) explains, 'the interest in the expansion of local economies arises from the existence of capitalist/worker/stage agency interests in the appropriation of profits/wages/taxes in particular places.' The fourth defining feature of the NUP has been an interest in the types of policies pursued by the territorial alliances. While there is evidence of diversity, there are also some common features: 'policies have the usual 'good business climate' menu of tax abatements, cutting 'red tape' and securing the necessary infrastructural investments' (Cox and Jonas 1993, 12).

The nature of this partial, geographically uneven, variegated but apparently commonplace set of transitions from an 'old' to a 'new' urban politics has perhaps best been captured by work on entrepreneurial urbanism. Writing over twenty years ago, Harvey (1989, 4) argued that recent years had seen the emergence of 'a general consensus…throughout the advanced capitalist world that positive benefits are to be had by cities taking an entrepreneurial stance to economic development.' In striving to examine the inter-relationship between the process of urbanization and capitalist social relations and accumulation, Harvey's (1985; 1989) seminal work drew directly on Baltimore and indirectly – through comparison – a number of other cities in the industrialized global north, particularly those in the UK and the US (Ward 2011).

Drawing upon Cox's (1993; 1995) and Harvey's (1989) intellectual interventions, a series of studies have followed that have strived to examine conceptually, empirically and methodologically the ways in which this generalized transformation towards a new politics of entrepreneurial urbanism has occurred across cities of the industrialized global north, and to a lesser extent, the global south. Six themes in particular run through this literature. First, increased attention has been afforded to the changing spaces, scales and subjects of the state (Jones 1997; 1998; Peck 2001; 2003; Brenner 2004). Rejecting claims about the 'hollowing out' of the state, much of this work has sought to underscore the ways in which recent decades have witnessed a qualitative process of state restructuring (O'Neill 1997). The edges of the state have been renegotiated as its various constituent parts have become involved in a myriad of different types of territorial alliances. Drawing a firm line around where the state stops, starts and stops again has become increasingly complicated. Activities that were once performed inside the state are now just as likely to be done outside.

Instead the state's role has been recast as one of a facilitator, with a whole array of indicators designed to evaluate performance, often at a distance. Internally the state has also been restructured. More traditional ways of decision making have been replaced by new ways of organizing activities. New teams and units have been formed, in the process challenging traditional ways of working, such as through formal committees. For Leitner (1990, 147) we have witnessed:

> ...a form of private entrepreneurialism that is characterized by a distinctive set of institutional arrangements and practices, and which attempts to apply the outlook and techniques of private sector management.

Some public sector professional demarcations have been transgressed in the process, with elements of traditional jobs such as architecture, engineering, and planning combined to form new types of entrepreneurial 'redevelopment' officials (Painter 1998).

The second theme in this work takes up the issue of who is involved in territorial alliances, 're-designing urban governance' in the words of Jessop (1997, 34). It has detailed the nature and the extent of the changes in the institutional arrangements in place to govern cities (Boyle and Hughes 1994; Goodwin and Painter 1996; Cochrane 1999; Imrie and Raco 1999; Ward 2000). Studies have revealed how increasingly the interests of labour have been trumped by those of capital, the emphasis of the state shifting from addressing social inequalities to creating the conditions for capital accumulation in ways that privilege profits and taxes over wages.

Related to this, the third theme that runs through much of the entrepreneurial urbanism literature has emphasized the changing agenda, interests and identities involved in territorial alliances and the discursive and material pre-conditions for the participation of different agents (Cox and Mair 1988; Cochrane et al. 1996; Jessop et al. 1999; Peck and Tickell 1995; Valler and Wood 2004). This draws attention to the discourses and representations, and the politics over their mobilization and use, associated with contemporary entrepreneurial modes of urban governance (Jessop 1997; 1998; McCann 2002; Ward 2003b). Reflective of the wider 'cultural turn' in human geography and beyond, those working on the politics of urban economic development have become increasingly sensitized to the non-materiality of political practices. If Cox and Jonas (1993) rightly emphasized the materiality of the NUP, then work on this theme has both emphasized the non-material and sought to think through the relationship between the two. Or, put another way, it has explored 'the relations between the political economy of place and the cultural politics of place' (Hall and Hubbard 1996, 162). One element of this has been the re-imaging of cities, which Jessop (1997; 1998) has written about in terms of the changing practices of the state. This has involved local government leaders spending more time on place promotion, investing in new cultural projects and focusing on selling the city in terms of new lifestyles and experiences, cajoling, manipulating and stimulating the attachments and emotions individuals feel towards cities. Methodologically it has meant paying greater attention to the important of discourse, ideology and language in the NUP (Wilson 1996; 1998), building on Cox's (1993; 1995) initial formulations.

Turning to the fourth theme that characterizes this literature, there has been an increasing acknowledgement of the range of scales represented in 'urban' territorial alliances (Amin and Graham 1997; Brenner 1999). This quite clearly draws on work by Cox (1998a; 2001). On the one hand this work has strived to reveal the range of geographical scales present in contemporary territorial alliances of one sort or another, and has drawn directly from respectively Harvey (1989, 6) and Cox (1998a, 19):

> The shift towards entrepreneurialism in urban governance has to be examined...
> at a variety of spatial scales – local neighbourhood and community, central
> city and suburb, metropolitan, region, nation state, and the like.

> Local politics appears as metropolitan, regional, national, or even international
> as different organizations try to secure those networks of associations through
> which respective projects can be realized.

For those working in this tradition, geographical scale continues to have strong intellectual purchase. Even acknowledging and allowing for the multiplicity of scales that are present in any single 'scale' – local, regional etc. – the ontological purchase of the scalar vocabulary remains undiminished (Brenner 2004; Jonas 2006). On the other hand, others have sought to go further, and to re-think the language of geographical scale. Reflective of a larger debate between those who propose different ways of conceiving space, work in this field has highlighted the increasingly open, porous and inter-connected configuration of territorial entities (Massey 1993; Amin et al. 2000; Amin 2004). So, for Allen and Cochrane (2007, 1163) it is important to appreciate both the relational as well as the territorial elements bound up in the 'local' in the local politics of economic development:

> it would seem that there is little to be gained by talking about...[local]
> governance as a territorial arrangement when a number of the political elements
> assembled are not particularly...[local]...in any traditional sense. Many are
> 'parts' of elsewhere, representatives of political authority, expertise, skills, and
> interests drawn together to move forward varied agendas and programmes. The

sense in which these are...[urban]...assemblages, rather than geographically tiered hierarchies of decision-making, lies with the tangle of interactions and capabilities within which power is negotiated and played out.

The fifth theme running through contemporary work on entrepreneurial urbanism and the politics of local economic development has been that which emphasizes the restructuring of the built environment. It is argued that new kinds of landscapes have emerged, as strategies to market and promote cities consist of a variety of urban design elements. As Hubbard (1996, 1444) puts it, 'place marketing is inevitably accompanied by a fabrication of the landscape, which can therefore be seen as both an expression and a consequence of attempts to re-image the city.' New downtown redevelopments appear to puncture a growing number of the industrialized cities of the global north. Here we can think not only of the iconic developments in some cities, such as the Guggenheim in Bilbao, but also other equally significant, more mundane constructions, such as new convention centres, gyms, museums and other investments that constitute the physical resuscitating of the centres of cities as entertainment complexes and that contribute to the improving of the business climate (Cox and Jonas 1993).

The sixth and final theme in this vein is that most recent work acknowledges the role of the environment in the politics of local economic and regional development. Emphasizing the inter-relationship between cities, the environment and capital accumulation, this work has sought to consider a series of issues around spatial fixes and territorial alliances (While et al. 2004; Jonas et al. 2007; 2010; While et al. 2010). Taking seriously issues of carbon control and sustainability, it has attempted to theorize evolving urban economy-environment relations in cities around the world in 'terms of an ensemble of governance practices, strategies, alliances and discourses that enables the local state to manage, though not necessarily resolve, seemingly conflicting economic, social and environmental demands at different scales of territoriality' (While et al. 2004, 549).

These six themes reveal the insights, which have been many. The emphasis has been squarely on territory and the state. Nevertheless, that is not to say that amongst this work there has not been a sensibility to other ways of conceiving of space. There has. Kevin Cox's work suggests thinking about opening up the local – looking elsewhere for local politics – in two important ways. First, is the sense that what happens in terms of territorial alliances in one locality is shaped by what happens in another locality or at another geographical scale. As he has put it recently, 'there is both horizontality and verticality in the relations drawn on in the construction of institutional fixes' (Cox 2010, 220). Terms such as 'non-local' refer to a more general sense of something happening beyond the immediate locality and are used in some cases, while in other examples it is the metropolitan and the national that are named to convey a sense that local relations are shaped and structured by processes occurring at other geographical scales. The following are illustrative:

...social processes and struggles within localities are significantly determined by the nonlocal social relations of local actors: by the circulation of capital, by central state policies, by migration—indeed by multifarious processes occurring at wider scales—as well as by sets of localised social processes occurring elsewhere (that is, in other localities) (Cox and Mair 1991, 197)

...local politics is a misnomer. ...much of local politics is not about localised social structures per se. Rather, insertion of localised social structures in wider spatial and scale divisions of labour means that local politics very often centres upon the way the locality is to be defined relative to the wider world and upon the ways in which subsequent action taken locally can suspend any contradictions between local actors and that wider world (Cox and Mair 1991, 202)

The result is that what is commonly referred to as 'urban politics' is typically quite heterogeneous and by no means referable to struggles within, or among, the agents structured by some set of social relations corresponding unambiguously to the urban (Cox 2001, 756)

The second way Kevin Cox's work suggests thinking about opening up the local is through an acknowledgement and an appreciation of both absolute and relational space. Cox (1998b, 41) has argued that under 'certain circumstances it is useful to talk about the local and the global in a relational rather than absolute sense.' Through most of his own work he has been committed to an approach that emphasizes territoriality (of state structures, of the politics of economic development, of investments and so on), which resonates with much of the work produced by others in this field. Nevertheless, he has been explicit that both [relational and territorial conceptualizations of space] 'have their purposes' (Cox 1998b, 41). In arguing that 'urban politics has become 'globalised' (Cox 1995, 213), he claims that in part the local exists in relation to the global: theirs is a relational relationship in which locally-dependent alliances seek to respond to restructuring tendencies elsewhere. He begins to hint at a relational urban politics, although not strongly enough for some (DeFelippis 1999). In the next section of this chapter I take Cox's fledgling relational urban political geography and consider one, potentially fruitful, intellectual advancement.

Assembling the 'New Urban Politics' II: Inter-city Policy Networks and Policy Tourism

Consultancy firms...manage to make business from writing ...local identity scripts, because each locality paradoxically seeks uniqueness by copying others – but by being 'the best'. The US definitions are now transported to localities across the Atlantic to invent new local identities...which break with definitions appropriate to past localised social structures and roles in spatial divisions of labour (Cox and Mair 1991, 207)

'In order for the local business coalition to promote...territorially defined... identities and distinctions effectively and thus secure for themselves the emergent powers of locality as agent', Cox and Mair (1991, 206) claim, 'they have to be fostered as the basis of both material interest and personal identity.' The means by which this is done is not just a matter of what takes place within a locality. In the quote with which this section begins, Cox and Mair (1991) are remarkably apposite. They highlight the role of private consultancy firms who play an important role in uprooting a policy, program or strategy in one place and replacing it somewhere else. In their case they write about Bradford's *Bouncing Back*, Dundee's *City of Discovery* and Glasgow's *Miles Better*: three UK examples of the beginning of a fashion that persists today of territorial alliances in localities running campaigns around evocative and emotional strap-lines. Fast forward fifteen years and many cities and towns in a number of nations find themselves in the grip of creativity fever from which there appears to be no known cure. Florida's (2002) writings on the creative class and the creative city have taken the processes behind Cox and Mair's (1991) observations to a higher plain. Recent years have seen what Harvey (1989, 10) observed as the 'repetitive and serial reproduction of certain patterns of development' intensify and multiply.

Inadvertently perhaps, Cox and Mair (1991, 207) drew our attention to the ways in which policies and programs appear and reappear in geographically distant localities. They highlight the involvement of consultancy firms and write about how 'local identity scripts' are, in their words, 'transported' between the US and the UK. It is perhaps not a surprise that even then it was not just consultancy firms that were involved, nor was it only about policies being exchanged between the US and the UK. Many other agents were involved with varying geographical reaches, bringing a number of cities around the world into a large matrix of policy circulation. And the last couple of decades appear to have witnessed an expansion in the *policy transfer community* – those agents involved in the movement of policies from one place to another. Or, put another way, 'the practice of policy transfer is on the rise' (Hoyt 2006, 223). According to Peck (2003, 228-229):

> The cumulative effect of a range of developments – the internationalization of consultancy firms; the broadening of policy remits of trans-national institutions; the formation of new policy networks around think tanks, governmental agencies and professional associations; and the growth of international conferencing and 'policy tourism' – has been to proliferate, widen and lubricate channels of cross-border policy transfer.

Using the example of Business Improvement Districts it is possible to consider two ways in which other places figure in the place-based politics of economic development. The first is through the role of inter-city policy networks to facilitate the movement of policy models from one locality to another. There is a relatively long history to some formal inter-city networks, such as twinning, which in the UK can be dated back to the end of the Second World War (Clarke 2009; Grosspietsch 2009). Cities would 'twin' with another city or town and undertake a series of joint cultural and social programs. In the US the 'people to people initiative' was launched in 1956 by President Eisenhower as the Sister Cities Program (Zelinsky 1991). Both the UK and US schemes were designed at a particular juncture, with cities in the West keen to reinforce their cultural and social values through entering into formal relationship with cities elsewhere. UK and US cities were twinned with cities from a range of countries. More recently the emphasis has moved away from disseminating a particular political vision and towards sharing good practice around economic development. For example, in the case of Chicago, whose first 'sister city' was Warsaw in 1960, the last decade and a half has seen the re-focusing on economic development and inward investment (http://www.chicagosistercities. com/). More generally, over the last few decades there has been a proliferation of state-sponsored economic development networks of differing geographical focus and reach, including different sorts of practitioners, such as architectures, engineers and planners.

It is in and through this networked context that the Business Improvement District model has been moved from one locality to another, within and across national borders. In some cases the BID model has been moved through existing networks, such as those organized more broadly around local economic development. In other cases specific networks have been established around city centre and downtown revalorization. Multiple territories are connected, made proximate, through the formation of these networks. The International Downtown Association – physically located in Washington but the centre of a network of national downtown trade associations and convener of an annual conference – has been at the centre of the BID program's internationalization (McCann and Ward 2010). As it puts it:

> Founded in 1954, the International Downtown Association has more than 650 member organizations worldwide including: North America, Europe, Asia and Africa. Through our network of committed individuals, rich body of knowledge and unique capacity to nurture community-building partnerships, IDA is a guiding force in creating healthy and dynamic centers that anchor the well being of towns, cities and regions of the world (see http://www.ida-downtown.org).

According to the IDA the BID model is one of the most successful ways of resuscitating the conditions of downtowns the world over, for capital, state and, less directly perhaps, workers. According to the recent IDA President, David Feehan, 'the IDA is proud of the role it has played in the resurgence of downtowns in the US and Canada…through partnerships in Europe, the Caribbean, Australia and Africa, IDA is expanding its resources and knowledge base even more' (http://www.ida-downtown.org). Its partners include the Association of Town

Centre Management (ATCM) in the UK, Business Improvement Areas of British Columbia (BIABC) in Canada, Caribbean Tourism Organization (CTO) in the West Indies, and Central Johannesburg Partnership (CJP) in South Africa. Neil Fraser, the Executive Director of the CJP describes the role of the IDA as 'a true leader in bringing together city practitioners and specialists from North America and around the world' (http://www.ida-downtown.org). The network involves territorial alliances of different geographical scales. National alliances and city alliance co-exist as part of the network, echoing Cox's (1998a, 4) work on 'spaces of engagement' in which he argues that spatially fixed, territorial 'agents are participants in a much more spatially extensive set of exchange relations than those contained within the bounds of a particular place.'

Through various face-to-face events – conferences, institutes, seminars and workshops – and through distributed educational documentation circulated through their networks, the IDA and national trade associations educate public and public-private sector downtown policy-makers and practitioners on the returns of the BID model. They emphasize the rationale behind 'attracting in new investment and so enhancing the circulation of value through their particular [geographical] markets' (Cox and Jonas 1993, 12), emphasizing how BIDs can oversee the creation and maintenance of a 'good business climate' (Ward 2007a). Together with private consultancy firms, think-tanks and national and local governments, the activities of the IDA and its associated networks have served to convince the local government and locally-dependent capital of the virtues of the BID model. Successful US examples, such as New York, Philadelphia and Washington are invoked to national and local government around the world (Cook 2008). One locality's set of experiences are brought into relational proximity with another, such as places with as diverse social structures as Columbus, Ohio, in the US, Coventry in England, Milwaukee, Wisconsin, in the US and Tokyo in Japan.

The second means by which other places figure in the place-based politics of economic development is through the growth of policy tourism as a normalized way of learning for locally-dependent government agents. There are two types of policy tourism – *event-led* and *visit-led policy tourism* (Ward 2011) – and in this chapter we focus on the latter. This is defined as visiting, touring and learning from localities that have become known for their approaches to particular issues. There is a history to these sorts of visits of course, particularly in urban planning. In the UK, for example, since the 1950s the professional trade associations of architects and planners have regularly organized such trips. The emergence of mega-events and other such cultural and sporting infrastructural investments as a means of energizing local and regional economic development in recent year also lies behind its proliferation. Manchester's Olympic and Commonwealth Games Bids in the 1990s were assembled through various examples of policy tourism involving visits to Atlanta, Barcelona and Sydney (Cook and Ward 2010). What has intensified in recent years is the visit's qualitative nature. New national and supra-national organizations have emerged to co-ordinate them. A whole social infrastructure has been established to facilitate these exchanges, as these visits have become more professional and more output-oriented:

> Cities that become popular destinations for incoming delegations of policy actors develop protocols and packaged narratives for dealing with their visitors in a way that is efficient for the host and also edifying and enjoyable for the guests (McCann 2011: 118)

Within each area of policy, whether it is be crime, education, environment, health, housing, or of course economic development, there are most favored destinations for those agents who are keen to learn as a means of translating general 'models' into policies or programs for their own localities. These are cities and towns that have been represented as being particularly successful and from which other localities are diagnosed as being able to learn. The waterfront redevelopment of Baltimore in the 1980s and the downtown redevelopment of Barcelona in the 1990s are two iconic cases in point. These examples have discursively and materially shaped the local economic development pathways and trajectories of a number of cities around the world (Nasr and Volait 2003; Healey and Upton 2010). More recently Freiburg in Germany has become constructed as a city from which others can learn, specifically its emphasis on an 'ethical, eco-friendly and healthy lifestyle' (Donald 2009, 48).

The policy tourism tours take in key sites or spaces in localities, major infrastructure developments, new public spaces, residential developments: physical examples of the host city's successes. By being there and seeing 'evidence' agents are able to distil and interpret the possible lessons to be learnt for their own cities. Show-and-tell tours, walk-and-talk activities and before-and-after visual displays serve to reinforce the means through which visiting agents can translate the evidence they have generated – photographs, notes etc – into tangible suggestions. These are then relayed back to other agents in their home localities, feeding into and shaping the production of territorial strategies of the sort identified by Cox (1995) in his NUP work.

The case of the making mobile of the BID model is replete with examples of policy tourism, perhaps not surprisingly. Three examples will suffice. First, various local government agents in Coventry and London visited the US East-coast BIDs during the mid 1990s. The aim was to see and to learn what was going on, with a view first to introducing the model into the UK before establishing BIDs around the country (Travers and Weimar 1996; Ward 2006; Cook 2008). Second, in 1995 the Central Johannesburg Partnership and International Downtown Association organized a tour to the UK and the US for Johannesburg's public and private sector officials. The purpose was 'to visit...sites and learn from international experiences in order to set up practices and legislation for a CID [City Improvement District] in Johannesburg' (Peyroux 2008, 4). Subsequently the Central Johannesburg Partnership (CJP) was established and has taken its place alongside other representatives of capital, the state and labor in an alliance governing the city. In the third example the late 1990s saw a series of 'urban' policy documents of different sorts published in the UK (Department of Environment, Transport and the Regions 1999; 2000). They each focused political and practitioner attention on the role cities should be encouraged to play in driving national economic growth. These documents were replete with examples of policy tourism. Central government ministers, such as John Prescott, and senior officials from various national government departments were regular visitors to New York and Philadelphia. They were keen to see the BID model in action. Subsequently a series of other green and white papers – necessary so that the UK government could make legislative changes – were introduced at the end of the 1990s and the beginning of the 2000s. This was required because the UK state's scalar division of labour required the creation of an appropriate national financial and legal framework before BIDs could be established in localities. During this period there was a sustained creation of favorable 'importing' conditions. Various 'transfer agents' operating at and across a range of 'spaces of engagement' (Cox 1998a), such as national think tanks, regional development agencies and local authorities visited examples of existing US Business Improvement Districts. Reports from these visits were fed into and shaped the decision-making process (Ward 2006; Cook 2008). The creation of English BIDs was finally announced in 2001, and the final piece of the legal framework was agreed in 2004, allowing new sorts of territorial alliances to be established in many localities to oversee the enhancement of value through their 'local' economies. Subsequently almost one hundred English, Scottish and Welsh localities have sought to establish Business Improvement Districts, many but not all, successfully.

Conclusion

This chapter has reviewed the contributions of Kevin Cox, alongside those of David Harvey and others, to understandings of the New Urban Politics (NUP) and local dependence. His formative work, on his own and with colleagues, shaped the development of English-speaking urban political geography. As a personal aside, I was a graduate student in the mid-1990s. Some of his seminal contributions were already published, others were not yet out. It was intellectually very exciting. His legacy can be seen in the writings of those working in the field today. I re-read these groundbreaking papers in writing this chapter. Their impact remains undiminished.

Of course there have been theoretical developments over the proceeding twenty years. This chapter has used the lens of entrepreneurial urbanism to sketch out the intellectual contours of the work that has taken Cox's NUP work as its jumping off point. It is a rich and diverse set of contributions. It shares some features and is divided by others. One area of work tentatively flagged by Cox (2001) but that has not really been advanced in subsequent years is that on what Cox (1998b, 19) referred to as 'locating the local'. If terms such as 'local' or 'urban' were ever taken for granted, and this chapter has argued that they were not in much of Cox's (1998a; 2001) work, then that time has now surely passed. Instead the where in 'urban politics' has slowly but surely begun to be opened up for analysis, often from a range of theoretical standpoints.

With this in mind, the chapter has used the example of the movement of the Business Improvement District model from one country to another, and one city to another, to consider the issue of 'where' goes into the local politics of economic development. BIDs are territorial alliances whose primary function is to ensure a good business climate – clean streets, higher retail infrastructure investment, safer shopping environments etc. An initiative driven by a combination of capital and the state, BIDs have played a not inconsequential role in resuscitating and revalorizing city centers and downtowns in many cities and towns. A Coxian approach to territory, the state and urban politics continues to be extremely illuminating in such examples. For example, it reveals why businesses that are differently locally dependent are predisposed to get involved in such territorial alliances. It also details the discursive and the material rationales for participation in these sorts of alliances by capital, the state and labor.

This is fine as far as it goes…which is a long way, of course. Yet what is largely absent from many NUP accounts is the role ascribed to comparisons and references to other places as part of territorial politics. The struggles within localities over particular economic development pathways and trajectories are ones in which reference is made and re-made to other localities. It is not just the circulation of capital and the circulation of people that matter, as highlighted by Cox and Mair (1991). It is the circuits, channels, networks and webs that exist to connect different localities and in and through which cities – 'as local alliances attempting to create and realize new powers to intervene in processes of geographical restructuring' (Cox and Mair 1991, 208) – make up policy that also matter. This means conceptually two things. First, it is the nature of the social relations *between* localities that warrant further study. Which agents are involved in the movement of policies from one place to another and with what consequences? Recent work has sought to address these questions, through advancing an agenda for 'research into the spatial, social, and relational character of globally circulating urban policies, policy models, and policy knowledge' (McCann 2011: 107). This approach asks questions of more traditional means of conceiving of 'urban politics', whether 'old' or 'new'. Second, the material outcomes in one locality matter in contingent ways to what happens in another locality. What happens in one locality is significantly shaped by the 'nonlocal social relations of local actors…by sets of localized social processes occurring elsewhere (that is, in other localities)' Cox and Mair (1991, 197). Localities are implicated in each others' pasts, presents and futures in a way that challenges more traditional ways of conceiving of 'urban politics', again whether 'old' or 'new'.

Addressing both these theoretical and methodological challenges has already begun (Ward 2006; 2007; 2011; McCann 2007; 2011; McCann and Ward 2010; 2011; Cook 2008; Peck and Theodore 2010; Prince 2010; Robinson 2008; 2011).

It is to be hoped that it is one of many new strands of intellectual thinking that builds on the foundational NUP work of Cox and his colleagues, taking urban political geographical theory into exciting and fruitful directions in the twenty-first century.

References

Allen, J. and Cochrane, A. (2007), 'Beyond the territorial fix: regional assemblages, politics and power', *Regional Studies* 41, 1161-75.

Amin, A. (2004), 'Regions unbound: towards a new politics of place', *Geografiska Annaler* 86B, 33-44.

Amin, A. and Graham, S. (1997), 'The ordinary city', *Transactions of the Institute of British Geographers NS* 22, 411-29.

Amin, A., Massey, D. and Thrift, N. (2000), *Cities for the Many not for the Few* (Bristol, Policy Press).

Brenner, N. (2004), *New State Spaces: Urban Governance and the Re-scaling of Statehood* (Oxford, Oxford University Press).

Boyle, M. and Hughes, G. (1994), 'The politics of urban entrepreneurialism in Glasgow', *Geoforum* 25, 453-70.

Clarke, N. (2009), 'In what senses 'spaces of neoliberalism'? The new localism the new politics of scale, and town twinning', *Political Geography* 28, 496-507.

Cochrane, A.(1999), 'Redefining urban politics for the twenty first century', in A. E. G. Jonas and D. Wilson (eds), *The Urban Growth Machine: Critical Perspectives Two Decades* Later (Albany NY, State University of New York), 109-24.

Cochrane, A., Peck, J. and Tickell, A. (1996), 'Manchester plays games: exploring the local politics of globalization', *Urban Studies* 33, 1319-36.

Cook, I. R. (2008), 'Mobilising urban policies: the policy transfer of US Business Improvement Districts to England and Wales', *Urban Studies* 45, 773-95.

Cook, I. R. and Ward, K. (2010), 'Relational comparisons: the assembling of Cleveland's waterfront plan', Imagining Urban Futures Program Working Paper 9. Available at: http://www.sed.manchester.ac.uk/geography/research/urbanfutures/output.htm [accessed 14 April 2010]

Cox, K. R. (1989), 'The politics of turf and the question of class', in J. Wolch and M. Dear (eds), *The Power of Geography: How Territory Shapes Social Life* (London, Unwin Hyman), 61-90.

Cox, K. R. (1991), 'Questions of abstraction in studies in the New Urban Politics', *Journal of Urban Affairs* 13, 267-80.

Cox, K. R. (1993), 'The local and the global in the new urban politics: a critical view', *Environment and Planning D: Society and Space* 11, 433-48.

Cox, K. R. (1995), 'Globalisation, competition and the politics of local economic development', *Urban Studies* 32, 213-24.

Cox, K. R. (1998a), 'Spaces of dependence, spaces of engagements and the politics of scale, or: looking for local politics', *Political Geography* 17, 1-23.

Cox, K. R. (1998b), 'Representation and power in the politics of scale', *Political Geography* 17, 41-4.

Cox, K. R. (2001), 'Territoriality, politics and the 'urban'', *Political Geography* 20, 745-62.

Cox, K. R. (2010), 'The problem of metropolitan governance and the politics of scale', *Regional Studies* 44, 215-27.

Cox, K. R. and Mair, A. (1988), 'Locality and community in the politics of local economic development', *Annals of the Association of American Geographers* 78, 307-25.

Cox, K. R. and Mair, A. (1991), 'From localized social structures to localities as agents', *Environment and Planning A* 23, 197-213.

Cox, K. R. and Jonas, A. E. G. (1993), 'Urban development, collective consumption and the politics of metropolitan fragmentation', *Political Geography* 12, 8-37.

Cummings. S. (ed.) (1988), *Business Elites and Urban Development* (Albany NY, State University of New York Press).

DeFilippis, J. (1999), 'Alternatives to the 'New Urban Politics': finding locality and autonomy in local economic development', *Political Geography* 18, 973-90.

Department of Environment, Transport and the Regions (DETR), (2000), *Our Towns and Cities – The Future: Delivering an Urban Renaissance* (London, The Stationery Office).

Donald, A. (2009), 'Comment', *Blueprint* December, 48.

Fainstein, S. (1991), 'Rejoinder to questions of abstraction in studies in the New Urban Politics', *Journal of Urban Affairs* 13, 281-87.

Florida, R. (2002), *The Rise of the Creative Class ... and How it's Transforming Work, Leisure, Community and Everyday Life* (New York, Basic Books).

Goodwin, M. and Painter, J. (1996), 'Local governance, the crises of Fordism and the changing geographies of regulation', *Transactions of the Institute of British Geographers NS* 21, 635-48.

Grosspietsch, J. (2009), 'More than folk and food music? Geographical perspectives on European town planning', *Geography Compass* 3, 1281-1304.

Hubbard, P. (1996), 'Urban design and city regeneration: social representations of entrepreneurial landscapes', *Urban Studies* 33, 1441-61.

Hall, T. and Hubbard, P. (1996), 'The entrepreneurial city: new urban politics, new urban geographies?' *Progress in Human Geography* 20, 153-74.

Hall, T. and Hubbard, P. (eds), (1998), *The Entrepreneurial City: Geographies of Politics, Regime and Representation* (Chichester, John Wiley & Son).

Harvey, D. (1985), 'The geopolitics of capitalism', in D. Gregory and J. Urry (eds), *Social Relations and Spatial Structures* (Macmillan, London), 128-63.

Harvey, D. (1989), 'From managerialism to entrepreneurialism: the transformation in urban governance in late capitalism', *Geografiska Annaler* 71B, 3-17.

Healey, P. and Upton, R. (eds), (2010), *Crossing Borders: International Exchange and Planning Practices* (London, Routledge).

Hoyt, L. (2006), 'Importing ideas: the transnational transfer of urban revitalization policy', *International Journal of Public Administration* 29, 221-43.

Imrie, R. and Raco, M. (1999), 'How new is new local governance? Lessons from the United Kingdom', *Transactions of the Institute of British Geographers* 24, 45-63.

Jessop, B. (1997), 'The entrepreneurial city: re-imaging localities, redesigning economic governance, or restructuring capital?' in N. Jewson and S. MacGregor (eds), *Transforming Cities: Contested Governance and New Spatial Divisions* (London, Routledge), 28-41.

Jessop, B. (1998), 'The narrative of enterprise and the enterprise of narrative: place marketing and the entrepreneurial city', in T. Hall and P. Hubbard (eds), *The Entrepreneurial City: Geographies of Politics, Regimes and Representation* (Chichester, John Wiley and Sons), 74-99.

Jessop, B., Peck, J. and Tickell, A. (1999), 'Retooling the machine: economic crisis, state restructuring, and urban politics', in A. E. G. Jonas and D. Wilson (eds), *The Urban Growth Machine: Critical Perspectives Two Decades Later* (Albany NY, State University of New York Press), 141-59.

Jonas, A. E. G. (2006), 'Pro scale: further reflections on the 'scale debate' in human geography', *Transactions Institute of British Geographers* 31, 399-406.

Jonas, A. E. G. and While, A. (2007), 'Greening the entrepreneurial city: looking for spaces of sustainability politics in the competitive city', in R. Krueger and D. Gibbs (eds), *The Sustainable Development Paradox: Urban Political Economy in the United States and Europe* (New York, Guilford), 123-53.

Jonas, A. E. G., While, A. and Gibbs, D. (2010), 'Carbon control regimes, eco-state restructuring and the politics of local and regional development', in A. Pike, A. Rodriguez-Posé and J. Tomaney (eds), *Handbook of Local and Regional Development* (London, Routledge), 283-94.

Jones, M. R. (1997), 'Spatial selectivity of the state? The regulationist enigma and local struggles over economic governance', *Environment and Planning A* 29, 831-64.

Jones, M. R. (1998), 'Restructuring the local state: economic governance or social regulation', *Political Geography* 17, 959-88.

Leitner, H. (1990), 'Cities in pursuit of economic growth: the local state as entrepreneur', *Political Geography Quarterly* 9, 146-70.

Logan, J. R. and Molotch, H. (1987), *Urban Fortunes: The Political Economy of Place* (Berkeley CA, University of California Press).

Massey, D. (1993), 'Power-geometry and a progressive sense of place', in J. Bird, B. Curtis, T. Putman, G. Robertson and L. Tickner (eds), *Mapping the Futures: Local Cultures, Global Change* (London, Routledge), 59-69.

McCann, E. (1995), 'Collaborative visioning or urban planning as therapy? The politics of public-private policy making', *Professional Geographer* 53, 207-18.

McCann, E. (2002), 'The cultural politics of local economic development', *Geoforum* 33, 385-98.

McCann, E. (2007), 'Expertise, truth, and urban policy mobilities: global circuit of knowledge in the development of Vancouver, Canada's 'four pillar' drug strategy', *Environment and Planning A* 40, 885-904.

McCann, E. (2011), 'Urban policy mobilities and global circuits of knowledge: towards a research agenda', *Annals of the Association of American Geographers* 101, 107-30.

McCann, E. and Ward, K. (2010), 'Relationality/territoriality: Toward a conceptualization of cities in the world', *Geoforum* 41, 175-84.

Nasr, J. and Volait, M. (eds), (2003), *Urbanism Imported or Exported? Native Aspirations and Foreign Plans* (Chichester, Wiley Academy).

O'Neill, P. (1997), 'Bringing the qualitative state into economic geography', in R. Lee and J. Wills (eds), *Geographies of Economies* (London, Edward Arnold), 290-301.

Painter, J. (1998), 'Entrepreneurs are made, not born: learning and urban regimes in the production of entrepreneurial cities', in T. Hall and P. Hubbard (eds), *The Entrepreneurial City: Geographies of Politics, Regimes and Representation* (Chichester, John Wiley and Sons), 259-74.

Peck, J. (2001), 'Neoliberalizing states: thin policies/hard outcomes', *Progress in Human Geography* 25, 445-55.

Peck, J. (2003), 'Geography and public policy: mapping the penal state', *Progress in Human Geography* 27, 222-31.

Peck, J. and Tickell, A. (1995), 'Business goes local – dissecting the business agenda in Manchester', *International Journal of Urban and Regional Research* 19, 55-78.

Peck, J. and Theodore, N. (2010), 'Mobilizing policy, models, methods and mutations', *Geoforum* 41, 169-74.

Peyroux, E. (2008), 'City Improvement Districts in Johannesburg: an examination of the local variations of the IDB model', in R. Pütz (ed.), *Business Improvement Districts. Ein neues Modell aus Governance-Perspektive von Praxis und Stadtforschung* (Geographische Handelsforschung, 14, Passau, LIS Verlag), 139-62.

Prince, R. (2010), 'Policy transfer as policy assemblage: making policy for the creative industries in New Zealand', *Environment and Planning A* 42, 169-86.

Robinson, J. (2008), 'Developing ordinary cities: city visioning processes in Durban and Johannesburg', *Environment and Planning A* 40, 74-87.

Robinson, J. (2011), 'Cities in a world of cities: the comparative gesture', *International Journal of Urban and Regional Research* 35, 1-23.

Stone, C. and Saunders, H. T. (eds) (1987), *The Politics of Urban Development* (Lawrence, Kansas, University of Kansas Press).

Stone, C. (1989), *Regime Politics: Governing Atlanta 1946-1988* (Lawrence, Kansas, University of Kansas Press).

Stone, C. (1991), 'The hedgehog, the fox and the New Urban Politics', *Journal of Urban Affairs* 13, 289-97.

Travers, T. and Weimar, J. (1996), *Business Improvement Districts: New York and London*. The Greater London Group, London School of Economics and Political Science (London, London School of Economics).

Tunström, M. (2007), 'The vital city: constructions and meanings in the contemporary Swedish planning discourse', *Town Planning Review* 78, 681-98.

Valler, D. and Wood, A. (2004), 'Devolution and the politics of business representation in Britain: a strategic – relational approach', *Environment and Planning A* 36, 1835-54.

Ward, K. (2000), 'A critique in search of a corpus: re-visiting governance and re-interpreting urban politics', *Transactions of the Institute of British Geographers* 25, 169-85.

Ward, K. (2003a), 'Neo-liberal 'turns', entrepreneurial urbanism and the limits to contemporary urban re-development', *City* 7, 201-11.

Ward, K. (2003b), 'Entrepreneurial urbanism, state restructuring and 'civilising' East Manchester', *Area* 35, 116-27.

Ward, K. (2006), ''Policies in motion', urban management and state restructuring: the trans-local expansion of Business Improvement Districts', *International Journal of Urban and Regional Research* 30, 54-75.

Ward, K. (2007a), ''Creating a personality for downtown': Business Improvement Districts in Milwaukee', *Urban Geography* 28, 781-808.

Ward, K. (2007b), 'Business Improvement Districts: policy origins, mobile policies and urban liveability', *Geography Compass* 2, 657-72.

Ward, K. (2010), 'Entrepreneurial urbanism and Business Improvement Districts in the state of Wisconsin: a cosmopolitan critique', *Annals of the Association of American Geographers* 100, 1177-1196.

Ward, K. (2011), 'Entrepreneurial urbanism, policy tourism and the making mobile of policies', in G. Bridge and S. Watson (eds), *The New Companion to the City*, (Oxford, Wiley Blackwell), forthcoming.

While, A., Jonas, A. E. G. and Gibbs, D. (2004), 'The environment and the entrepreneurial city: searching for the urban 'sustainability fix' in Manchester and Leeds', *International Journal of Urban and Regional Research* 28, 549-69.

While, A., Jonas, A. E. G. and Gibbs, D. (2010), 'From sustainable development to carbon control: the eco-restructuring of the state and the politics of urban and regional development', *Transactions Institute of British Geographers* 35, 76-93.

Wilson, D. (1996), 'Metaphors, growth coalition discourses and black poverty neighborhoods in a US city', *Antipode* 28, 72-96.

Wilson, D. (1998), 'Progress report: The politics of urban representation', *Urban Geography* 19, 531-42.

Zelinsky, W. (1991), 'The twinning of the world. Sister cities in geographic and historic perspective', *Annals of the Association of American Geographers* 81, 1-31.

PART III
STATE, TERRITORY AND DIFFERENCE

Chapter 9
Structure, Agency and South Africa – Some Influences of (and on) Kevin Cox[1]

Jeff McCarthy

Background: Why South Africa?

As an analytical theme, territory, state and urban politics invites myriad possibilities in terms of international case studies. Why, then, in the Anglo-American context, should one reflect specifically upon South Africa? A significant number of research studies in urban politics do, but for those who have not been to South Africa, it may not be especially clear why.

South Africa after all has a population that is only a very small fraction of that of Africa as a whole (less than 5 per cent). Moreover, India and China, to choose but two cases, have populations each more than twenty times that of South Africa, and yet they each have attracted – at least until the last decade – probably much the same coverage as South Africa in the professional journals pertaining to urban politics.

A starting hypothesis on the attractiveness of South Africa is that, at least for the Anglophone world, South Africa has presented an accessible (e.g. English-speaking) laboratory upon which to revisit many of their own internal conflicts. South Africa – metaphorically speaking – loudly 'blares' these conflicts out, in almost exaggerated format. Especially for social researchers interested in class-based conflicts, whilst in Britain for example there may be a *penchant* for subtlety about such conflicts, South Africa – even more so than in America –'is where it all hangs out'.

Class inequalities are pronounced in Africa generally, at least by the standards of North American or European norms. The main reasons for these patterns lie in the configuration of labour and skills markets. The highly skilled tend to be internationally mobile, whereas such mobility is much more difficult for manual labourers; and the latter are in over-supply in the countries Africa generally. In consequence, levels of material inequality are stark, making the potential application of class analysis almost self-evident. Moreover, South Africa has some big cities, roughly comparable in scale and sophistication to those of Brazil or

1 The author wishes to acknowledge the editors' useful advice in making revisions to this chapter. In addition he thanks the editor of South Africa's *Mercury* newspaper for permission to make citations from her newspaper.

Mexico, but more accessible in linguistic terms. Looked at in these terms, the Anglo-American academic interest in South Africa for the class analysis of urban issues is perhaps not so hard to understand after all.

Indeed, this is perhaps especially so for those with a Marxist intellectual perspective. Certainly Cox (2002) makes no secret of this in his textbook *Political Geography: Territory, State and Society;* but the interest in South Africa amongst Marxist intellectuals in the Anglophone world is by no means restricted to him. Partly this is because in South Africa, Marxism is not just about academic analysis, and theory. As Johnson (2009) has recently pointed out, for example, one third of the South African cabinet is now made up of senior members of the South African Communist Party (SACP). This makes Marxist approaches to economic development a very real prospect for actual implementation in South Africa, and Marxist academics are amongst those in the ascendancy in policy-influencing circles in South Africa, at the time of writing.

However, many academics do not find a neat symmetry between Marxist theory and the policy and practices of the SACP. Johnson (2009, 66) for example opines that, in African context, Communist Party membership and rhetoric usually conceals a trend of "effortlessly evolving towards plutocracy while wrapping themselves in the hammer-and-sickle and mouthing leftist rhetoric". Whilst Johnson (2009) could be seen as hardly ever having been sympathetic to Marxism anyway, his article in the journal *New Left Review* is paralleled in many ways in a response by longstanding Marxist analyst Bond (2009). The latter is rather more sympathetic to the SACP, but also negative on what he terms as the "the rise of a grasping BEE [black-economic-empowerment bourgeoisie], the failure of basic social provision, soaring unemployment and vast inequalities" (p. 75).

Whether or not one cares to agree with either or both of the above, the point is nevertheless taken that South Africa is not simply of interest to Marxist theorists, but is a very practical affair relating to the relationships between the state, power, capitalist accumulation and socialism. Most of the remainder of this article is devoted to reflection on the implications of this for understanding Kevin Cox's work in one particular geographical context.

Cox and South Africa – A Note on Method and Changing Context

Against the background that we have just sketched, Kevin Cox is hardly exceptional in being both interested in South Africa and Marxism. However the geographical content of such a combination of interests is rare, and in Cox's case also even influential upon certain outcomes in the country, particularly those aspects pertaining to urban politics. Nevertheless the specifically Marxist component of the confluence of interests between Marxism and South Africa appears to have really only matured in Cox's (2009) post-2000 work.

To demonstrate this change over time and the reasons for it, in much of what follows, the method that has been followed is partly biographical. It is recognized that Kevin Cox would likely be uncomfortable with such a method, because he is often personally self-effacing, and also because he has tended intellectually to emphasize structure over agency in much of his work. Be that as it may, this method has been assessed by the present author as the most efficient way possible for him, in a short span of words, to convey both the importance of Cox's works and the complexities in its application in South Africa, to outside readers.

The aspect of application raises an important methodological point. Perhaps the main difference in approach to theory between human and physical geography is that in the former case the theorist can – even if unintentionally and in limited ways – change the very domain he or she is studying. As in climatology, we can – in human geography – tell a good theory 'if it works' in practice; but the advantage (and complexity) that human geographers have over their climatologist colleagues, is that by developing a good theory one can also change previously predicted outcomes. This is for example what Marx (1845) meant in his *Theses on Feuerbach* when he wrote "The philosophers have interpreted the world. The point however is to change it."

To this we may add a further point; that the agents of such change are real, live, individual human beings – people with first names and surnames, all with virtues and with vices; and these people are playing out their intentions through malleable conceptual frameworks – but not of course, as Marx would say, according to circumstances of their choosing. Some, for example, may be playing out their intentions in libraries or in seminars; others may be doing so in trade unions and urban social movements; and yet others within state bureaucracies.

I have elaborated my own understandings of how such varying circumstances interact with different conceptual understandings of the same realities, and with practical or political engagement in more general terms elsewhere (McCarthy 1991). In essence, this perspective would lead me to see Kevin Cox as on a something of a consistent trajectory over time as a Left-influenced observer of social structures throughout much of his life. However, one can also observe how his perspectives evolved, and influenced other observers and more specifically some actors engaged in socio-spatial re-structuring in South Africa.

What I suggest is that, in relation to South Africa (and indeed probably other subjects), Cox moved from a centre-Left position in the 1970s where he influenced a category of South African (let us call them neo-liberal) actors on how to view the socio-geographic structures evident in apartheid South Africa. In time however (about from the early 1980s onwards) Cox moved on to where he developed more unambiguously Left (and Marxist-structuralist) concepts – initially apparently for their own sake, but again he probably unconsciously influenced a new category of actors working on the restructuring of South Africa (now with ostensibly more socialist intent). More recently still, since about the year 2000, Cox moved on to a point where he projected his Marxist concepts onto his observations of socio-geographic restructuring in post-apartheid South Africa. Here he retained residues of a Marxist-structuralist perspective, but this had evolved into what he now termed as an historical-geographical-materialist approach, which allowed him to deal more with specific times (or periods) and places. In the meantime, there were other influences bearing upon groups of actors in South Africa who had been influenced by Cox's evolving concepts and analyses at various stages. Many of these were also going about the restructuring of post-apartheid South Africa, or analyzing it, in ways that differed from those which Cox had developed post-1980, and more especially post-2000.

On most occasions the outcomes of these activities and perspectives tended to work in parallel or in tandem with each other in the evolution of South Africa into a post-apartheid format. However, on occasion these various actors also came into conflict, in the process revealing some important lessons about relationships between theory and practice. These same conflicts also possibly implicitly highlight the salience of Cox's (2002) and Cox and Hemson's (2008) more recent works pertaining to what he termed as difference and identity in South Africa.

Overview of Influences: From Centre-Left Perspectives and Application to Urban Apartheid to Marxist-structuralist Perspectives on Post-apartheid Restructuring

In this section I provide a brief overview of the evolution of Cox's perspectives and influences, and in the section to follow we dig more deeply into what some conflicts amongst such influences might reveal.

Cox's (1973) early work on urban politics – in particular his short book *Conflict, Power, Politics and the City* – was well-known to a few subsequently influential South African academics during the 1970s. This book could be styled as a product of his involvement in centre-left academic and political debates about cities in the USA and Britain during the late 1960s and early 1970s. In the event, together with Harvey's (1973) *Social Justice and the City*, Cox's (1973) book was probably the most influential upon a small group of critical human geographers of the 1970s in South Africa, including the present author, who found his way to The Ohio State University (OSU) partly under the influences of reading Cox's early works.

The emphasis upon jurisdictional fragmentation as an instrument for the perpetuation of distributional inequities in Cox's (1973) early work rang more than a few bells for those working with the socio-economic realities of the *apartheid* city. Hypothetically, the *apartheid* government liked to justify (to itself at least) its policies as a work-in-progress project towards 'separate-but-equal' conditions, whereas objective researchers could see contrary realities and forces at work. In many respects, these realities appeared to resemble those recounted by Cox (1973) and Harvey (1973) and are recorded as such in some South African urban geographical studies of that time (McCarthy, 1978). It was largely for these reasons that Kevin Cox found several South African graduate students knocking on his door during the 1970s.

Later, partly because of his having had South African postgraduate students, Kevin Cox in turn made a number of visits to South Africa from the early 1980s onwards, often giving guest lectures or seminars in academic departments (especially in Durban where three of his former doctoral students were resident). At that stage he did not force his emerging theoretical perspectives onto South Africa. Rather, he tended to reflect to South Africans, in theoretical terms, what he had learnt from his mainly American research experiences.

As time progressed, however, he did translate his South African experiences into his teaching at OSU, and also into aspects of his research. In the published word, this was most widely evident in his textbook *Political Geography: Territory, State and Society* (Cox 2002), where South African examples are a significant element of the book. Here South Africa features most strongly in his discussions of "territory and the politics of difference"; by this time Cox had moved from his centre-Left analytic position to more Marxist observations on South African social structures. More recently still, in relation to his interest in identity, Cox collaborated with David Hemson now of South Africa's Human Sciences Research Council (Cox and Hemson 2008), and this work will be referred to in the penultimate section of this chapter.

Finally, as part of his most recent so-called historical-geographical materialism perspective, Cox (2009) has most recently authored important unpublished research on patterns of post-apartheid restructuring in South Africa, in which he recounts growing poverty and class inequality in the country, and a faltering pattern of capitalist accumulation, amongst other considerations.

The Nature of Influences

In the process of this journey Kevin Cox both directly and indirectly influenced a number of academics and activists in South Africa. The direct influences were upon those who read his works in South Africa, and also amongst a few graduate students who studied under his supervision at OSU, thereafter returning to South Africa, or visiting it and researching it. In his book *Political Geography: Territory, State and Society,* Cox (2002, xii) for example cites in his Preface (amongst others) a number of people with South African connections in this regard: "There are many people who have over the years stimulated me…Not least are former graduate students…Jeff McCarthy…Felicity Sutcliffe…Mike Sutcliffe…Murray Low …and Andy Mair", all of whom either lived in or visited South Africa, and who subsequently wrote on it. Cox (2002, xii) however also wrote in the same Preface that, amongst the various influences upon him, the Marxist geographer David Harvey has been the strongest: "He is the one above all who has shown the way forward" (Cox 2002, p. xii).

One work by Harvey that apparently influenced Cox's (2002) *Political Geography: Territory, State and Society* was Harvey's (1996) *Justice, Nature and the Geography of Difference.* Here Harvey (1996) coined the phrase 'historical-geographical materialism' to refer to his methods, which Cox (2002) also deploys in his more recent general texts and specific writings on South Africa (Cox and

Hemson 2008; Cox 2009). Another common denominator to both works is an interest in human identities, and perceptions of differences between communities. Strikingly, Harvey (1996, 21) points out in the first chapter of his aforementioned book that its own point of departure in this regard was reflection upon significant differences of perspectives amongst academics and activists, all of whom at the beginning of an Oxford project thought they had in common largely Marxist purposes with regard to the reconstruction of a specific locality (the Cowley plant in Oxford). The present article too reflects on some of these activist/academic interfaces, but in a South African context, as a way of exploring one set of avenues of the diffusion, adaptation and amendment of Cox's ideas.

In Kevin Cox's case it is the ideas that matter most, and it is also important to recognize from the outset that he never intentionally sought to influence practical politics in South Africa, either whilst in South Africa, or when elsewhere in the world.

Nonetheless, probably unbeknown to him, Kevin Cox's class perspectives on urban politics (together with its acknowledged quality) made his work – even that of the 1970s and early 1980s – interesting to people involved with South African opposition movements, especially those components of it with a socialist perspective, and in urban affairs.

A few examples of this were evident to the present author during the early 1980s, one of which is chosen for purposes of illustration of both direct and indirect influences upon categories of actors of influenced by Cox's earlier centre-Left perspectives and his intermediate Marxist-structuralist perspectives.

Direct Impacts and Indirect Consequences and Feedback

Maharaj and Narsiah (2002) would probably qualify as actors/observers in South Africa indirectly influenced by Cox earlier and intermediate perspectives, as we shall elaborate later. They point out that so-called progressive approaches to urban geography began in South Africa in the late 1970s, and then converged with popular mobilization against apartheid during the early 1980s into what they term as the "critical urban geographies of the 1980s". Here, they say, "the seminal contribution was perhaps McCarthy and Smith's (1984) book *South African City: Theory and Analysis in Planning,* which made a case for a structural Marxist approach to the study of South African cities" (Maharaj and Narsiah 2002, 89). The latter book and other works of the present author at about that time (McCarthy 1982; McCarthy and Swilling 1985) were clearly conceived under Marxist-structuralist influences received primarily from Cox, but also under influences of anti-apartheid activists and urban social movements in South Africa at that time.

The present author was not a member of either the (now ruling) African National Congress (ANC) or of the South African Communist Party (SACP), but he was actively involved in the United Democratic Front (UDF) during the

1980s. The UDF, in turn, was widely regarded as 'the internal wing' of the ANC (Ellis and Sechaba 1992), even if that – in the present author's perspective – is a mis-reading of how it actually formed and developed (in the present author's view, it was more a localized response to internal crises).

In any event, it is true that the UDF was often overlapping with especially SACP activists in its activities during the 1980s, and this is where Cox's work possibly first found its way inadvertently into South African urban politics. We should not over-emphasize such often indirect influences (subsequent, more direct influences for example on/via Mike Sutcliffe were likely much stronger), but the cases are nevertheless important partly for what they illustrate about the complexity of relationships between theory and practice.

The book *South African City* was partly inspired by the author's collaboration in the early 1980s with the Durban Housing Action Committee (DHAC) which subsequently became a leading affiliate of the UDF in Durban. DHAC, in turn, was an umbrella social movement bringing together local civic associations opposed to the (then white elected) Durban municipality, and these civics often sought the technical advice and assistance of the present author, amongst others, in their protest activities aimed at de-legitimizing and de-stabling apartheid rule.

The present author's doctoral thesis, supervised by Cox, had explored the interface between behavioural and organizational considerations, and protests about declining neighbourhood conditions in American cities (see for example Cox and McCarthy 1982). This, in turn led to an interest in relationships between neighbourhood activism and urban social movements (McCarthy 1981). On return to South Africa, he began applying some of this thinking outside of the universities, which soon brought him into contact with urban social movements in Durban. Specifically, the present author became engaged in *pro bono* support to the Clairwood Rateayers and Cato Manor Resident's Associations amongst others, some of which were affiliates of the DHAC.

The Secretary of DHAC then was Pravin Gordhan (who incidentally has since gone on to become South Africa's Minister of Finance). The present author first met Pravin Gordhan in 1983, a year or so after arriving back in Durban after a brief interlude at Rhodes University in Grahamstown, during which time the *South African City* book, referred to above, was initially penned.

How the present author's own (and Cox-influenced) perspectives or engagements were influential on DHAC is difficult to say. Nevertheless what can be said with certainty is that, over time, the present author learnt a lot from the latter (and especially Gordhan) about applying global theory to South African realities. Consequently in the Preface to the book *South African City – Theory in Analysis and Planning* we not only acknowledged Cox as one who had assisted in improving the book, but also explicitly concluded acknowledging "a number of community activists in Durban and elsewhere who have provided us with insight into what it really means to struggle for livable environments in South Africa" [mentioning people by name in print in the context of a Right-wing police state at the time was considered dangerous to their health].

Post-apartheid Urban Restructuring – Direct but Differentiated Impacts?

Also referenced in the Preface credits to the *South African City* book was Mike Sutcliffe. He became a major political actor in South Africa who was more evidently and much more directly influenced by Kevin Cox than say were DHAC activists or Maharaj and Narsiah (2002), with Sutcliffe's doctoral thesis having been supervised by Cox. Sutcliffe is at the time of writing the current (2004-2010) City Manager of the Ethekwini Municipality (greater Durban), and former head of South Africa's Demarcation Board which drew up the post-apartheid regional council and municipal boundaries.

In an interview published in the Durban newspaper, *Sunday Tribune,* on March 1, 2009, Mike Sutcliffe explicitly credited "the Marxist geographer, Kevin Cox" as an important influence upon his own thinking and work. That work – especially in practical terms – has not been inconsiderable, and has earned him rare awards for example from the Association of American Geographers for distinguished contributions to public service.

Sutcliffe nevertheless recently came into public conflict both with critical academics, and with activists in Left-wing urban social movements, largely around issues of identity and the process of urban reconstruction in the city which he now administers. These conflicts possibly highlight the importance of what Cox (2008; 2009) has most recently come to focus upon in South Africa – namely relationships between politics and identity, as they are situated within contestations around variable class interests within processes of capitalist accumulation.

Perhaps the most striking recent instance of these conflicts in the Durban area has been a set of exchanges around the so-called Warwick Triangle (WAT) area's redevelopment. These have been between Sutcliffe and a range of others, including a leading South African critical human geographer, Brij Maharaj (Professor and Chair of Geography at the University of KwaZulu-Natal (UKZN)). Maharaj, as is explained below, was also marginally influenced by Cox's works in his formative academic years, but also has something of an activist background and more recently has been aligned with social movements opposing some of the municipality's urban reconstruction plans for Durban's Warwick Avenue Triangle (WAT) area.

During the 1990s, Maharaj and colleagues wrote research articles critical of the capitalist accumulation biases of post-apartheid urban reconstruction programmes initiated by the municipality in Durban (Maharaj and Rambali 1998). At much the same time, another article by Maharaj (1999) reviewed the history of the Warwick Avenue Triangle area of Durban, which extolled its working class communitarian virtues and explained how a multi-racial identity was maintained in this area for decades, despite the best efforts of the then (apartheid) Durban municipality to destroy it. That paper traced the history of integrated residential development in the area and examined how slum clearance laws, the Group Areas Act and urban renewal programmes were used by the municipality to undermine the area, despite attempts by the residents to resist removal.

As Grest (2002) has observed in the socialist oriented South African journal *Transformation,* one of the reasons that WAT has acquired such a high level of resonance was that it represented a premonition during the apartheid era of what post-apartheid citizenship might be like:

> The notion of citizenship is both complex and contested, and its practice, especially in the context of the local area which is the focus of our discussion is equally so. Citizenship is one of the key ideas of contemporary South African politics. Its development holds out the promise of a better life for South Africans denied citizenship under the apartheid regime and is the subject of daily struggles of millions for a fuller life...The political reforms of the 1980s [creating four sub-categories of South African citizenship based on race] created the necessary space in the [WAT] Triangle of anti-apartheid community organisations linked to the United Democratic Front and pledged to combat...[municipal displacement and disruption of the area] (Grest, 2002, 41-42).

When the Durban municipality in 2009 appeared to put developers with shopping mall and taxi rank construction plans ahead of such ideals, this is when Sutcliffe (2009a; 2009b) and Maharaj (2009a; 2009b) and many other Durban academics apparently ran into their most serious public confrontation. Some further background about poverty and urban social movements in contemporary South Africa should help to place further discussion of the Sutcliffe/Maharaj differences, below, into some context.

As regards social movements in South Africa in 2009, it is probable that any senior urban administrator in post-apartheid in South Africa would sometime run afoul of these, such are the dynamics of popular expectations versus objective resource limitations. Indeed, by the third quarter of 2009, many democratically elected municipalities were quite literally under siege, especially in poorer, middle sized municipalities in the interior of the country.

The issues embraced by such movements varied. However, perhaps it was symptomatic of the state of affairs near the time of first preparation of the present article (mid-2009) that the main social movement challenge to the Durban municipal administration was coming from three sources: Those protesting at poverty and unemployment, which as Cox (2009) shows is growing rapidly in scale and depth in South Africa; at municipal displacement of self-employed street and market traders; and at the loss of local identities in the post-apartheid WAT context.

These protesters included the apparently hungry WAT people who in July 2009 stormed into food stores in central Durban, partly in protest about their being displaced as informal traders in the Warwick Avenue area by a planned formal shopping centre and associated set of taxi ranks approved by the municipality. After storming the stores, these protestors then ate the food *in situ* in these major chain stores, before being arrested and chastised, *inter alia,* by municipal officials. The *Mercury* newspaper's record of these events was as follows:

...about 100 people, members of the SA Unemployed Peoples Movement, were arrested for looting Durban city centre branches of Shoprite and Pick n Pay yesterday. The group's chairwoman, Nozipho Mteshane said they would continue their action until the government took them seriously. 'This is just the tip of the iceberg. I cannot stop the people because they are angry. We handed in a memorandum of demands to the city [municipality] a week ago and gave them seven days to respond and they have not'... 'We want the government to provide the unemployed people with a R1 500 a month basic income grant', she said. Onlookers at the Shoprite store on Dr Pixley Seme (West) Street said members of the group ate roast chicken, chips and other goods inside the store. Heavily armed police arrived and closed both stores. The looters inside the stores were then arrested...Municipal manager Michael Sutcliffe said the looting should be condemned. 'There seems to be a political element in this. It's true they handed in a memorandum last week and we know there is a lot of unemployment and poverty, but they are not the poorest of the poor, which is why we feel there are other elements involved. (*Mercury* newspaper, July 23, 2009, p. 3, Article '100 rampage through chain stores')

The "poorest of the poor" is of course a relative term. There are people in South Africa truly at the bottom of the pile (mostly in rural areas) and who are poorer than those arrested, but their incomes are probably half those of the chastised for illicit food-eating; and – for purposes of illustration – perhaps 2 per cent that of a senior academic; 0.5 per cent of that of a senior municipal official or a South African Cabinet Minister; or about 0.05 per cent of the income of a leading national businessman. Be that as it may, amongst the grievances presented to the municipality along with the memorandum referred to above, was the Municipality's support for a new formal sector shopping centre in the Warwick Junction area of Durban that would displace informal traders. This project, in turn, became the focus of intense public conflict between a number of critical academics based at UKZN (including Maharaj to be discussed below) and Michael Sutcliffe, the Municipal Manager.

In response to academic criticism mainly of the planning process at Warwick Junction, Sutcliffe (2009a) wrote an article published in the *Mercury* newspaper on June 15, 2009 entitled '*Now that the academics have woken up, its time they learnt the facts*', in which methodological issues were raised about the accuracy of UKZN researcher's observations on the WRT area, and plans for its redevelopment, as well as the differences between urban reconstruction in apartheid as opposed to post-apartheid times. He pointed out that the Municipality had for long wanted to build freeways over the WAT area, but had been prevented from doing so due to a lack of funds. Luckily in 2009 however they were able to draw upon national government funds as a result of improvements in transportation needed to facilitate South Africa's hosting of the 2010 FIFA World Cup.

We have been fortunate that because of the 2010 windfall in funding, we have been able to get the R1.2 Billion require to restructure roads around Warwick.

But there are social costs too. We have had to relocate thousands of people as we develop new roads...Over the past eight years we have relocated more than 1000 traders, in part to accommodate road and other construction projects...The differences between forced removals under apartheid and the relocations we do now are stark...Under apartheid there was no constitutional framework guiding what can and can't be done...(Sutcliffe, 2009a).

In many ways, this was fair and objective comment, but the fears of many academics were not allayed. Maharaj for example (2009a) argued that: "In both the apartheid and democratic eras, politicians have used and abused research for their own ends" (*Mercury* newspaper, June 18, 2009, p. 14, Article 'In defense of scholar's research on Warwick'*)*. In a subsequent academic seminar paper by Maharaj (2009b) he implied surprise that the municipality seemingly could be supporting property developers at the expense of informal traders and a strong legacy of civic organization against forced removals in WAT. In that paper, he argued the main issues under contest in the WAT area were the Municipality's plans to destroy an historic market, displace poor traders and deny them their livelihoods, in contrast to supporting the bigger business interests behind the Warwick Mall Pty Ltd (Maharaj 2009b). Whilst the ANC provincial government structures were eventually forced to intervene and mediate between the municipality and the morning market traders, the traders themselves (with whom Maharaj, 2009b, appeared to be more aligned) claimed such mediation had not yielded the desired effect. According the *Mercury* newspaper of October 21, 2009, the Chairman of the Early Morning Market Association, Harry Ramlal, whose members remained opposed to the construction of the mall claimed that:

The municipality is not concerned about poor people and is undermining informal traders. None of the informal traders in the precinct support the development which will benefit large businesses and not the informal traders.

Our interest here is less in the detail of allegation and fact than it is in differences in perspective and theoretical framework in addressing the facts. Hypothetically Sutcliffe and Maharaj should have been starting from similar conceptual points of departure. How did they arrive at such different perspectives in this case? Maharaj (2009b) believed there was substantial continuity with the practices of local government in Durban in respect of WAT in 2009 and what the same institution had done during the 1940s in actually pioneering *apartheid*. Whilst Maharaj was not academically supervised by Cox, his doctoral thesis on the local state and the implementation of urban apartheid in Durban is replete with references to Cox's work, and the same is true of much of his prolific journal publication since then. In addition he has collaborated in research with some of Cox's former students, including Murray Low around analyses of the incomplete realization of democracy in post-apartheid Durban (Low, Ballard and Maharaj 2007).

In part these and other studies probably shaped his sensitivity to the WAT case, as did his work on the critical evaluation of growth coalition projects in Durban. Maharaj and Ramballi (1998) for example focused on the Point Redevelopment Programme (a waterfront renewal initiative) and the International Convention Centre in Durban, both of which were key municipally-supported interventions designed to stimulate the tourism industry and thus, ostensibly, job creation. They concluded that the public-beneficial effects of these interventions were relatively weak, and that whilst most of the funding came from local government, most of the benefits accrued to private developers and hoteliers. In this they effectively confirmed an hypothesis advanced by another former Cox student Andrew Mair, when he was on a visit to Durban in 1988, and which he published in a local newspaper at the time (much to the ire of the then white-elected local municipality, which had contrived such plans, and which then roundly denounced Mair in response in the press).

To return to our conceptual problematic: Why, then, the differences between Sutcliffe (2009a; 2009b) and Maharaj (2009a; 2009b)? Why should Maharaj (2009b) stress apparent similarities between pre- and post-apartheid urban reconstruction; and Sutcliffe (2009a) point to the differences? At the most obvious level the differences could be those of institutional location. In *academia* abstractions are important; and, as Harvey (1996, 23) reminds us there are differences between "what it might mean to be loyal to abstractions rather than to actual people". In addition, in municipalities there are bureaucratic and constitutionally defined imperatives to serve 'the public interest' in ways that might inadvertently injure certain constituencies; and a question Sutcliffe (2009a; 2009b) raises is why academics should pick on certain areas like WAT specifically to demonstrate their apparently humanistic concerns.

An hypothesis we advance in the penultimate section of this paper is that much could be explained here though appreciating the importance of differentiated concepts of citizenship, since for one protagonist it is an historical premonition of post-apartheid citizenship that most mattered for WAT; and for another it is a here-and-now constitutionalist view. With that in mind, it is to Cox's recent own reflections on the ambiguities of citizenship in post-apartheid South Africa that we turn to next.

Cox, Hemson and Historical-geographical Materialism

In the present author's assessment, in many respects Cox's deepest insights on South Africa have been his most recent (Cox and Hemson 2008; Cox 2009). In the first of these cases, Cox collaborated with David Hemson, whose own history as an activist-cum-academic is also not irrelevant to the subject/s at hand. Hemson was a long-standing trade unionist who was once controversially expelled from the ANC ostensibly for his militant leftist tendencies (Ellis and Sechaba 1992). As both a trade unionist and social scientist, he retained his Marxist perspectives, and in collaborating with Cox in recent research work they (Cox and Hemson 2008) drew upon Mamdani's (1996) notions of the bifurcated colonial state in Africa, as well as the notions of historical-geographical-materialism, to analyze Durban dockworker's political loyalties. Cox and Hemson's (2008) method is to start with an open mind in looking at an array of data on migrant dockworkers and their political loyalties in KwaZulu-Natal, and arrive at the conclusion that the differentiated citizenship of such workers ('subjects' to a chief in their rural areas, yet citizens of a post-apartheid South Africa in the urban areas) leads to ambivalent loyalties. Moreover, they establish a regional bias to the expression of such ambivalences in political terms (e.g. in voting behaviour) amongst the so-called peasant-workers of KwaZulu-Natal (those from the more extensively chieftain-dominated northern areas being less ANC).

This work was based upon material from the pre-Zuma Presidency era, however, and indications are from the last South African elections that that the phenomena described by Cox and Hemson (2008) has been significantly undermined by a Zulu with traditional orientations now being placed at the helm of the ANC. Moreover, the 2009-era ANC has brought with it much stronger trade union and communist party influences than was the case in the past. Nevertheless, as Cox (2009) avers, the tasks ahead, developmentally, for the ANC are daunting, if for no other reason than that the skills base of the economy seems so fragile, and also that this base coincides with increasingly challenged concepts of citizenship and identity in South Africa.

At one point in his extensive review of trends leading up the present in South Africa, Cox (2009) makes a point which might seem surprising in isolation – that South Africa might have been better off if it had been colonized by the Japanese rather than the British. The reason he makes this point is that, unlike South Korea to whom Japan outsourced aspects of industrial development (and for which they needed to cultivate Korean skills), the British did not see such a need but rather focused upon extractive industries (e.g. mining, agriculture) where the width of skills required was modest, but where migrant, unskilled labour needs were high, the supply of which was facilitated by the bifurcated state to which Mamdani (1996) refers in his book *Citizen and Subject.*

Cox (2009) argues that scarce skills concentrated amongst whites and a small black middle class now lie at the crux of widening distributional inequalities and stunted economic growth, whilst the new nationalist project of the ANC is increasingly pushing it in a direction of demolishing or diminishing symbols of 'White' South Africa. Cox (2009) therefore writes of the "remarkable tit-for-tat" of replacing symbols of white identification with citizenship with those of black nationalism, and the contradictions this in turn places the state under with regard to the potential further loss of skills for example through emigration.

This brings us to Cox's (2009) latest and 'big picture' perspective on South Africa. In a chapter of his manuscript *South Africa and the Long History of Globalization,* entitled 'Globalisation and the decolonisation of South Africa: A hiding to nothing?' Cox (2009, no page nos.) opens by writing:

The sub-title of the last chapter was 'the end of the beginning.' Churchill said it at a certain point in the Second World War and clearly wanted to convey a sense of optimism about the outcome, while at the same time girding the British people to greater effort. I used it to refer to the overthrow of apartheid in South Africa. Apartheid was the colonial state taken to an extreme, so its overthrow meant something. But can one be as optimistic, even guardedly so, about the eventual outcome as Churchill was when talking about the progress of the war?

After some fifty pages of statistics on widening class inequality, stumbling economic growth, and new patterns of politicisation, Cox (2009) ends up with a negative prognosis, not too dissimilar from the non-Marxist Johnson's (2009) *New Left Review* analysis referred to earlier in this chapter. He recognizes that the ANC is going about the restructuring of old structures in creative ways, but Cox now sees through his historical-geographical materialist lenses slim room for manoeuvre. Cox (2009, no page nos.) finally compares the ANC's project with that of the former National Party and concludes as follows:

[The National Party] were blessed by the fact that their economic uplift project applied to a relatively small proportion of the total South African population: no more than about 12% in 1948. And of course, they were blessed by the fact that the global economy experienced a major period of boom during the first twenty years of their rule. All white boats could rise and did. Afrikaner ones rose more rapidly but not to the point that English-speaking whites felt seriously put out and would have considered emigrating.

The position that the ANC finds itself in is altogether more daunting. Blacks and especially Africans have been on the 'wrong' side of the racial divide and so lack the capacities that Afrikaners could benefit from. It is also a program of economic uplift that applies to a much, much larger fraction of the population. And global economic circumstances don't help. The National Party had the degrees of freedom that would allow a racialized interpretation of South African society. The ANC, if, and paradoxically, it is to bring about de-racialization and therefore decolonization, does not have that luxury.

There would of course probably be a number of those, either directly or indirectly influenced by Cox, and engaged in transforming South Africa today, who would dispute the ominous sound of that last sentence. But then, as Harvey (1996, 23) would ask when reflecting upon similarities and differences between activists and academics: "What is it that constitutes a privileged claim to knowledge and how we can judge, understand, adjudicate, and perhaps negotiate through different knowledges constructed at very different levels of abstraction under radically different material conditions?"

Conclusions and Questions

The breadth of the subject considered here inevitably raises as many questions as it does answers.

To start with some (approximate) answers to the questions set near the outset, Kevin Cox clearly has had both practical and intellectual impacts on South Africa. In the first instance, for example, it would seem improbable that Mike Sutcliffe would have become Chair of South Africa's municipal demarcation Board or City Manager of Durban had he not studied under Cox. To a lesser extent, someone like Maharaj, South Africa's leading critical 'human geographer of colour', would not likely have been as attracted to human geography or would have developed the interests within it that he did without at least indirect influences from Cox.

On the other hand, such relationships are not simple and can even be contradictory, as we have pointed out in this essay. Cox himself also changed his perspectives not only on South Africa, over time, but also on theory and epistemology. The same is true of others he affected. The present author, for example, went through something of an half-U movement, starting with Cox as a centre-left analyst, moving with him to Marxist-structuralism in the early 1980s, and then moving away again to centrist concepts and centre observations on restructuring post-2000 (see for example Bernstein and McCarthy 2002; and Robinson, McCarthy and Foster 2004). Others originally directly influenced by Cox have also presumably evolved differently, and their own personalities and perspectives have been asserted in their works on South Africa (see for example Kitchin 2004; Kitchin and Ovens 2009), often in as much applied as academic ways.

Perhaps the most refreshing aspect of all of this is its unpredictability, and variety – "people making their own histories but not (always) according to circumstances of their choosing". The common thread perhaps in it all – including in Cox and in all those discussed – is an interest in urban structure and restructuring, and in urban economics and/or policy of some type. Whilst they might not always have agreed given different perspectives and political positions over time, in one way or another urban political economy and South Africa as domains have caused them, and likely still will cause them to a degree of jostling interaction, some of which makes a difference to actual outcomes in South Africa; and others to the development of more global abstractions as (Harvey, 1996) would have put it.

To conclude: Did Kevin Cox find South Africa or did South Africa find him? The short and un-theorized answer is a little of both, but the more one reflects on the evidence it seems the latter was the stronger force (South Africans finding him). And then, when they found him, they used at least part of what they learnt from him to change their own environments, and to teach others here, though not always in ways that Cox himself would necessarily have been optimistic about!

References

Bernstein, A. and McCarthy, J. (2002), *Johannesburg – Africa's World City: A Challenge to Action* (Johannesburg: Centre for Development and Enterprise).

Bond, P. (2009), 'In power in Pretoria?' *New Left Review* 58, 75-82.

Cox, K. R. (1973), *Conflict, Power and Politics in the City: A Geographic View* (New York, McGraw Hill).

Cox, K. R. (2002), *Political Geography: Territory State and Society* (Malden, MA, Blackwell).

Cox, K. R. (2009), *South Africa and the Long History of Globalization*, Columbus, OH: Department of Geography The Ohio State University, Unpublished book manuscript.

Cox, K. R. and Hemson, D. (2008), 'Mamdani and the politics of migrant labour in South Africa: Durban dockworkers and the difference that geography makes', *Political Geography* 27, 194-212.

Cox, K. R. and McCarthy, J. J. (1982), 'Neighbourhood activism as a politics of turf: A critical analysis', in Cox, K. R. and Johnston, R. J. (eds), *Conflict, Politics and the Urban Scene* (London, Longmans), 196-219.

Dobson, R., Skinner, C. and Nicholson, J. (2009) *Working in Warwick: Including Street Traders in Urban Plans*. Durban, University of KwaZulu-Natal School of Development Studies.

Ellis, S. and Sechaba, T. (1992), *Comrades Against Apartheid: The ANC and South African Communist Party in Exile* (Bloomington, Indiana University Press).

Grest, J. (2002), 'Urban citizenship and legitimate governance: The case of greater Warwick Avenue and Grey Street Urban Renewal Project, Durban', *Transformation* 48, 38-58.

Harvey, D. (1973), *Social Justice and the City* (London, Arnold).

Harvey, D. (1996), *Justice, Nature and the Geography of Difference.* (Malden, MA, Blackwell).

Johnson, R. W. (2009), 'False start in South Africa', *New Left Review* 58, 61-74.

Low, M., Ballard, R. and Maharaj, B. (2007), 'Dilemmas of representation in post-apartheid Durban', *Urban Forum* 18, 247-64.

Maharaj, B. (1999), 'The integrated community apartheid could not destroy: The Warwick Avenue Triangle in Durban', *Journal of Southern African Studies* 25, 249-66.

Maharaj, B. (2009a), 'In defense of scholar's work on Warwick', *Mercury,* 18 June, p. 14.

Maharaj, B. (2009b), *Post-apartheid contestations: the struggle for the Warwick market in Durban: Proceedings of the School of Politics Seminar UKZN* (Durban, University of KwaZulu-Natal, School of Politics).

Maharaj, B. and Narsiah, S. (2002), 'From apartheid apologism to post-apartheid neoliberalism: Paradigm shifts in South African urban geography', *South African Geographical Journal* 84, 88-97.

Maharaj, B. and Rambali, K. (1998), 'Local economic development strategies in an emerging democracy: The case of Durban in South Africa', *Urban Studies* 35, 141-48.

Mamdani, M. (1996), *Citizen and Subject* (Princeton, Princeton University Press).

Marx, K. (1845), *Theses on Feuerbach* [Translated in Marx, K. and Engels, F. (1938) *The German Ideology*] (London, Lawrence and Wishart).

McCarthy, J. J. (1978), *Residential Growth in Durban: A Spatial Analysis* (Durban, University of KwaZulu-Natal. Unpublished Master's thesis).

McCarthy, J. J. (1981), 'Research on neighbourhood activism: review, critique and alternatives', *South African Geographical Journal* 63, 107-31.

McCarthy, J. J. (1991), 'Theory, practice and development: A geographical perspective', *Theoria* 78, 93-114.

McCarthy, J. J. and Smit, D. P. (1984) *South African City: Theory in Analysis and Planning* (Cape Town, Juta).

McCarthy, J. and Swilling, M. (1985), South Africa's emerging politics of bus transportation, *Political Geography Quarterly* 4, 235-49.

Kitchin, F. and Ovens, W. (2009), *Land Management and Spatial Planning in Towns and Cities.* (Pretoria, Urbanlandmark).

Kitchin, F. (2004), 'Expanded public works programme project ideas', *Innovation Insights* 3, 1-11.

Robinson, P., McCarthy, J. and Forster, C. (2004), *Urban Reconstruction in the Developing World* (Sandown, Johannesburg, Heinemann).

Sutcliffe, M. (2009a), 'Now that the academics are awake its time they learnt the facts', *Mercury,* 15 June, p. 6.

Sutcliffe, M. (2009b), 'Need to check facts of Warwick Triangle project before making criticisms', *Mercury,* 11 June, p. 8.

Chapter 10

Political Geographies of Capitalist Development in South Africa

Alistair Fraser

Introduction

Few geographers have sought to use the insights of Marxist Geography with as much intensity as Kevin Cox. As many of the contributors to this book demonstrate, Cox has committed a lot of his intellectual energy into using Marxist theories to develop a radical, innovative and indeed imaginative form of urban political geography. Cities in the advanced capitalist 'Global North' have been his primary research laboratories. But other, not-so-narrowly urban sorts of spaces have also shaped his evolving relationship with Marxist Geography – and I would suggest that South Africa is most definitely paramount among them. As I discuss in this chapter, Cox has discovered in South Africa a wide range of tantalizing geographical patterns, such as the country's unique urban geography, the extant explanations for which he has not found entirely satisfying. Looking to geographers such as David Harvey, as well as to other sources of inspiration in Geography, particularly Doreen Massey, Cox has forged a rich alternative theoretical framework to explain the peculiar nature of South Africa's capitalist development. The resulting ideas have interacted with research he has conducted on migrant workers and various other collaborations with former students. Together with his teaching, these research projects have deepened his understanding of South Africa and its uniqueness; but Cox has also sought to reveal the country's more general significance for how we understand the production of space. Cox has therefore used South Africa as a research laboratory for understanding geography; and geography to understand South Africa.

My research on the country's unfolding land question intersects with, and in key respects draws upon, Cox's understanding of South Africa. To a large extent, this is because he was my academic advisor while I studied for my Doctorate at The Ohio State University. And like other Cox students, his theoretical and conceptual innovations have heavily influenced my work. My aim in this chapter is to highlight some of these influences. In particular, I want to discuss how my take on South Africa has unfolded with the help of Cox's sharp thinking about the methodology of collecting empirical data. I therefore provide some examples of Cox's advice to me when I was in the field, which I use to argue that a key part of his skill – and something other geographers should strive to emulate – has been his openness to experiment with empirical realities towards finding new research questions that can ultimately shed light on the abstract issues that excite the discipline. My point, then, is to emphasize an aspect of Cox's *practical approach* to geographical research that risks going unnoticed amidst the celebrations of his conceptual contributions.

Kevin Cox, South Africa, and Geography

South Africa's recent history is exceptional. Of central importance here is the apartheid system which prevailed between 1948 and 1994. Apartheid was a strategy of territorial domination and fragmentation, the likes of which the world had never seen before in terms of its intensity and depth. It was based on cementing and re-casting various aspects of the country's geography. For example, apartheid pursued the strict division of already-segregated urban areas according to racial classification; the renewal and implementation of multiple laws and regulations that governed how people could move throughout the country; and the consolidation of native reserves into 'independent' homelands. Production of and control over space was germane to the apartheid project.

Not surprisingly, especially in the context of disciplinary interest in the production of space (Lefebvre 1991), South Africa has generated a lot of interest among geographers, including from some who were born and lived under apartheid (e.g., Paula Meth, Jeff McCarthy, Jennifer Robinson and Michael Sutcliffe), but also many others and not least Kevin Cox (Photo 10.1). Cox's interest in South Africa spans four decades. He first went there in 1983. In part, he was drawn by some South African students he had trained at The Ohio State University; but the principal cause was an invitation from the South African Geographical Society. He visited Johannesburg, Cape Town, and Durban; and what he found got him profoundly interested. He once recalled to me his amazement at the place and the way it had taken shape: '*Just fascinating!*' And it is fascinating; it is an extraordinary experience to weave one's way around the country for the first time. I did this in 2003, almost a decade into the post-apartheid era. When Cox first went there, of course, the apartheid state was under pressure but surviving. He would have been taking notes, asking questions, mulling it all over. And then, in a bookshop near Wits University in Johannesburg, he bought Luli Callinicos' (1980) *Gold and Workers* (Cox 2010, pers. comm.). Callinicos' book, which combines a Marxist reading of South Africa's capitalist development with a Howard Zinn-style people's history methodology and presentation, has continued to shape Cox's thinking about South Africa; and it is one of the main texts he uses in his undergraduate classes on South Africa. What Callinicos showed so clearly was just how important it was to the white rulers of South Africa that they produce a certain type of geography: how, for example, a labour market had to be forged via hut taxes; how people's movements had to be controlled; how land had to be taken and social relations re-cast. All of this sparked Cox's imagination. Apartheid – and the geography that it drew upon and produced – left an impression.

Photo 10.1 **Kevin Cox in Limpopo Province, South Africa (Author, May 2005)**

But in the 1980s, around the same time Cox began thinking in depth about South Africa, there was something else going on that would have had an impact on Cox and his relationship with South Africa: the discipline of Geography was changing. Geography was shedding its positivist legacy for new perspectives. Amongst the key developments, a new, more radical, more left-leaning and Marxist type of Human Geography was emerging. Cox followed this set of changes and was excited by the new concepts and ways of seeing space; these changes in the discipline must have been on his mind when we visited South Africa that first time and then subsequently thereafter. Indeed, as I want to suggest in this chapter, key conceptual developments in Geography have influenced his approach to South Africa. Any study of Cox's take on the country bears this out. In what follows, then, I highlight two ways that changes in Geography intersected with Cox's understanding of South Africa and discuss how that interaction has helped Cox develop a rich understanding of South Africa's peculiar form of capitalist development.

South Africa Through the Lens of Historical-Geographical Materialism

My first example refers to David Harvey's influence on Cox's thinking about South Africa. Harvey drew attention to the importance of capitalist accumulation in the making of diverse geographies *and* the centrality of space in the making of capitalism. He used Marx and Marxist theories to do so, but he also argued that those influences – versions of Marx's historical materialist approach – were inadequately geographical. Time, not space, was the key to Marx's explanatory framework; it was '*historical*' materialism because recognizing the historical development of society through different modes of production enabled an alternative future to be theorized. In contrast to this, Harvey found that, the 'spatial dimension to Marx's theory of accumulation under the capitalist mode of production has for far too long been ignored' (Harvey 1975, 9). His project, then, was to theorize how geography mattered in capitalist accumulation (Harvey 1982; 1985). In the process, Harvey developed an understanding of 'historical-geographical materialism' (hereafter, HGM) that could improve explanations of capitalist development *and* promote the place of Geography within social scientific inquiry as a whole.

Cox is one of the many geographers who have used the ideas underpinning HGM to further their research. One key outcome of this endeavour is his concept of 'local dependence', which is a development of Harvey's notion of the contradiction between geographical fixity and mobility. Local dependence comes into play when capital invested in a particular locality cannot easily move and so depends on a continuing flow of value through the local economy; when local governments 'depend on a local tax base'; and when workers 'depend on localized social relations' (for an overview, see Cox 2009). The concept helped geographers explain the significance of local-scale politics, even at a time when it might have seemed that extra-local relations were all that mattered (think: globalization). And the focus on local dependence and the spaces of engagement that emerge as a result of that dependence reinforced other developments in geography that encouraged interrogation of concepts of geographical scale. For Cox, then, spaces and places in the Atlantic core of contemporary capitalism were at the heart of his intellectual engagement with HGM, but he also worked closely with others interested in spaces outside the core, such as Bae-Gyoon Park, who under Cox's supervision examined the political geography of capitalist development in South Korea, looking at territorial struggles around development and how they were reflected in national level politics (Park 2008).

South Africa stands in stark contrast to these sorts of places because capitalism there has developed in a *uniquely* racist manner. It was capitalism, but not as Harvey theorized it, nor as Cox would have known it, even though he would have been familiar with racial segregation in parts of the United States (put simply, South Africa's development was racist in a much deeper way). The urban question in South Africa, for example, appeared as a racial question, as did questions about the land and agrarian development, or about the powers that the state or capital could wield. Issues of race always had to be placed alongside the process of capitalist accumulation. And in numerous ways, the country's geography reflected this odd marriage of racism and capitalism. There was the geography of group areas in the cities; the striking prominence of compounds and hostels in the townships; the prevalence of migrant labour; and the displaced urbanization in the native reserves/homelands/Bantustans. The challenge with which Cox sought to grapple was to develop an understanding of and explanation for the peculiarly racist way that capitalism developed. Not surprisingly, given the influence HGM has had on Cox's work as a whole, a key part of his approach has been to combine Harvey's take on HGM with inspirations such as Luli Callinicos and work by authors such as Dan O'Meara (e.g. see O'Meara 1983; 1996) to piece together an HGM-like theory that can improve how we understand South Africa. And the key to seeing why his view of South Africa's capitalist development is historical-*geographical* materialist rather than just historical materialist (which obviously has applicability, as scholars such as O'Meara have demonstrated) is his focus on the way space and its production has been central to the trajectory of capitalist development in South Africa.

As Cox has made clear in his teaching and in writings on South Africa (e.g. see Cox, Hemson and Todes 2004; Cox and Hemson 2008; Cox 2010; on Zambia, see Cox and Negi 2010), the most crucial consideration in understanding South Africa's odd geography of racial domination is the problem of securing labour power that capitalists had to confront from the outset of industrialization. First the mining sector and then manufacturing faced enormous difficulties in securing enough labour power and at a suitably low cost. In their efforts to resolve the problem, South Africa's capitalists sought to construct novel geographical arrangements. One of these was a system of migrant labour which drew in workers from rural parts of South Africa and from other countries. In other contexts, of course, industrialization and the expansion of capitalist social relations would have meant urbanization. But while this happened in South Africa, the level of urbanization was seriously curtailed via a set of policies known as 'influx control'. Under influx control measures, the arrival of black workers to the city was encouraged but those workers were not allowed to bring their families. The advantage here for the mines and for industry was that wage demands could be held back if labour power was reproduced in rural areas, in the reserves, and away from the inevitably-more-expensive city. This system of migrant labour, backed up by the archipelago of reserves, therefore helped to reduce the wage demands of black workers. A particular geography was constructed. Labour power could be secured, but not with the level of permanent settlement that a Marxist theory of urban development might have expected – and certainly not as Marx had witnessed when he theorized capitalist development in Western Europe.

Other arrangements also emerged from the effort to secure labour power at a suitably low cost. For example, industry's success in sourcing labour power posed problems for the agricultural sector, which was also confronted with the challenge of finding sufficient labour. Thus, at the same time as there were calls for influx control in the cities, many white farmers called for laws that would limit the numbers of Africans who could leave the countryside; that is, laws to enable 'efflux control'.

In all these efforts to secure labour power under specific conditions – and whilst managing tensions between different (and in the sense that they all had problems securing labour power, competing) branches of capital in South Africa – there has been the South African state. Up until 1948, the state was focussed on protecting white interests generally, but it advanced a much more racist agenda after the National Party won the 1948 election. Among numerous other changes, the new 'apartheid' state sought to change the status of the archipelago of native reserves from reserves to 'quasi-independent states' or Bantustans. There was a serious degree of racial thinking here: it was, after all, about advancing a programme of 'separate development', albeit one that would continue to give capital access to labour power. But promoting separate development was also always about limiting black urbanization; that is to say, about reducing what the state might have to spend on housing and infrastructure whilst retaining access to black labour. Once again, therefore, the challenge of securing labour power at a suitable cost helped shape the country's geography, the general structure of which remains to this day, even if the reserves, as such, have gone.

What Cox emphasizes about capitalist development in South Africa, then, is a clear sense of the extent to which a wide, diverse, complex, and overlapping geography was constructed to boost certain sectors of capital, even if at the expense of others, and dictate the terms under which the majority of South Africa's population would live. In his efforts to get to grips with this geography, Cox has pursued an understanding of South Africa that embraces an analysis of the spatial dynamics, dimensions, and indeed the tensions of accumulation. It follows from this that all other critical aspects of the country's peculiar development – such as the racial character of the state's actions or the peculiar racial form of urban development – can only be grasped by placing them in relation to the geography of accumulation. Race is central to understanding the place; but its centrality needs to be seen as a product of the way capitalism developed and in particular the battle that capitalists have faced in securing *the* key commodity in capitalist societies: labour-power. Clearly, then, insofar as Cox's take on South Africa places the tensions of accumulation in the centre, it is inspired by Marxism and we can detect Harvey's influence inasmuch as Cox sees the geography of capitalism as an integral part of the accumulation process. So far, so banal: what else should we expect from one of Marxist Geography's key thinkers? Yet there should be no doubt that other, less strictly Marxist influences have had a role to play in his theoretical understanding of South Africa.

Capitalist Order... and the Chaos of Space

South Africa fascinates Cox because its geography has been so peculiar. But South Africa is also of interest because clearly in evidence is way capitalists and the state have shaped the country in far-reaching and enduring ways that facilitate accumulation in general but also specific branches, such as mining and agriculture. In this sense, the material is all-important to an understanding of South Africa; the tensions of accumulation matter. But this is emphatically not to say that Cox is blind to other processes. Rather, Cox is quick to note that South Africa is a place in which accumulation has built upon the geography of difference; a geography that is intimately bound up with the specific racial politics of colonialism. Thus, what Cox emphasizes in his thinking on South Africa is a much more *social constructionist* stance than what some geographers might imagine he would stomach. In this regard, a prominent source of inspiration has been Doreen Massey's evolving approach to Geography and the production of space; an evolution, moreover, that occurred during the years that Cox developed his ideas about South Africa.

What Cox adopts from Massey (e.g. 1994; 1999; 2005) is a recognition that *combinations* of processes (including and in addition to accumulation) play a significant role in the production of space. Of particular significance here are Massey's ideas about the power of the 'happenstance'. Here is the key quote:

> There is always an element of 'chaos' in space. It is a chaos which results from those happenstance juxtapositions, those accidental separations, the often paradoxical character of geographical configurations, in which – precisely – a number of distinct trajectories interweave and, sometimes, intersect. (Massey 1999, 284)

According to Massey, then, space is always simultaneously produced by the 'chaos' of the accidental – this is the 'chance of space' (Massey 2005, 111-17) – alongside order, such as the logics of accumulation or the easy-to-grasp logics that lead states to act in favour of industry or finance or whichever sector is in trouble. Distinct processes of chaos and order meet up in a place and interact. Accumulation matters, as South Africa demonstrates, but it is not alone.

I want to suggest that Massey's view on the production of space helps Cox get to grips with the peculiar marriage of capitalism and racism that took shape in South Africa. Put simply, some key features of South African society might not have emerged if capitalist logics were strictly adhered to. Consider job reservation policies. These policies forged a racialised economy that artificially boosted white wages. But while job reservation protected the incomes of white workers and depressed black wages, it also limited the size of the domestic economy, hence 'eliminating possibilities of economies of scale in anything but those most basic wage good industries catering to a black demand' (O'Meara 1996, 172). Job reservation was counter-productive from the perspective of many domestic capitalists. Another example of South Africa's development not adhering to capitalist logics was the specifically racial character of the urban question. This was also far from inevitable: black urbanization was feared, curtailed, and shaped (via segregation) by white-ruled governments in part because of settler ideologies and racial prejudices. It need not have done so, but it did because race mattered in South Africa.

What these examples highlight is the extent to which the 'order' of capitalist accumulation met up with the 'chaos' of the accidental – and for Cox, as of course for many others, colonialism was central to explaining this. In particular, processes designed to separate Europeans and Africans, to take land, or control how Africans moved through the country, 'depended on the assumption of difference between the European...and the African: as it turned out, the assumption of a racial difference' (Cox 2010, no page nos.; my emphasis). And all of this hinged on the accidental, far from inevitable colonial '*social construction* of native peoples as uncivilized, inferior, technically inept, lazy, childlike' (ibid., my emphasis). What I want to draw attention to here is the fact that Cox incorporates this social constructionist point in large part because he sees a place for Massey's reasoning alongside the more rigid, even (as I suspect he would acknowledge!) dogmatic form of Marxist geography with which we associate him. There is, then, a fair bit of room in Cox's view of geography for the accidental, the chance occurrence, or what Massey (2005) refers to as the 'throwntogetherness' of space. Accumulation matters – and, for Cox, it matters a lot! But the production of space is not simply a product of the tensions accumulation conjures up. South Africa demonstrates this quite clearly and it has therefore helped enrich his understanding of and approach towards researching Geography. Of course, it is entirely possible that any interrogation of South Africa's geography would result in an approach that entails integrating a degree of sensitivity to the logics of accumulation with an appreciation of local circumstances and the specific way accumulation meets up with other social forces. But I find it useful to see Cox's willingness to incorporate the 'chance of space' into his much more Marxist approach as a reflection of his engagement with changes that have occurred in the discipline in the same period as his understanding of South Africa has taken shape. Like his interaction with Harvey's HGM, Cox has found in Massey's approach to space a set of useful ideas, concepts, and pointers and in South Africa a place where he can clearly see how they have been at work. What I now want to discuss is the way Cox's take on South Africa has influenced my work there.

Land Reform in South Africa

My work in South Africa has dealt with aspects of the country's land question. In particular, my doctoral dissertation research explored numerous aspects of the government's land reform programme as it unfolded in the northeast of the country, especially in and around a commercial farming district known now as Levubu (Figure 10.1).

The main focus of my work was on the restitution of land rights to communities who had been dispossessed in the late 1930s by the pre-apartheid state. In this regard, I spent a lot of my time researching the Ravele claimant community, whose ancestors were forcibly removed from their land around Levubu in 1938 and given a smaller, inferior piece of land 10km to the north and adjacent to the present-day village of Mauluma, which is located in the former Venda native reserve. Since 1938, and reflecting the limited opportunities available to black South Africans living in the reserves, the Ravele people have relocated throughout the wider region. Many went to the gold mines in and around Johannesburg. But some did

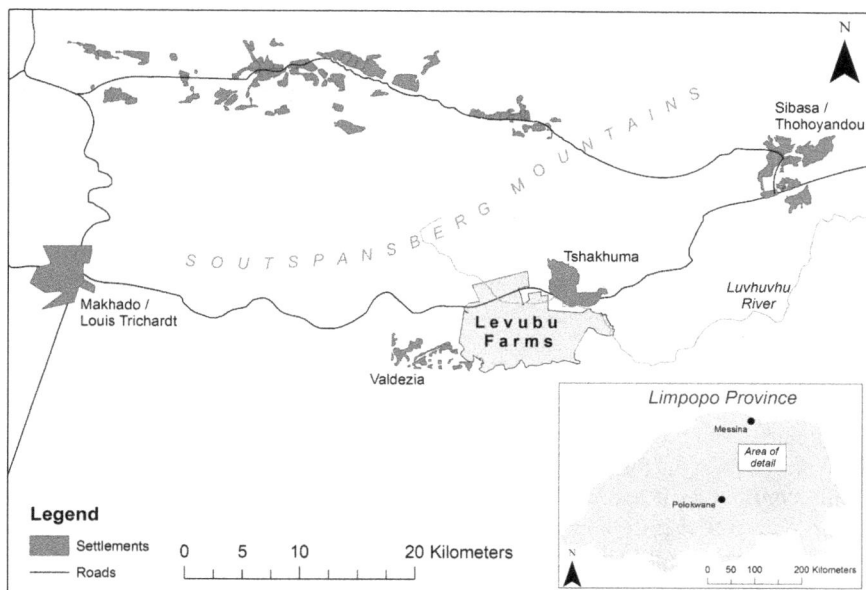

Figure 10.1   The Levubu area of Limpopo Province, South Africa

stay in Mauluma, not least because some among the Ravele traditional leaders became key players in the Venda homeland administration, which was established in 1979.

When apartheid ended and the new democratic government expressed its interest in restoring land rights, a group of the Ravele people, led by their traditional leaders in and around Mauluma, sought restitution of their land rights in Levubu. The overall process was time-consuming and long drawn-out. My research sought to examine as much of this process as possible. In one part of the work, I spent three months conducting interviews with leading claimants, ordinary beneficiaries, and members of the community who were affected by the claim. A key question was whether the 'community' of claimants, as recognized by the government, was united; and if not, then why not? I also sought contrasts with their claim by examining claims by other communities that were further on or behind in the restitution queue. What quickly became clear was that the Ravele people were in line to hit the 'restitution jackpot', that is, unlike many other 'communities' claiming restitution, the land from which they had been removed had been transformed into a highly productive and profitable agricultural zone. The white commercial farmers on the Ravele land had drawn on years of government support to transform the area into a technologically sophisticated and intensively-farmed environment producing export-quality avocados, mangoes, macadamia nuts, and citrus. Even if restitution meant the Ravele beneficiaries would receive only a small portion of an annual surplus from their restituted farms, that income would doubtless make a positive difference if it was used, as some of the leaders suggested, on education bursaries for children of the beneficiaries. This was the 'jackpot' which other claimant communities could not expect to receive if they ever had their land rights restored – many other pieces of land under claim in the wider area were of use for low-density cattle farming but not much else.

Another part of the research entailed tracking and interpreting the government's ideas about how to restore land rights without negatively affecting production on the commercial farms in Levubu. Certainly, government officials I interviewed expressed serious concerns that they must avoid ruining Levubu; and given international media representations of South Africa's malaise, including comparisons between its land reform and the fast track process in Zimbabwe to the north, such concerns were justified. The problem was that the intended beneficiaries had little or no experience of operating commercial farms; their ideas for what to do with the land were probably not going to ensure that production would continue as it had under the white farmers. The government's officials on the ground were therefore under pressure to restore land rights but only with great care. It was a sensitive process – and one that was far from easy to research. By the time I began my field work it was becoming clear that the government was leaning towards a proposal to force beneficiaries into so-called 'strategic partnerships' with some Limpopo-based agribusinesses. These deals would apparently ensure that production would continue under a profit-sharing agreement, but they would also lay out a future in which the beneficiaries would eventually assume full control over their farms. That, at least, was the plan (see Fraser 2007a; 2007b).

A final part of my research was about understanding the stance of the white farmers whom the government intended to pay off and have move on. I explored the stance of some of the Levubu farmers who were angling to shape and take advantage of the government's plans for partnerships; and worked on the actions of the farmers who were bluntly refusing to sell (Fraser 2008). This latter element led me to consider the activities of white farmers amidst land reform *and* the phenomenon known in South Africa as 'farm attacks', during which thousands of rural whites – including some in the areas in which I was doing my research and indeed one whom I had interviewed – had been killed. One element of the farmers' approach to farm attacks has been a voluntary paramilitary force/rapid response unit, which patrols white-owned farms and areas surrounding them. In addition, some farmers run farm security events in which they teach attendees how to use a wide range of weapons and how to patrol and defend their properties (see Fraser 2010).

Cox's Conceptual Contribution

As the preceding discussion noted, my research in and around Levubu involved a wide range of actors and demanded that I deal with some of the classic tensions that have shaped South Africa's capitalist space economy. Here, I want to draw attention to some of the ways that Cox's conceptual framework played a role in shaping how the research was defined, how it occurred, and how it was subsequently worked upon.[1] There are two issues here.

First, Cox may have had other concepts in mind at the time, but as I think back to 2004 and my arrival in South Africa to conduct the fieldwork, the most significant concept in my view was territoriality. As Cox had stressed I should understand it, thinking about territoriality did not just mean considering any sort of action intended to affect the content of an area, as per Sack (1983); but rather the actions of *certain* types of actors, specifically those involved in accumulation. This was because Cox sought to understand a place through the lens of HGM. This entails getting to grips with what capitalists are doing, what they want to but perhaps cannot do, and what obstacles are either in their way or are in the process of being removed. More generally, at issue is getting to grips with the contradictions and tensions that the capitalist accumulation process throws up in a specific place. In turn, this means paying special attention to those capitalist actors who are geographically immobile, more reliant on the local economy, and hence more liable to act territorially. In my case, therefore, Cox's influence steered me towards a focus on the commercial farmers whose land the government intended to purchase. Did some view themselves as immobile or did they see opportunities in leaving; and did those differences matter in the land reform process? What actions were the farmers undertaking? What tensions were apparent and what was their source? In other words, what were some of the micro-scale political geographies of land restitution?

There were, of course, a wide range of other issues involved in land restitution in South Africa, not least the ways in which the government was interacting with the beneficiaries. As with my work on the white farmers, Cox made a significant contribution to the way my research conceptualized these interactions. One question was why the claimants had agreed to the partnership schemes which were thrust upon them by government officials. It seemed like they were acquiescing too much; not holding out for a better, more realistic deal. The government's plan was for all of the beneficiaries' land to be operated under the strategic partnerships. But the beneficiaries could have demanded that they were only run on some, rather than all, of their land. There were some white farmers in Levubu who were willing to sell but stay on the land as tenants of the beneficiaries. Such an arrangement would have guaranteed some income for the beneficiaries alongside the riskier partnership scheme. Another option was for the beneficiaries to push the government into accepting that they could farm some of the land for food security purposes, for example by removing some of the older, less productive fruit trees and replacing them with food rather than cash crops. Instead of pushing for these options, however, my research revealed that the community's leadership, which was strongly associated with the traditional leaders, was leaning towards the partnership without fully taking into account all of the risks. They were gambling; in essence, taking the restitution jackpot they were about to receive

---

1   Of course, this is not to link Cox to any of my conceptual flaws!

and placing a 'double-or-nothing' bet that the partnerships would yield (what to me, at least, were unrealistically) positive returns. What was so interesting about this situation was that traditional leaders – sons and nephews of Venda's decentralized despots, as Mamdani (1996) viewed them – were making a major comeback in the new post-apartheid era. Rather than the end of apartheid marking the end of colonialism, processes such as land restitution called attention to the continuation of colonialism – or, as Gregory (2004) saw it, a 'colonial present' (see Fraser 2007b). A question with which I had to grapple was why the leaders were allowed to recover such influence. What Cox pushed me to theorize was the dilemma facing the South African state insofar as it was under pressure not to disrupt accumulation but yet deliver on some of the promises for redistribution which it made to the electorate. Part of the state's solution to this dilemma was to secure a lower cost of borrowing on international money markets; borrowings that the state could then use to invest in the cities or spend on infrastructure and hence help to create employment. And one way it fought to achieve this goal of cheaper borrowing was to pursue 'market friendly' solutions to challenges such as restoring land rights in Levubu. And if achieving support for such market friendly solutions entailed mobilizing traditional leaders, then so be it. Hence, the traditional leaders pushing for a sub-optimum solution to restitution were empowered by the state's determination to negotiate South Africa's vulnerable geo-historical position relative to the globalizing economy; that is, its place within the 'geopolitics of capitalism' (Harvey 1985).

Cox's Methodological and Empirical Contribution

Beyond Cox's conceptual and theoretical contribution, I should also like to note that my work on South Africa has been shaped by the sharpness of mind with which he approaches empirical issues and his willingness (and, indeed, encouragement) to experiment methodologically. Consider, for example, that one piece of advice to me was that, upon arriving in my study area, I should not prioritise visiting government officials involved in land reform, nor focus on land rights NGOs active in the area – two possible sources that I expect many an academic advisor would have emphasized. Rather, Cox's advice was that I should head straight for the local banks and speak with the bank managers about what was happening about land reform in the surrounding area. They would have a stake in the accumulation process and a perspective on the politics of local economic developments in the area. It was excellent advice. The banks were indeed worried about what was going on, active in encouraging some farmers to take a leading role in land restitution, and willing to point me in the direction of key figures in the white farming community. Some of the people I then contacted – including some prominent commercial farmers – proved instrumental in the subsequent research; and I cannot avoid thinking that being referred to them by the bank managers must have helped. Obviously, then, I benefited from Cox's thinking about the fieldwork and about South Africa.

But his attention to the empirical was closely connected to his conceptual understanding of South Africa. At issue was 'local dependence', which as I have discussed earlier was a concept he had developed with reference to his research in North America. Levubu was a key exporting area; many businesses in the wider area – as much as 30 per cent according to one of the bank managers – relied on production there. Land restitution was placing some local capitalists at risk; the banks were therefore involved. I explored many of these tensions as my research unfolded. Land reform was on the horizon and it was making an impact. Some farmers simply got out of agriculture as soon as they could. Others struggled on, refused to sell, and fought the process. The terrain on which I conducted this research was highly uneven but Cox's interest in paying attention to the dilemmas faced by capitalists, whether they were locally dependent or more mobile, definitely helped me to find my way.

A second way that Cox influenced my fieldwork was the emphasis he urged me to place on getting to grips with the white farmers' spatial imaginaries. He wanted me to ask what their horizons were; what they saw ahead; where they saw themselves locating should things go wrong in South Africa; what they intended doing to protect their investments. For Cox, the issue was whether the skills of the white farmers were going to stay in South Africa; whether they were preparing to exit; whether their contribution to the country's peculiar form of capitalist development would continue. His emphasis was on thinking about the long-term impact of land reform. The methodological approach he encouraged me to use was the semi-structured, open-ended interview. I conducted these interviews with farmers in the area and transcribed them almost immediately. The interviews were extraordinary enough; but equally amazing to me was that Cox wanted to read these transcripts in detail and would even go so far as to insert excited comments and type out page-length notes and bullet points on what the interviews might mean for the project and for South Africa. His interest in what the farmers were saying and doing about land reform, and what they said they could see ahead, in turn pushed me onwards. As with my visit to the bank manager, Cox helped me identify novel ways to approach the research; ways that he believed would yield insights. His interest in the empirical was shaped by his framework – in this case, and reflecting the influence of Harvey and Massey on his thinking, seeing imaginaries as a key way to understand how change is understood and then made.

A final example of Cox's empirical sharpness refers to a period towards the end of my research. I was going to have some afternoons free; some down time in which I could pursue related mini-projects (perhaps material for teaching purposes). I had noticed that very few trees were surviving in and around the former Venda homeland. Out of sheer necessity, people were trimming and felling trees, to such an extent that the landscape was denuded, even barren. It was also apparent that poverty shaped the type of agriculture that developed in Venda, as opposed to the type of agriculture the white farmers 10km to the south pursued. I discussed these contrasts with Cox. He suggested that I take some photographs of these different landscapes and then run a short survey among blacks and whites in the area to see what they might associate with each sort of photo. I followed his advice and gave the survey a trial run. Unfortunately, it simply did not work. Perhaps my questions were poorly crafted, perhaps the photographs were not clear; but for whatever reason I did not get a good feel about the work. I abandoned it. But I have always been struck by Cox's willingness to experiment with those materials. He was open to the possibility that something might come of it. He could imagine the abstract concepts at work: ideas about landscape, competing notions of what home looks like, the spatial imaginaries and horizons of black and white South Africans. There was – and is – an extraordinary sharpness to his thinking; the empirical matters and he is keen to find a method that will help him reveal data that can shed light on the abstract. These are traits that all geographers would do well to imitate.

Conclusion

Cox found in South Africa a fascinating place to do research; a laboratory of sorts. He pursued a sort of revised regional geography there, one that seeks to understand the place in its own right. Of course, like others interested in South Africa, he has turned to Marxist-inspired theories to explain the place. And like others, he has kept the struggle to secure labour power at the centre of his analysis. He has, therefore, built a theoretical understanding of South Africa that stands up to Marxist scrutiny. But what Cox has also sought to do is come at South Africa with spatial concepts in mind. He has pursued a geographical understanding of South Africa. He found a peculiar geography and has sought to explain it.

But given South Africa's peculiar form of capitalist development, he has inevitably been forced to draw numerous contrasts with the arenas in which most of his work occurred. This in turn has led him to use South Africa as a vehicle for developing his understanding of geography as a whole. In trying to understand South Africa, then, he has asked how space and place in general are produced. As I have noted, the theoretical possibilities of using HGM have been most apparent to him, but he has not been quite so dogmatic as to stick only with the view of space that HGM sets forth. Rather, Cox has used South Africa as a vehicle for coming to terms with the role of the accidental in the production of space. Capitalist logics matter, but they are not enough to explain how space emerges. As my work in South Africa tries to demonstrate, for example, the logic of creating a national space economy in which accumulation can continue has affected the government's approach to restitution in Levubu and led it to create novel arrangements. The strategic partnerships established in Levubu were hybrid entities in which market-led and more stentorian state-led influences were blended to produce outcomes that subordinated the interests of land reform beneficiaries to the interests of capitalist accumulation nationally. So we can find the logics, the order. But as recent events in Levubu suggest, the accidental still makes its way into the frame. At the time of writing (January 2011), the partnerships have unwound – in part because the agribusinesses involved in the partnerships were poorly managed and went bankrupt after credit from their banks was refused. The state's faith in 'market-friendly' solutions to the land question was misplaced; as such, many of the tensions around land reform in Levubu remain unresolved and are (worryingly) festering. Order and chaos; the logic and the accidental meet up, just as Cox has sought to theorize with respect to South Africa and space more generally.

South Africa has changed since 1983, when Cox first went there...and for the better. But many of the features that excited Cox remain. The country still has an urban question that is tied up with accumulation and race. Migrant workers retain footholds in the former homelands. Competition for labour power between different branches of capital remains important. More generally, addressing the tensions that South Africa's capitalist development throws up continues to entail the production of space. What Cox demonstrates so vividly in his teaching and research on South Africa is the gains to be made from a concerted, intense, and yet broad and extensive engagement with understanding how these persistent features of a place might matter.

References

Callinicos, L. (1980), *A People's History of South Africa* (Johannesburg, Raven Press).

Cox, K. R. (2009), 'Local economic development, politics of', in R. Kitchin and N. Thrift (eds), *International Encyclopedia of Human Geography*, 239-44.

Cox, K. R. (2010), 'Module two', *Geography 608: South Africa: Society and Space* [online] Available at: http://www.geography.osu.edu/faculty/kcox/g608/module2.doc (Accessed November 5, 2010)

Cox, K. R., Hemson, D. and Todes, A. (2004), 'Urbanization in South Africa and the changing character of migrant labour', *South African Geographical Journal* 86(1).

Cox, K. R. and Hemson, D. (2008), 'Mamdani and the politics of migrant labor in South Africa: Durban dockworkers and the difference that geography makes.' *Political Geography* 27, 194-212.

Cox, K. R., Hemson, D. and Todes, A. (2004), 'Urbanization in South Africa and the changing character of migrant labour', *South African Geographical Journal* 86:1, 7-16.

Cox, K. R. and Negi, R. (2010), 'The state and the question of development in Sub-Saharan Africa.' *Review of African Political Economy* 37:123, 71-85.

Fraser, A. (2007a), 'Hybridity emergent: geo-history, learning, and land restitution in South Africa', *Geoforum* 38, 299-311.

Fraser, A. (2007b), 'Land reform in South Africa and the colonial present', *Social & Cultural Geography* 8, 835-51.

Fraser, A. (2008), 'White farmers' dealings with land reform in South Africa: Evidence from northern Limpopo province', *Tijdschrift voor Economische en Sociale Geografie* 99, 24–36.

Fraser, A. (2010), 'The craft of scalar practices', *Environment and Planning A* 42, 332-46.

Gregory, D. (2004), *The Colonial Present* (Oxford, Blackwell).

Harvey, D. (1975), 'The geography of capitalist accumulation: a reconstruction of the Marxian theory', *Antipode* 7, 9-21.

Harvey, D. (1982), *The Limits to Capital* (Chicago, University of Chicago Press).

Harvey, D. (1985), 'The geopolitics of capitalism', in D. Gregory and J. Urry (eds), *Social Relations and Spatial Structures* (London, Macmillan), 128–63.

Mamdani, M. (1996), *Citizen and Subject: Contemporary Africa and the Legacy of Late Colonialism* (Princeton NJ, Princeton University Press).

Massey, D. (1994), *Space, Place, and Gender* (Minneapolis, University of Minnesota Press).

Massey, D. (1999), 'Spaces of politics', in D. Massey, J. Allen and P. Sarre (eds), *Human Geography Today* (Cambridge, Polity Press), 279-94.

Massey, D. (2005), *For Space* (London, Sage).

O'Meara, D. (1983), *Volkskapitalisme: Class, Capital, and Ideology in the Development of Afrikaner Nationalism, 1934-1948* (Cambridge, Cambridge University Press).

O'Meara, D. (1996), *Forty Lost Years: The Apartheid State and the Politics of the National Party, 1948-1994* (Randburg, South Africa, Ravan Press).

Park, B-G. (2008), 'Uneven development, inter-scalar tensions, and the politics of decentralization in South Korea', *International Journal of Urban and Regional Research* 32, 40-59.

Sack, R. (1983), 'Human territoriality: A theory', *Annals of the Association of American Geographers* 73, 55-74.

Chapter 11

'Everyday Life is Situated': Politics, Space and Feminist Theory

Kim England

A few years ago, I was invited to participate in a session organized around the theme of this book at the 2008 Association of American Geographers' Annual Conference in Boston, Massachusetts. session organizers (Andy Jonas and Andy Wood) suggested it was a "propitious moment in which to examine the influence of Kevin Cox's work on urban and political geography." At that point it had been 20 years since Kevin's important paper with Andy Mair "Locality and Community" had been published in the *Annals* and 10 years since his "Spaces of dependence, spaces of engagement" appeared in *Political Geography*. It was also two decades since I finished my PhD with Kevin as my PhD advisor. When I first arrived at The Ohio State University (OSU) there were no women on the regular faculty. This was typical of too many departments at the time, as was made clear in a watershed publication in the emergence of feminist geography in the US. Jan Monk and Susan Hanson (1982) published their manifesto, 'On not excluding half of the human in human geography' around the time I arrived at OSU. Monk and Hanson challenged the sexist biases in geography's supposedly neutral assumptions, theories and methods (giving plenty of examples) and made the case for "the profound social change that would be wrought by eliminating sexism" in Geography (1982, 11).

Once it became clear to me that I wanted to become a feminist geographer, Kevin while initially somewhat perplexed and in need of convincing was supportive of my intellectual forays, some of which for him surely seemed random and impetuous. It was he who first directed me to the Monk and Hanson piece. Kevin was, of course, no feminist geographer (and is still not!), nor has he ever claimed to be. I consider it a mark of his intellectual security (and brilliance) that he was comfortable enough to guide my choice of research topics, without insisting on steering me towards urban political 'territory' more familiar to him. In that process we did not always agree on (and perhaps still don't!) what sites, scales and practices count as 'political' and which topics get counted as 'political geography' (and who decides what counts!). As an advisor he was incredibly generous with his time – prepared to delve into literatures that were new to both of us and discuss (or was it argue?) with me about the strengths, weaknesses and usefulness of what we read. I greatly benefited from his sharp intellect, his insistence for clarity of thought and high quality writing, as well as his remarkable, seemingly encyclopedic memory for pieces of scholarship he had read in areas well beyond his own (like Marxist feminist theory). In so many meetings we'd be discussing ideas and an unexpected turn in our conversation would remind him about an article in some journal I had not yet heard of. I would then scurry off to the library in search of what almost always turned out to be a gem. Kevin himself has produced an enviable number of publications that are gems. These include the 1988 "Locality and Community" *Annals* piece and the 1998 "Spaces of dependence, spaces of engagement" in *Political Geography*. Together these pieces capture the impact of Kevin's impressive contributions to urban and political geography, and I use them to structure my reflections in this chapter.

Local Dependence, Spatial Entrapment and Feminist Theory

When I was a graduate student, most of Kevin's work focused on theorizing and investigating the politics of local economic development, and especially the place-based conflicts and business coalitions that arise in this process. The ideas he and Andy Mair developed around 'local dependence' stem from asking why a particular set of superficially unconnected firms and business interests in a particular locality would come together with the local state to form strategies aimed at securing local economic growth. To address this, they extended David Harvey's arguments about the contradiction between the mobility of capital and the necessarily spatially fixed investment in the built environment required for production and capital accumulation (e.g. Harvey 1982; 1985). Their concept of local dependence "signifies the dependence of various actors – capitalist firms, politicians, people – on the reproduction of certain social relations within a particular territory" (Cox and Mair 1988, 307). Many of these 'various actors' are reliant on locally embedded social networks, based on "predictability, trust, brand loyalties and unique local knowledge" (p. 309), and these social relations require constant upkeep so that capital will continue to flow through them. At the same time, investments in the built environment are spatially immobile and tie a firm to a location which must prosper economically before the value of the spatially fixed investments is realized. The local state gets drawn it because it too relies on a territorially defined local tax base to be able to, for example, fund public services. Such actors then are especially interested in continued growth and investment in their locality and this shapes business strategies and government policy-making.

The concept of 'local dependence' has had a considerable impact on geography and beyond. A quick search on Google Scholar indicates the 1988 *Annals* paper has been cited almost 400 times. Most of the authors and the editors of this collection are among those who have cited it. I, on the other hand, have never cited this paper before now! Yet this paper is a key landmark in my intellectual history, symbolizing a major facet of my graduate training. Although I did not know it at the time, I was lucky enough to be a graduate student at OSU at the same time as a remarkable set of students, including "the three Andrews, Jonas, Mair and Wood" (Cox 1998, 4). This made for some lively and provocative graduate seminars with Kevin, animated discussions over beers and life-long friendships.

As I proceeded through graduate school it seemed to me that Kevin continually offered new research seminars based on different readings (and how extraordinary that was only dawned on me once I began preparing my own suite of undergraduate and graduate courses). Thus I, as did others, took seminars with Kevin almost all the way through my entire graduate career. Chunks of some of those seminars involved Kevin and Andy Mair sharing and working through ideas that resulted in their 'local dependence' concept. I recall receiving numerous typed mimeoed handouts about different aspects of their project with "comments?!" handwritten across the top. As I reflect on that time, I now have a better appreciation of how significant it was to experience them formulating many of their ideas in real time. As Kevin and Andy rehearsed and refined their ideas and asked for our feedback, it clear they did not agree on several points, and from time to time engaged in intellectual jousting with looks of exasperation on both sides. While I occasionally found this bewildering and intimidating, it was often entertaining, and I remain impressed by the collegial and open manner in which Kevin handled this obviously collaborative venture with Andy.

While I broadly defined myself in graduate school as an urban political geographer (after all I had read all that Marxist theory, urban growth machine, and territoriality literature), I did not fit squarely in that frame in ways that others working with Kevin did. Increasingly, I was drawn to feminist studies. I read debates about the emergence of feminist geography with relish; I sought out and took feminist theory classes. I read feminist critiques of traditional Marxist theory that explored the "unhappy marriage of Marxism and feminism" (Hartmann 1979). From Marxist theory I learned that capitalism was supposedly the first mode of production to be indifferent to the social identities of the people in the exploited class (all workers are exploited, and therefore all workers are 'equal' in the workplace), that capitalism developed without regard for gender, race, ethnicity, sexuality and so on. On the other hand, feminist theories taught me that pure capitalism, indifferent to the social identities of workers absorbed into the labor market enabling surplus value to be incessantly extracted in a continuous cycle of accumulation, had never existed. Through feminist theory I became aware that Marxist theory appeared oblivious to the significance of unpaid domestic labor occurring in the homes of workers, especially in discussions of use and exchange values. As Iris Young (1981, 52) argued:

> Such traditional women's tasks as bearing and rearing children, caring for the sick, cleaning, cooking, etc. fall under the category of labor as much as the making of objects in a factory. Using the category of production or labor to designate only the making of concrete material objects in a modern factory has been one of the unnecessary tragedies of Marxian theory.

So I realized that reproductive labor was a vital component of capitalism, necessary for the daily and intergenerational reproduction and maintenance of 'productive' laborers, helping to keep wages down and profits up.

I looked for scholarship that conceptually and empirically made links between reproduction, consumption and production, and ways that Marxist feminist theories were being integrated into geography. I was especially influenced by Linda McDowell and Doreen Massey's (1984) pioneering research on spatial and gender divisions of labor that highlighted women's historically and spatially differentiated experiences of paid work in various localities and economic sectors across England. Thus I became intrigued by feminist geographies of economic restructuring, labor markets and home-work linkages. For my dissertation I examined the role of local clerical labor markets in the changing geographies of office locations in American cities. This work developed out of my discomfort about stylized discussions in the literature about both clerical workers and white, married suburban women. I was troubled by the common portrayal of suburban mothers as helpless, even hapless victims, constrained by the suburbs; and how that veered too much into spatial determinism. I recoiled at descriptions that suggested that these women were too dim-witted to realize they were being exploited by 'capitalists'. I focused on conceptually and empirically exploring the popular view that white, suburban married women were a 'spatially entrapped' labor supply willing to accept low paid clerical work and the extent to which this entered into the location decisions of firms employing large numbers of clerical workers (England 1993; 1995).

Although it often seemed I was on a different though often parallel track from Kevin and most other students working with him, together we all delved into the intellectually rich and exciting world of spatial divisions of labor, Fordism/post-Fordism, socio-spatial dialectics, and critical realism. The discussion and debates about 'local dependence' in all those seminars with Kevin obviously shaped how I framed some of my ideas about spatial entrapment. While Kevin and Andy's concept of 'local dependence' was deployed in the context of the politics of local economic development, they did suggest that it was "applicable to a broader array of substantive interests, including industrial geography, labor mobility, the local state and the micro-geography of social life" (Cox and Mair 1988, 308). They include a lengthy discussion of 'the local dependence of people', where they argue that people as well as firms and local states are locally dependent.

> But people can also be locally dependent. Personal social interaction usually takes places in a localized socio-temporal context. Everyday life is *situated*. Children attend particular schools at particular times. Mutual aid is with particular neighbors. People attend particular churches at particular times. These practices tend to get routinized, and for very good reasons. Once settled, they not only facilitate realization of individual ends, but in addition they create a world of predictability and confidence. There is then resistance to change, including spatio-temporal change. Regardless of the precise social relationships at issue,

therefore, there is a material basis for people to be locally dependent. (Cox and Mair 1988, 312).

Some of my clerical labor markets research can be interpreted as extending the idea of the 'local dependence of people' and the 'micro-geography of social life' and showing that 'everyday life is situated'. My goal was to trouble the assumptions in geography, planning and urban studies literature that flowed from the apparent immobility (spatial entrapment) of white suburban women as evidenced by, for example, the short commutes of women, especially married mothers. I argued that spatial fixity is at the heart of women's (and men's) experiences of paid employment, but the 'spatial-entrapment-of women thesis' is an overgeneralization and over-simplification of that experience. By positioning women as knowledgeable agents enmeshed in localized social relations, short journeys-to-work should be viewed as one possible strategy to be adopted as part of what we now call work-life balance.

Seen through the lens of 'local dependence of people' such spatial strategies for work-life reconciliation will, to quote Andy and Kevin "usually take place in a localized spatio-temporal context" (p. 312). These include good child-care arrangements, the local school system, and low mortgage payments. It could also be that the clerical worker's job that others might condescendingly describe as low status, provides her family's health insurance or is the only source of reliable income. There may be, as Kevin and Andy suggest, "firm-specific practices and structures that the individual employee gets 'locked into', the availability of flexi-time or good day care facilities or a particular career ladder and promotion procedures not replicable elsewhere." (p. 312). In addition, women living with partners make residential and/or employment decisions that account for their partner's workplace as well as the needs of their children. These all serve to spatially limit women (and men's) options. As Kevin and Andy remarked, "Everyday life is *situated*" (1988, 312, original emphasis). This situatedness means that women have evolving networks of social relationships that produce the spatially sticky materiality of their everyday lives. "Within capitalism, people, like firms, construct relationships that are difficult to substitute and therefore difficult to replicate elsewhere" (Cox and Mair 1988, 313). Thus a particular web of localized socio-spatial relations may bind a person to a particular neighborhood, job and house. So that "although initially contingent, the workplace, the living space and the particular social system of everyday life which they jointly constitute tend to acquire for people a certain necessity" (Cox and Mair 1988, 313). In other words, fully understanding the materiality of people's everyday lives involves considering a multiplicity of overlapping, changing and often contradictory set of socio-temporal and spatial relations.

That 'everyday life is situated' has long been a theme for feminist geographers, although not employing the term 'local dependence' they consider the relative spatial immobility of certain social relations. Some have developed analyses that emphasize the interconnections between, and the relational geographies of home, neighborhood and the paid workplace. For example, in their extensive study of gender, work and space in Worcester, Massachusetts, Susan Hanson and Geraldine Pratt emphasize people's 'rootedness' in their exploration of the complex links between domestic responsibilities, occupational segregation, job search and residential choice (Hanson and Pratt 1995). Melissa Gilbert (1988) foregrounds issues of race as well as class and gender in women's place-based personal networks, arguing that "power should be conceptualized in terms of a multiplicity of interconnected, mutually transformative, and spatially constituted social relations" (Gilbert 1998, 596). More recently, Helen Jarvis (2005) explored the socially and materially embedded "infrastructure of everyday life" that shapes the work-life choices of middle-class families. And Kevin Ward and his colleagues explore how low-income women's "constrained juggling act" is spatially situated in the 'local' social relations of their urban working class community (Ward et al. 2007).

Broadly understood then, 'the local dependence of people' has a great deal of appeal. In many respects, what it captures is what animates many critical human geographers – investigating the material and representational connections between politics, power and space. The concept of local dependence has primarily been taken up by those interested in the political-economy of local development, most often with a focus on capital and the state, and to a lesser extent, labor. But for me that amplifies the ongoing emphasis in political and economic geography on capital, the state and labor to an extent that often feels like I'm being catapulted back into the Marxist-feminist critiques about reproductive labor that I first encountered in graduate school. Even after this many years it still needs repeating that feminist scholars have redefined what counts as 'political' in geography. Marginalizing or ignoring social reproduction can limit the theoretical and empirical power of any analysis of capital-state-labor relations. This has been forcefully argued by feminist geographers addressing debates on the social construction of scale, who make a case for finer scales such as the home and the body (e.g. Marston 2000; England 2003). For instance, Marston (2000, 232) notes that "the home as a socially produced scale – a scale that is thoroughly implicated in wider social, political and economic processes." Such refinements capture the full complexity of scale construction and challenge theories of scale as a hierarchical division of bounded territories (global, national, local, etc.) that allocates particular activities, practices and processes to a particular scales. Instead, scale is understood as relational and as a tangled web of networks, social relations and material practices operating across an array of scales.

Kevin, of course, has made important interventions into the debate on scalar politics. For him it is not so much the social construction of scale that is significant, but the construction of the *politics* of scale. His goal is to produce a rich and complex understanding of 'local politics' and to 'locate' local politics. In this endeavor he troubles the "areal concept of scale" (1998, 19) and instead suggests using networks as a metaphor and approaching scale as spatialized social networks. For Kevin, local politics is more than the politics of the local state (as in hierarchical divisions). Instead he theorizes local politics as rooted in a place but moving beyond the local jurisdictional boundaries to create "networks of associations" with localities and institutions at various scales. The framework he developed to demonstrate his ideas, which I turn to next, is one that *has* captured the attention of feminist scholars, who have used to explore such diverse topics as maternal health in Mexico (Mills 2006) and political action by Québec's women's movement (Masson 2006).

Spaces of Dependence, Spaces of Engagement and Bringing in the State

The 1998 "Spaces of dependence, spaces of engagement" piece is yet another heavy hitter in the citations department. Kevin offers an appealing framework around which to both analytically *and* empirically explore the production of local politics via the politics of space, scale and networks. 'Spaces of dependence' are "those more or less localized social relations upon which we depend for the realization of essential interests and for which there are no substitutes elsewhere; they define place-specific conditions for our material well-being and our sense of significance" (1998, 2). So people, communities and institutions are dependent on localized social relations for which there are few if any substitutes in other locations. That said, "…typically agents are participants in a much more spatially extensive set of exchange relations than those contained within the bounds of a particular place" (Cox 1998, 4). Thus the actual *content* of the politics of something highly localized can extend well beyond the territorial *form* of the local. Sustaining and defending the conditions that produce spaces of dependence often involves constructing networks of association with other actors and other centers of power. Through this process a different form of space is created. This is a space of engagement which Kevin defines as "the space in which the politics of securing a space of dependence unfolds. This may be at a more global scale than the space of dependence, as per the idea of 'jumping scales' but it may not be" (1998, 2). Indeed, he is rightly adamant that jumping scale is not unidirectional, and is not necessarily an upward shift of politics because "the world of politics is much more open than this" (1998, 3). To move away from a hierarchical understanding of scale, Kevin suggests conceptualizing the politics of scale relationally through networks of associations often connected across scales. He notes that "agents, experiencing a problematic relation to a space of dependence, construct through a network of associations a space of engagement through which to achieve some mitigation" (Cox 1998, 3-4).

When I first heard Kevin speak of his spaces of dependence/spaces of engagement framework I was immediately impressed with how he had sorted through and distilled a set of unruly ideas (about local politics, space and scale) and nicely captured them in this deceptively simple, but incredibly useful framework. Over the years, I have seen how others had adopted and adapted it, and come to appreciate its versatility. In working on this chapter I have used it as a lens through which to rethink some themes in my research (much in the same fashion as Kevin applied the framework to a series of disparate case studies). Here I put it into conversation with my work of welfare provision in the US. In a piece I wrote for Kevin's collection, *The Sage Handbook of Political Geography* (co-edited with Murray Low and Jennifer Robinson), I explored the political geographies of welfare provision and welfare reform using a feminist analysis of the state and welfare systems. I argued that the 'public' (as in the state) is deeply implicated in the 'private' space of home, and I also drew on the politics of scale literature to show that social and spatial relationships taking place *within* homes are closely tied to other geographic scales (England 2008). For the current exercise however I follow Kevin's lead and focus more centrally on the state and the creation of spaces of engagement via networks of associations.

In his Second New Deal of 1935-36, President Franklin D. Roosevelt signed in legislation that introduced the Works Progress Administration, the National Labor Relations Act and the Social Security Act. On the latter, in his message to Congress in June 1934, Roosevelt announced:

> I place the security of the men, women and children of the Nation first... (including) security against the hazards and vicissitudes of life. ...If, as our Constitution tells us, our Federal Government was established among other things, 'to promote the general welfare,' it is our plain duty to provide for that security upon which welfare depends.

Roosevelt then promptly set up the Committee on Economic Security (CES) to study economic insecurity and make recommendations for expansive federal legislation to offer economic security that was inclusive and national in scope. His reference to "the Nation" and citing the "promote general welfare" statement in the Preamble to the Constitution, not only indicates that as President the entire country is his space of *dependence*, but also that Roosevelt's assertion that "it is our plain duty" to provide economic security "upon which welfare depends" indicated that he saw his space of *engagement* to be the Federal system (including its division of powers between Federal, State and local government). The early plan was for Old Age Insurance to become a national program (which it did become), as close to universal as possible, and for public assistance programs (such as Old Age Assistance and Aid to Dependent Children) to be administered by States in line with extensive Federal guidelines and national standards. However, the legislation that Roosevelt finally signed in August 1935 was far more circumscribed; reflecting the debates and compromises made within the CES and Congress in the process of turning the Bill into an Act.[1]

---

1   The SSA was an omnibus bill that covered several programs, only one of which was 'social security' – Old Age Insurance (Title II) – as it is understood today, which was the only program that was fully Federal (and in fact the only program that had *not* already existed in some form at the State level). The others were Federal Grants-in-Aid to States and so were partially federally funded but state administered. The Grants to States included one to assist with each State's Unemployment Compensation laws (Title III), and then

Despite a Democrat controlled House and Senate, the Bill was in danger of not passing without the support of Southerners and thus concessions were made in order to secure their votes. Some conservative Southern Democrats (all white men, some of whom were well-established legislators and sat on key committees, such as the House Ways and Means Committee and Senate Finance Committee) were suspicious of the legislative proposals and were especially vocal in their opposition at the Congressional hearings (and though it is often overlooked, so were several conservative-oriented Northern Democrats).[2]

From the perspective of many Southerners, the suggestion of inclusive, federalizing Social Security programs was a threat to the social and economic order in their States – a threat to *their* spaces of dependence. As one Charleston newspaper editorial lamented "with our local policies dictated by Washington, we shall not have the civilization to which we are accustomed" (quoted in Katznelson 2005, 40). That 'civilization' included the regional economy of the South, where the competitive advantage relative to the industrial North included a cheap supply of African-American agricultural workers, primarily men, but women too (and of course, many African-American women worked for pitiful wages as maids and cooks, not only in the southern States, but elsewhere in the US too). Unemployment Insurance and public assistance (Aid to Dependent Children and Old Age Assistance) programs would be State administered, but the way this was originally proposed in the Bill was seen to threaten to limit large agricultural landowners' access to workers by offering alternatives to the low wages in agricultural and domestic work.

By proposing national standards of "reasonable subsistence compatible with decency and health" for the States to adhere to, Roosevelt's vision depended on a space of engagement to be built from below exploiting a variation of the idea of "networks of association" among the States (i.e. buy-in from Congress). In response, the Southerners created a counter-strategy around a network of legislators who in effect, worked to "defend, enhance the interests of those dependent on some particular place-specific conditions – to defend or enhance a space of dependence" (Cox 1998, 15). For example, a faction led by Senator Harry Floyd Byrd (representing Virginia) argued vociferously against the proposed national standards and opposed any provisions that there would be Federal sanctions against States that discriminated against African-Americans in public assistance programs. The language outlawing racial discrimination was eventually stricken from the Bill. Southerners also led the way to excluding agricultural workers and

---

others to enable States to furnish financial assistance to "needy individuals" (including Old-Age Assistance [Title I], Aid To The aged, blind, disabled [Titles X, VIV and XVI]) and to "needy dependent children" (Aid To Dependent Children [Title IV], and a set of other State programs collectively called Maternal And Child Welfare [Title V]).

2   Of course 'the Southerners' were not a monolithic group speaking in a single voice, some were very supportive of the Bill, but the views of the more conservative Democrats greatly shaped the debate and eventual content of the Social Security Act.

domestic workers from coverage under the social insurance programs (Old Age Insurance and Unemployment). As occupations are deeply raced and gendered, these exclusions were racist and sexist; this 'compromise' meant a huge proportion of African-American women and men were denied access to social insurance programs (Abramovitz 1996; Neubeck and Cazenave 2001).[3]

Southerners developed an argument that can be reinterpreted as criticizing the Federal Government for attempting to 'jump scale' to the State level by trying to take greater responsibility for 'welfare' via national programs and by imposing national standard guidelines on the States. This, it was claimed, violated the Tenth Amendment (Powers of the States and People, i.e. 'States Rights') of the Constitution which assigned responsibility for public welfare to the States and local governments. So Southerners blocked early versions of the Social Security Bill requiring States to provide categorical assistance that would establish public assistance programs (Old Age Assistance and Aid to Dependent Children) at levels "at least enough to provide a reasonable subsistence compatible with decency and health" following national standards. Such provisions were blocked until they were amended to let the States administer their own programs and set eligibility and benefit levels for public assistance in a framework of looser Federal guidelines. This along with the deletion of the anti-race discrimination provisions effectively meant that local race discrimination could remain part of a State's official practice. State governments could administer programs in a manner that added layers of eligibility requirements to those stated in Federal law and permitted local officials to implement rules with ample discretion (Quadagno 1994; Neubeck and Cazenave 2001).

My specific interest in the production of the Social Security Act is the ADC program. As with my suburban clerical workers project I am troubled by some accounts of the evolution of the Social Security Act that render ADC recipients as powerless victims of the state. As Kevin points out in a different context, "(t) he territorial reach of state agencies is imperfect. Even in the case of the most totalitarian of states, there are always spaces of resistance" (Cox 1998, 3). The final Social Security legislation left individual States with a great deal of discretion about who would receive ADC. So even though African-American mothers and children, especially in the South, were far more likely to be impoverished and live in single-parent families, they formed a tiny group of recipients in the first years of the ADC program (despite efforts by the federal Bureau of Public Assistance to increase their numbers). African-American mothers, local officers often determined, had plenty of employment opportunities as seasonal agricultural workers or domestic workers and so were 'employable mothers' in ways white

---

3   Subsequent amendments removed many of these restrictions. For example in 1939, 55 percent of the civilian labour force was covered by Old Age, Survivors and Disability Insurance (OASDI) programs, by the 1970s, 90 percent were, and in 2002 96 percent were (2004 Green Book, Committee on Ways and Means, 2004 House of Representatives, Table 1-7).

mothers were not. In western States, similar arguments were made about Latinas and Native Americans.

State governments (such as Alabama and Georgia) through local welfare officers intruded, often literally into welfare recipients' home and sexual privacy. Some States' laws were replete with exclusionary rules based on assumptions about the 'moral character' of welfare mothers. Several States had "suitable home" and/or "substitute father" laws covering ADC recipients that meant local officials could choose to cut off ADC to families if there was any suggestion of a "man in the house." Once cut-off a woman had to prove she was not in a relationship or end the relationship to be reconsidered for ADC, or alternatively get him to pay the bills and support the children. For if there was a "man in the house" he might be being supported, or at least subsidized, by ADC rather than making himself available as cheap agricultural labor. To ensure the 'good moral character' of recipients, local officials could make surprise home visits (often early in the morning or late at night) to look for evidence of 'inappropriate' behavior. There is ample evidence that local officials were more diligent in enforcing these rules with households headed by women of color (Quadagno 1988; Neubeck and Cazenave 2001; Solinger 2010).

Having been denied ADC either by eligibility requirements or straightforward discrimination, by the 1950s increasing numbers of African-American women (and other women of color) challenged their exclusion from, and began enrolling in, ADC (known as AFDC after 1962). From the early 1960s, inspired by the Civil Rights movement, feminist activism and other grass roots organizations, welfare recipients began organizing in different cities across the US. In the process they created a space of engagement based on a network of associations across the US, echoing Kevin's example of the Civil Rights movement:

> Those who fought for black civil rights could never have accomplished what they did by constructing networks of influence purely within particular Southern cities or States. Rather a much broader network embracing federal officials and an alliance of civil rights workers throughout the country had to be put together."
> (1998, 17)

Johnnie Tillman organized welfare mothers in Los Angeles in 1963, and eventually headed up the National Welfare Rights Organization. She argued that welfare was a basic right of citizenship, and later in the very first issue of *Ms Magazine* in 1972, she famously argued:

> The truth is that A.F.D.C. is like a supersexist marriage. You trade in *a* man for *the* man. But you can't divorce him if he treats you bad. He can divorce you of course, cut you off anytime he wants. But in that case, *he* keeps the kids, not you.

These local welfare rights groups moved to "construct networks with centers of social power that (lay) beyond their space of dependence" (Cox 1998, 17) as State-wide networks emerged in California, Michigan and Mississippi, among others. Through tactics of protest and disruption in a range of different locations and across a range of scales they were able to achieve important gains. Eventually the National Welfare Rights Organization (NWRO) was formed in 1967.[4] During the 1960s and 1970s the NWRO and other welfare rights social movements pushed for major changes in the rules governing welfare eligibility. For example, in 1968 the first welfare case heard by the Supreme Court (King v. Smith) overturned Alabama's 'substitute father' law that allowed benefits to be arbitrarily removed or reduced (Solinger 2010). This and other landmark US Supreme Court decisions finally established AFDC as a statutory entitlement. As a result, a State's decisions to deny or reduce public assistance became subject to due process of law protections.

Challenge for the Future

Kevin and I have had our tussles over what counts as political geography. From my perspective this arises from his faithful adherence to historical-geographical materialism, on the one hand, and my post-graduate school interest in feminist theories of difference and intersectionality, on the other. For example, the emails exchanges and conversations we had about two pieces I've written for collections he has put together in the last 10 years could be boiled down to "that's all very interesting Kim, but really it all comes down to class struggle and state power." And I didn't agree. He is a scholar with a remarkably agile mind and a piercing intellect – and still after over two decades he sends me journal articles, reads my papers (and continues to demand clarity of thought and high quality writing from me!), offers constructive (usually) criticism, and is supportive of my work. I offer my concluding comments in the spirit of continuing our conversations.

Kevin himself has declared "(t)he central institutional locus of the political is the state" (Cox 1998, 1). Analyses of state power have focused most on themes such as geopolitics, state regulation state sovereignty and electoral politics, which tend to be pitched at the global, national and local (as in the local state) scales. Feminist critiques have made it increasingly common to look at the ways that state power permeates other scales and the more 'mundane' aspects of everyday life (e.g. England 2003; Kofman 2007; Marston, 2000). For instance, as I have already suggested, the home is an important site and space of state control and one where numerous state institutions, practices and procedures are enacted and reproduced on a daily basis. Other geographers have also called for a deeper analysis of the

---

4   The NWRO was active from the mid-1960s to the mid-1970s. Since then, of course, AFDC has been dismantled (see, for example, England 2008). However, while curiously rarely acknowledged, organized welfare rights activism has continued since the mid-1970s, for example the National Welfare Rights Union was created in 1987 and has been active since (see Gilbert 2001; Boyer 2006).

politics of everyday life in the context of the social relations of the state. For example, Joe Painter (2006) calls attention to the prosaic aspect of state practices. As he remarks, the

> ...permeation of stateness into the everyday is evident in almost every area of social life. Giving birth, child rearing, schooling, working, housing, shopping, travelling, marrying, being ill, dying and countless other activities all involve us, to a greater or lesser extent, in relations with state institutions and practices, often in ways that are so taken for granted they are barely noticeable. (2006, 753).

Indeed, emphasizing the statization of social life, of everyday life helps keep a clear focus on the taken-for-granted and extensive spatial reach of state power. This is not to suggest that Kevin completely opposes such interpretations of the state, space and power. He remarks on how they have enriched theories of state-society reactions, helping to ensure that "the project of excavating the spatiality of state power is as vital as ever" (Cox et al. 2008, 89).

For Kevin the overarching social relation in that excavation is class (as in the Marxian relations of production and capitalist relations of domination). For example, in developing and embellishing on their concept of local dependence, and Kevin and Andy clearly prioritized a class-based interpretation. In a footnote they remark that "there are also ethnic and racial interpretations of spatial restructuring, which further complicate the issue. Here we look only at class, the interpretation most threatening to local business coalitions" (1988, 322). While I admit it might be unfair to point to a footnote in a paper written over two decades ago, this statement is very revealing of a 'class only' view of local politics. Even 10 years later, in the second of the two papers underpinning this collection, Kevin further remarks that "class politics can assume diverse forms: ethnic, racial, geographic" (Cox 1998, 2). My point is that Kevin tends to ignore other forms of exploitation and oppression, the non-economic and even non-capitalist ones (à la Gibson-Graham, 1996). Class (in the Marxist sense) is the power relation that matters most to Kevin. Ethnicity and race (and presumably gender, sexuality, and other relations of difference) are reduced to merely 'complicating the issue' or modifications to class relations. But class is *not* complicated by other systems of difference; it is fundamentally co-constituted with and through them, not merely modulated by them. Indeed to borrow Kevin's language, race politics can assume diverse forms: class, gender, geographic. Just as gender politics can assume diverse forms and so on and so on. Class intersects with the discourses, practices and processes associated with other non-economic social relations; and it does so differently in different situations, in different places and at different points in time. The adherence to historical geographical materialist visions of social processes means Kevin sidesteps theories that address social categories other than class and non-economic concepts of politics, power and agency that are also and always involved in producing actually existing political geographies.

This sort of critique is far from original to me, just as Kevin is not, of course, the only political geographer (or scholar of any sort for that matter) whose work can be thus criticized. But to make my point let me return to my case study of the Social Security Act. Of course a class analysis of this process is important (and in fact was one that I recall Kevin often using in his graduate seminars on Fordist-Keynesian state formation). Kevin might even argue that class was a necessary condition, and race, gender etc were contingent. But class as a system of exploitation and oppression is intertwined with other systems of inequality. For example, Neubeck and Cazenave (2001) offer a race-based analysis and point to "the racial state doctrine" that effectively legalized and legitimized the economic (i.e. class) but also social and political privilege of white people and the discriminatory practices maintaining that white privilege and white supremacy (e.g. the Plessey v. Ferguson decision upholding racial segregation under the doctrine of 'separate but equal'). They convincingly argue for the concept of 'welfare racism' as an analytical tool to chart the evolution of US welfare policy.

In fairness Kevin is not inured to such positions. Although state-capital-class relations, as per usual, remain the common denominator, his ongoing work on South Africa appears to have given him reason to modulate some of his own theorizing. For example, in a recent paper with Rohit Negi (2010), he explores the relationship between the state and the development prospects of sub-Saharan Africa. They frame their argument around a *capitalist* form of development (their emphasis), complete with references to Marx's *Capital: Volume 1*. And yet to quote them out of context, their argument is "more subtle and differentiated" than a simple application of classical Marxism. The difference that race makes to capitalist state formations is very evident in their argument, as is a slight nod to post-colonial theory.

Kevin is also clearly taking feminist work more seriously than in the past. In a 2005 unpublished paper, Kevin offers his view of the frictions between critical human geography (which he divides into two wings: 'political economy' and 'cultural') and Marxist geography aka historical geographical materialism. He flags a concern that some feminists "have turned their backs against class politics in favor of a politics of representation" (2005, 5) but later suggests that historical geographical materialism has benefitted from challenges from the cultural wing, including a more thoroughgoing analysis of meanings and identity politics. In the *Sage Handbook of Political Geography* he comments that a third of the authors are women (one of whom is me), and says this "marks something of the changes in the gender balance of the field" (2008, 19). He seems to find praiseworthy that "the contributions of feminist geographers have already set new agendas for political geography"; he gives examples of how feminists have decentered the state from discussions of power, brought attention to public/private space, and added questions of social reproduction to debates on the politics of scale. He (2008, 19) also suggests that "the task of bringing a feminist analysis to bear on all the core areas of political geography remains ... a challenge for the future." I hope this means he is pledging to be part of that challenge!

References

Abramovitz, M. (1996), *Regulating the Lives of Women: Social Welfare Policy from Colonial Times to the Present* (Boston, South End Press).

Boyer, K. (2003), 'At work, at home? New geographies of work and care-giving under welfare reform in the US', *Space and Polity* 7, 75–86.

Cox K. R. and Mair A. (1988), 'Locality and community in the politics of economic development', *Annals of the Association of American Geographers* 78, 307-25.

Cox, K. (1998), 'Spaces of dependence, spaces of engagement and the politics of scale, or: looking for local politics', *Political Geography* 17, 1-23.

Cox, K. R. (2005), 'From Marxist Geography to Critical Geography and back again', Department of Geography, The Ohio State University, http://geog-www.sbs.ohio-state.edu/faculty/kcox/Cox9.pdf (first accessed June 2011).

Cox, K. (2008) 'Introduction' to 'The Scope and Development of Political Geography' section,' in Cox, K. Low, M. and Robinson, J. (eds), *Handbook of Political Geography* (London and Thousand Oaks CA, Sage), 17-20.

Cox, K., Low, M. and Robinson, J. (eds) (2008), *Handbook of Political Geography* (London and Thousand Oaks CA, Sage).

Cox, K. R. and Negi, R. (2010), 'The state and the question of development in Sub-Saharan Africa', *Review of African Political Economy* 37, 71-85.

England, K. (2003), 'Towards a Feminist Political Geography?' *Political Geography* 22, 611-16.

England, K. (2008), 'Welfare provision, welfare reform, welfare mothers,' in K. Cox, M. Low and J. Robinson (eds), *Handbook of Political Geography* (London and Thousand Oaks CA, Sage), 141-513.

England, K. (1993), 'Suburban pink collar ghettos: the spatial entrapment of women?' *Annals of the Association of American Geographers* 83, 225-42.

England, K. (1995), '"Girls in the office": job search and recruiting in a local clerical labor market', *Environment and Planning A* 27, 1995-2018.

Flint, C. (2003), 'Dying for a 'P'? Some questions facing contemporary Political Geography', *Political Geography* 22, 617-20.

Gilbert, M. (2001), 'From the "Walk for Adequate Welfare" to the "March for Our Lives": welfare rights organizing in the 1960s and 1990s', *Urban Geography* 22, 440-56.

Gibson-Graham, J. K. (1996), *The End of Capitalism (As We Knew It): A Feminist Critique of Political Economy* (Cambridge MA, Blackwell).

Hanson, S. and Pratt, G. (1995), *Gender, Work and Space* (London and New York, Routledge).

Hartmann, H. (1979), 'The unhappy marriage of Marxism and Feminism: towards a more progressive union', *Capital and Class* 8, 1-33.

Harvey, D. (1982), *The Limits to Capital* (Oxford, Blackwell).

Harvey, D. (1985), *The Urbanization of Capital: Studies in the History and Theory of Capitalist Urbanization* (Baltimore, Johns Hopkins University Press).

Jarvis H. (2005), *Work/Life City Limits: Comparative Household Perspectives* (Basingstoke, Palgrave Macmillan).

Katznelson, I. (2005), *When Affirmative Action Was White: An Untold History of Racial Inequality in Twentieth-Century America* (New York, W.W. Norton & Company).

Kofman, E. (2007), 'Feminist transformations of Political Geography', in K. Cox, M. Low and J. Robinson (eds), *Handbook of Political Geography* (London and Thousand Oaks CA, Sage).

Marston, S. (2000), 'The social construction of scale', *Progress in Human Geography* 24, 219-42.

Masson, D. (2006), 'Constructing scale/contesting scale: women's movement and rescaling politics in Quebec', *Social Politics: International Studies in Gender, State and Society* 13, 462-86.

McDowell, L. and D. Massey, D. (1984), 'A woman's place?' in D. Massey and J. Allen with J. Anderson (eds), *Geography Matters!: A Reader* (New York, Cambridge University Press), 128-47.

Mills, L. N. (2006), 'Maternal health policy and the politics of scale in Mexico', *Social Politics: International Studies in Gender, State and Society* 13, 487-521.

Monk, J. and S. Hanson (1982), 'On not excluding half of the human in Human Geography', *The Professional Geographer* 34, 11-23.

Nuebeck, K. J. and Cazenave, N. A. (2001*), Welfare Racism: Playing the Race Card against America's Poor* (New York and London, Routledge).

Quadagno, J. (1994), *The Color of Welfare: How Racism Undermined the War on Poverty* (New York, Oxford University Press).

Raento, P., Minghi, J., Cox, K. R., Davidson, F. M., Flint, C. and Herb, G. H. (2010), 'Interventions in teaching political geography in the USA', *Political Geography* 29, 190-99.

Roosevelt, F. D. (1934), Message to Congress Reviewing the Broad Objectives and Accomplishments of the Administration. June 8, 1934. http://www.ssa. gov/history/fdrstmts.html (accessed June 2011)

Solinger, R. (2010), 'The first welfare case: money, sex, marriage, and white supremacy in Selma, 1966: a reproductive justice analysis', *Journal of Women's History* 22, 13-28.

Staeheli, L. A., Kofman, E. and Peake. L. J. (eds) (2004), *Mapping Women, Making Politics: Feminism Perspectives on Political Geography* (New York, Routledge).

Ward, K., Fagan, C., McDowell, L., Perrons, D. and Ray, K. (2007), 'Living and working in urban working class communities', *Geoforum* 38, 312-25.

Young, I. (1981), 'Beyond the unhappy marriage: A critique of the dual systems theory', in L. Sargent, (ed.), *Women and Revolution: A Discussion of the Unhappy Marriage of Marxism and Feminism* (Boston, South End Press), 43-70.

REJOINDER

Chapter 12

Territory, the State and Urban Politics: Some Reflections

Kevin R. Cox

Context

First of all let me say how much I appreciate the work of the editors and the chapter authors in putting together this collection of papers on the theme of 'territory, the state and urban politics.' It has been extraordinarily useful for me to read what has been written and to see my work in a different, more critical way, but always critical in a positive sense. This stimulation is longstanding, not least through the students I have worked with, some of whom have chapters in this volume. Likewise there are those peers – and in some instances their 'peerage' goes back a long way – who have always been so supportive and helpful. Whatever I might have accomplished owes so much to their own work.

I have been asked to provide a rejoinder to the chapters written for this volume. They are, of course, very varied in their respective foci and emphases. There are, though, some consistent themes and it is these which I wish to focus on, allowing me to reflect on some of the ideas being discussed, to clarify my position, and to revisit and reposition some of the different claims I have made. In putting together the book, the editors decided to highlight certain themes in my writings on urban politics, local economic development and state territoriality.

Given the centrality of the idea to my work, it seems appropriate to start out by making a few comments on the concept of local dependence. This idea was an important conceptual building block for much of my initial thinking around the theme of the politics of local economic development. I then want to move on to something which became quite central to my subsequent work on the state and the politics of scale: the territorial structure of the state, though this also picked up on earlier work like that in my book *Conflict, Power and Politics in the City* as well as with my growing interest in South Africa. South Africa, along with Great Britain, then became important to my interest in comparison; an interest that some of the contributors have noted. Quite how one frames these things can clearly change though, and that interest needs some re-visiting and its specificities re-worked. This is discussed in the third section of the chapter. Finally there are questions of method that have troubled me for a long time and which again need re-visiting and which overlap with, and seriously qualify my approach to, comparative study.

The Question of Local Dependence

Almost all the chapters in this book draw attention to the idea of local dependence and its utility in understanding local politics. It was an idea long in fruition and I benefited hugely at the time from talking it through with some outstanding graduate students from that period, including Kim England, Andy Jonas, Andy Mair and Jeff McCarthy. It should be admitted at the outset that David Harvey's (1985) arguments about the contradiction between mobility and fixity gave us confidence in this and to some degree all we did was develop his more general claims with respect to the more specific problem of the politics of local economic development. We fleshed it out and we explored its more concrete expressions. The notion of local dependence was then drawn on later in work on the politics of scale: something also implicit in Harvey's geopolitics of capital once the latter was laid out alongside a territorially structured state form. It remains a useful concept and one that is still important to my thinking, but as Allan Cochrane makes clear in his chapter in this book, there are also questions that need to be addressed. One of his concerns is that by theorizing local politics in terms of local dependence one risks marginalizing the role of non-local agents and agencies who may, in fact, be more important for local politics than any of those who are locally dependent in the sense that Andrew Mair and I specified in our original paper; something apparent in his work with John Allen on assemblages (Allen and Cochrane 2007; 2010). I think that this is absolutely correct. One expression of this is the way in which central states, in virtue of their own scale-specific local dependence come to have enhanced interests in those cities or regions defined as vital to the country's economic health as a whole. There is some element of this in current British policy towards London and the Southeast. This may also mean an alliance between national and local interests as Delphine Ancien emphasizes in her chapter in this book on the relation between the City and the British state.

This also works, as John Allen and Allan Cochrane have emphasized, at sub-national scales: how more regional interests, in the form both of state agencies and civil society, get pulled into what we often take for 'local politics.' Allen and Cochrane discuss this in terms of relatively fleeting forms of arrangement but it is also apparent in more enduring spatial divisions of labor that have important scalar features. I am thinking here of what Andy Wood (1997) and I termed 'the local economic development network' which functions as the mediator of inward industrial investment. It brought together the more regionally-based electric and gas utilities with more local chambers of commerce and local governments. As Alan Townsend and I (2005) later demonstrated there is something very similar in Great Britain.

In short, local dependence needs to be accorded a more scalar interpretation. The qualifier 'local' should be understood in relative rather than absolute terms.[1]

---

1 On reading some of the chapters in this volume I thought that this had not always been entirely grasped. Within metropolitan areas local governments are 'local' but within

In the same way, the politics of scale is not necessarily bottom-up; it can also be top-down as more central branches of the state seek to mobilize the more local for their own purposes. Similar considerations apply to multi-locational corporations. While their revenues depend on the efficient functioning of respective spatial divisions of production as a whole, some sites in those divisions will be more crucial than others, be less substitutable, and so will be more likely to elicit intervention in the local should the occasion arise.

Allan Cochrane also suggests that in the work on local dependence and local politics there may have been a tendency to neglect issues of reproduction. Again, I think that there is some point here but a response can be partly folded into my discussion above of the scalar aspects of local dependence. The first thing to note is the necessary relation between production and reproduction. As a result there is a history of capital intervening in the reproduction of the workforce all the way from the model communities of the nineteenth century to current employer anxieties about housing prices in places like Silicon Valley and Seattle. Second, because of the way issues of housing and health policy have often been shunted upwards to the national level the local politics of reproduction can be a result of local reaction to more centrally instigated initiatives. There are some classic instances of this in Great Britain. Housing policy is largely national. Historically, in order to counter the possibility of local housing shortages and concerns about inflationary pressures – local dependence at the national scale at work, in other words – the distribution of new housing has been planned top-down. But it is one thing to tell the County of Warwickshire to absorb so many new houses and quite another to determine where they should go: first to distribute them among the five constituent districts and then the even more fraught process of finding room within those districts.

There are ways in which the application of the idea of local dependence can be taken further, therefore. There are also some confusions that could usefully be confronted. In particular it overlaps with and is often equated to spatial entrapment; the sort of relation – or putative relation – that Kim England addressed when writing of gender and the journey to work (1993). In contrast to local dependence the notion of 'entrapment' is a situation that has no offsetting advantages for those 'entrapped.' It does not match the sorts of local dependence typically at stake in the politics of local economic development. The fixity of social relations for firms that local dependence draws attention to is a result of a socialization of production – a local division of labor, shared means of production – which facilitates accumulation. The fixity that goes along with this necessary socialization can be a

---

municipalities, so too are neighborhoods and they also can (e.g.) have their locality-specific interests attempting to structure the movement of value at larger scales to their advantage and pushing for change in state structures, as in the demand for changing from at large to ward elections. Regions, too, are 'local' with respect to the state and should be understood in that sense; something very clear in discussions of the geopolitics of contrasting state structures as will be discussed below.

problem when wider geographic divisions of labor start to shift as with the crisis in so many local economies in the Midwest and the Northeast of the US during the economic crisis of the late '70s and early '80s. But it isn't necessarily so.

On the other hand, we should note how this socialization of production distributes its advantages unevenly. For the most part it is a socialization for capital rather than for labor. So as to continue to take advantage of it, capital has at times sought to fix workers in place. Unemployment compensation programs were preceded by charity organizations which helped keep workers around until the next upturn in business. State encouragement of homeownership has worked in the same direction, though that was only one reason for it.[2]

Spatial entrapment in this case can be referred to a power asymmetry within the immediate sphere of production. Production, though, clearly has wider conditions and consequences. Two in particular are relevant to my argument here. The first is the technical division of labor and the variations in income that it generates. The second is the chronic insecurity of the wage worker: but again there is some differentiation in that instance that corresponds in part to positions in the technical division of labor. These have significant implications for spatial entrapment, echoing Massey's remarks (1993) on power geometries.

To take the technical division of labor first, the way it is expressed in the geography of labor markets has important implications for spatial entrapment. The vast majority of the working class is limited to very local labor markets (Gordon 1995). Much of the information about job vacancies tends to move by word of mouth. Alternatively there are the want ads in the local newspaper. This is in contrast to those who are credentialed in various ways. They are more likely to access job possibilities through trade journals and consequently tend to enjoy greater choice in where they live. This covers a wide range of positions, from teachers and nurses at one end through engineers to financial directors and marketing managers at the other. In short, the vast majority is highly dependent on local labor market conditions.

To some degree these effects are magnified by local housing markets. Housing markets tend to be very local indeed, fluctuating across space and time in accord with changes in local labor markets. The vast majority of those who find themselves in depressed local economies can then be doubly trapped: first by a lack of credentials that inhibits a speculative leap into a job market elsewhere; and second by an inability to retrieve money from the sale of an existing home

---

2   For example, Topalov's comments on nineteenth century bourgeois reform movements (my emphasis): "Even if in conflict about means and priorities, the various reform groups converged on a consistent and rather well-known pattern of transforming working-class life styles. They wanted to set up the conditions for a rational use of time and wages, enforce steady attendance at work, restrict 'idle' time lost from production and home life, suppress all waste of money and reorder all consumption behavior to an ordered maintenance of the labour force, and promote providence and thrift. *They wanted to make occupation and residence more stable.*" (1985, 260).

that would allow them to buy into the more buoyant housing market conditions of areas where jobs *are* available. For the more credentialed, on the other hand, there may be some wage and salary leverage to cushion the effect.

Within local labor and housing markets other effects take over. Insecurity regarding future employment prospects, concerns that extend to one's children, result in a struggle for advantage in what Andy Jonas and I (1993) referred to as 'spaces of collective consumption.' Again, those privileged in the technical division of labor are also advantaged in the struggle for access to the better schools and to housing in areas where values are increasing. Exclusionary processes come into play through a mobilization of land use planning law and opposition to particular planning decisions. The children of the urban poor are trapped in the less desirable schools. Some of the urban poor may also struggle to access employment in burgeoning suburban labor markets, as in theories of spatial mismatch.

These processes have implications for party political alignments. In a classic paper, Mike Savage (1987) pointed out the implications of variations in local labor and housing markets and subsequent spatial entrapment for party political support in early '80s Great Britain. There is also a long history of suburban exclusion in metropolitan housing markets that tends to conform to party political alignments. The attempt of the Conservative Party at the last British election to take advantage of discontent with Labour Party land use decisions is only the most recent instance of this (Young and Kramer 1978). This then suggests something about the nature of party political support and its geography. A case can be made for viewing the support bases of the different parties as coalitional in form: coalitions of the spatially entrapped or of those who gain from the entrapment of others. For most, local labor and housing markets are crucial conditions of their standard of living. Mike Savage in the article referred to above, noted how this variation influenced the geography of support for Labour and Conservative Parties respectively. Labour's program of macro-economic expansion worked to its favor in those parts of the country dominated by depressed local economies, but much less so in London and the Southeast where economic conditions were more buoyant.

I do not want to make too much of this. Partisan alignments are clearly more complex. In the US so-called 'cultural' issues are significant along with racial identities, though that is not to ignore the relations they may have to local economic conditions. In the British context one thinks here of the racism that the British National Party has been able to take advantage of in Great Britain's rustbelt areas. Likewise there are the effects of party identifications that, while often equally localized, have much longer histories than those of local labor markets. People vote Labour in part because they were born into Labour households and in areas where to vote otherwise was virtually unheard of. Issues of spatial entrapment, therefore, have to be factored into accounts of voting geography but only as part of a more complex set of effects, perhaps in the sort of stratified form envisaged by Massey (1983) when talking about gender and class.

Likewise, and as Kim England reminds us in her chapter, ideas of spatial entrapment can flirt with ones of spatial determinism. Her own research (1993) on women's journey to work serves as an effective response to that sort of equation. Women, she showed, were nothing if not ingenious in putting together quotidian routines that allowed them to break out of seeming spatial limits imposed by their double role. The result was that their journey-to-work patterns were very similar to those of men; i.e., those who were supposedly less spatially entrapped. The variety of strategies through which people cope with spatial entrapment is a research theme that should find wider applicability in the same way that the idea of local dependence has.

The Territorial Structure of the State

A number of the contributors draw attention to the relation between local dependence and the territorial structure of the state. This was something which became quite central to my work on the politics of scale: how the creation of new state powers at a particular level of the state, local or central, might be a response to the demands of the locally dependent. Although it was touched upon in some of my earlier work on local economic development and localities (for example, with Andy Mair and Andy Jonas), struggles around access to the state's territorial structures was conceptually much more to the fore in my subsequent work on spaces of engagement and the politics of globalization (Cox 1998). It is also very clear in Delphine Ancien's chapter in this book: she shows how the Greater London Authority lobbied the British state for new planning powers so as to deal with the constituent boroughs and so help mitigate the housing question that it saw as key to the continuing viability of London's financial services industry.

On the other hand, my interest in the territorial structure of the state precedes my work on the politics of scale by many years. In the early 1970s I was particularly interested in what was known in the US as the metropolitan fiscal disparities problem: fiscal disparities between local governments and particularly between central city and suburbs. This was documented and discussed in my book *Conflict, Power and Politics in the City* but the idea of local dependence as a crucial condition was long in the future. In the same way, and as Jeff McCarthy points out, this interest in the geography of territorial fragmentation, or 'jurisdictional fragmentation' as I significantly referred to it at that time, gained substantial reinforcement from a growing interest in South Africa during the 1980s. This, incidentally, is a challenge to the perspective on the territorial structure of the state that took shape subsequent to my work on the politics of scale; something I try to address below.

In thinking about the territorial structure of the state, and as a way of dealing with the state's organizational form, I have found it useful to draw upon a territorialized version of a typology originally suggested by Bob Jessop (1990). He conceives this in terms of three distinct dimensions: inputs from civil society, as in elections; what he calls withinputs or the state's internal organization as, for example, in the form of its division of labor; and its outputs in the form of particular policy interventions. Table 12.1 suggests how these three dimensions can be given a territorial interpretation.

Table 12.1   Dimensions of state structure

DIMENSIONS OF STATE STRUCTURE	CONCEIVED A-TERRITORIALLY	CONCEIVED TERRITORIALLY
INPUTS	Elections	The territorial aspects of electoral organization: ward/at large; FPTP/PR; primary/non-primary systems
	The social bases of party support	The territorial bases of party support:
		• Regional parties
		• Parties as coalitions of the
	Lobbying	locally dependent
		Territorially-specific lobbies: Core Cities; Council for the Preservation of Rural England; neighborhood organizations; Northeast-Midwest Congressional Coalition
THROUGH-PUTS	The government's division of labor: Departments, Agencies	The state's territorial division of labor: local/central branches of the state and their powers and responsibilities
	The division of powers	
OUTPUTS	Forms of intervention: financial; legal.	• Territorial targeting: depressed area policy; enterprise zones
		• Land use zoning
	The public/private boundary	• Redistribution of state revenues to local governments in conformity statutorily determined criteria
		• Determination of local government boundaries; annexation law
		• Determination of voting districts
		• Metropolitan governance

One of the virtues of this spatialization is that it allows the identification of some unity between the various contributions to this book. It also helps me to revisit some of the work which I engaged in a long time ago and then discarded, perhaps prematurely; in particular I have in mind my early work on voting geographies which Ron Johnston and Charles Pattie have so generously discussed in their chapter. I have indicated above how we might re-imagine the territorial basis of party politics. The table also suggests ways in which we might start to conceive the subject matter of political geography. As I have set it up here, it refers to the state but it does not take too much imagination to see how it might be adapted to the political geography of metropolitan areas, supra-national organizations like the EU or even more diffuse forms of quasi-state organization.

It is, however, primarily descriptive: institutional or formal, as Bob Jessop put it. It says very little about process except what is implicit in the sequence of inputs/within-puts/outputs. Jessop had his own way of dealing with this. Clearly in terms of its territorialized content it needs to be understood as part of some spatialized social theory and here I think that Harvey again provides some useful guidance. What I have in mind here is first of all Harvey's (1985) work on what he called the 'geopolitics of capitalism'. In that work he assumed the state. It is, however, not difficult to see how it could emerge from the tensions surrounding the accumulation process as it unfolds in a spatial context where the contradiction between fixity and mobility has to assume significance. In short the state can be conceived as a structure of social relations designed to facilitate the realization of interests in the accumulation process where its territorial character is one of its essential aspects. This occurs even while the class character of accumulation and the tensions it generates can assume more concrete territorial forms, as in the cross-class alliances that Harvey referred to. State territorial structures then form a condition for furthering the conflicts surrounding accumulation: facilitating, limiting and then becoming objects of transformation as the contradictions intensify. Attention can focus on any number of aspects of state territorial structure: systems of representation, the state's territorial division of labor, or new forms of territorial targeting as the coalitions of the locally dependent join forces.

In foregrounding the contradiction between fixity and mobility, and when attempting to understand the territorial structure of the state, it is important not to exaggerate the role of bottom-up forces. This, in retrospect, is one of the lessons of my South African experience. Under apartheid territorial fragmentation assumed quite remarkable proportions. There were, of course, the homelands with significant powers of self-government. In metropolitan areas the African townships came under the jurisdiction of so-called Bantu Administration Boards or BABs and not under that of the 'white' city on the periphery of which they were typically constructed. In the early '80s the townships would then be the recipients of many of the powers of the old BABs under the Black Local Authorities Act. These fragmentations, though, had very little to do with local dependence as it has typically been conceived. Much more important was the way in which they were the legatees of an institutional fix for South Africa that had slowly emerged during the early part of the twentieth century in order to facilitate the country's insertion into the international division of labor, and then reinforced under apartheid. If local dependence was an issue in this, and it was, then it was the dependence of the gold mining companies on cheap African labor if their massive investments in very deep mines were to be realized and, in turn, the dependence of the South African state on subsequent revenue streams. This reinforces my earlier comments about the scalar forms of a local dependence that should be construed in relative rather than absolute terms: so in this instance the local is represented by various agents in South Africa and the more global, the international division of labor.

This brings me to the important topic of variability in territorial structures. State territorial structures clearly do differ; some are more decentralized than others, for example. This helps to shed light on variations in state practice, as well as on the social forces sustaining those structures. A theme which has interested, even obsessed me over the years has been the contrast between the American politics of local and regional development and its trans-Atlantic cousins (Cox 2004a; 2004b). The American instance of immensely powerful local growth coalitions engaged in a territorial competition with growth coalitions elsewhere, then entering into alliances with some as they seek some sort of relief from state or federal governments is quite *sui generis*. It always was and, in my view, remains so even while there have been attempts in Western Europe to stimulate from the top-down, local, grass-roots development initiatives (Jessop, Peck and Tickell 1999). Yet what is put together in terms of coalitions between business and local government around programs designed to stimulate local economic development is still a pale reflection of the American case. The sort of imbrication between growth interests and local political representatives that is taken for granted in the US is likewise, and with some qualifications like that provided by the French *cumul des mandats,* barely perceptible.

I used to think that this was because of contrasting structures of territorial interests. In the US growth coalitions coalesce around a clear set of locally dependent interests. These include, first of all, the gas and electric utilities which, in virtue of federally imposed service areas beyond which it has been difficult to expand, are very dependent on the growth of local demand. Second have been the local media empires, often comprising a locally-owned and operated newspaper, a radio station and possibly a TV station: a reflection of a decentralized media structure that is owing in large part to the continental scale of the country; there are no truly national newspapers except possibly the *Wall Street Journal* and, at a stretch, *USA Today.* Thirdly, one would have to include the developers. A lot of development is very hands-on. It depends on a detailed knowledge of a local market and connections with banks, sub-contractors and local governments (Wood 2004). And finally, there are the local governments themselves, which depend very considerably for their revenues on locally generated property, sales and income taxes. In Western Europe, and with the possible exception of real estate developers,[3] there is nothing quite like

---

3   On the British case Adams, Leishman and Watkins (2012) provide evidence of the significance of networked relations of trust among the land buyers of major homebuilders. For the most part these are constructed locally but they also have to develop relations with the London-based agents of government departments that have land holdings. The firms for which they work, moreover, tend to be regional or national in scope. The problem that they confront and the reason for which the networks are important is that of intense land scarcity rather than that of local demand which tends to dominate in the US. This means that, unlike the American case, they have no interest in the formation of or support of local growth coalitions. New housing will sell anywhere; the problem is securing the land.

this. It is not difficult, therefore, to make out a case for this particular set of interests as accounting for the utter exceptionality of the American case.

I am now inclined to think, though, that this is only a part of the story. Rather, contrasting state structures have to be weighed in the balance and may, in fact, be of determinant significance. The territorial structure of the American state is extraordinarily decentralized. It is not just that it is probably the most radical federation in the world, assigning very significant powers and responsibilities to the states, or that those states have, in their dubious wisdom, chosen to delegate many of those powers to local governments. This certainly creates opportunities for local growth coalitions to exercise leverage since state governments can depend on exactly the same sorts of large scale investments that they also cherish. But in addition the representational system is also significantly territorialized. To even get nominated for the Senate or Congress, would-be candidates have to run the gauntlet of the primary system, and that means obligations to local coalitions of forces. Once elected, they are expected to do things for the District or State, and the structure of the federal state[4] allows them to do precisely that. This works partly through the committee system. Legislators get to sit on those committees which deal with legislation that might have particular bearing on home districts or states. Once there they can amend or block the pending legislation. When it is passed on by the committee for a vote in the House or Senate, then the relative weakness of party discipline means that once again, one can often vote, in effect, for one's constituency. The pressures towards and the possibilities of action on behalf of what local growth coalitions want can therefore be very considerable.

This, of course, is very different from the states of Western Europe. These tend to be much more centralized and local government powers are circumscribed by a much more rigorous central supervision as well as being supported financially by a redistribution of revenue from the center. Committee systems are much weaker, with many of their functions taken over by the Cabinet, which is like a grand committee of committees. And once a bill passes to the floor of legislative assemblies, then there are strong pressures for it to pass, inciting a level of party discipline foreign to the American state. Accordingly the opportunities for more local or regional pressures to be expressed at the central branches of the state are much more limited. They cannot be accommodated as they are in the US by bipartisan coalitions. If the pressures are too strong to be contained within the parties then regional parties tend to form; again in sharp contrast to the US.

What this suggests to me is an alternative explanation for the peculiar practice that is the American politics of local and regional development. Certainly the strong bottom-up forces rooted in the locally dependent interests of the utilities, the developers, the local media and local government help to sustain a highly territorialized state form. But that state form antedates the local dependence of the utilities, which only came about subsequent to the anti-trust concerns at the

---

4   As well as the states.

turn of the last century. It likewise antedates the full blossoming of the modern media emporia and the post-war expansion of local government revenue needs. The significance of the American state form, rather, is that it has provided an opportunity structure for locally dependent interests to advance their agendas. Without it, they would have had to rely on different avenues of access, possibly promoting regional parties or support at the center for national policies affecting taxation and subsidy programs that would work to their advantage.

Still, there is no escaping local dependence as I point out in my chapter elsewhere in this book. Local governments in Western Europe may indeed get most of their revenue from central governments and in a way that provides little incentive for territorial competition, but that simply displaces the pressures onto the central state and the accumulation process at a national scale. Central states have to intervene in top-down fashion, through the urban and regional planning machinery and through major infrastructural projects which while local, have important externalities of more national scope, if that process is to be facilitated.

The Role of Comparison

A number of the contributors to this book, including Delphine Ancien, Mark Goodwin and Jeff McCarthy, have commented on my interest in comparative studies. To a degree it comes almost naturally to someone who spent his formative years in Great Britain and then has had a career in the United States. In many ways the two countries are staggeringly different and were even more so when I first arrived in 1961. Serendipity has clearly played a role. I might easily not have stayed in the United States. If I had not then I would probably never have had the pleasure of advising graduate students from South Africa. In his chapter in this book Jeff McCarthy describes how this advising relationship led in turn to an interest in that country. My first visit was in 1982 when apartheid was still in place, even while there was talk about 'reforming' it. I was overwhelmed by the experience. Ever since, South Africa and what it has stood for – a settler state, racial identities which have seemingly (only seemingly) overridden class, a complex, multi-faceted territorial politics – has been an important part of my research horizon: an extraordinary stimulus to thinking through the relations of the abstract to the concrete and vice versa.

It is not surprising, therefore, if comparison has occupied an important place in my thinking and in my research. The discussion of the comparative politics of local and economic development in the previous section is a case in point. I am also thinking of the work that I did with Andy Wood (1997) on what we called the local economic development network in the US. Later research with Alan Townsend (2005) in England brought to light something very similar in functional terms though with interesting institutional variations. This is to talk about comparisons between countries. I have also looked at inter-urban comparisons as a means of shedding light on structures and outcomes in the American politics of local economic development. This goes back to my early work (1993) with Andy Jonas on Columbus (see also Cox 2010).

Even so, I am now no longer so sure of where as a methodological approach comparative study fits in. It certainly has a history in the social sciences that is worth recounting and which sheds light on how we might practice human geography. The 1950s and the 1960s witnessed an efflorescence of cross-national studies in the social sciences, particularly in political science and to a lesser degree in sociology.[5] Comparison was also carried on within countries in what Dogan and Rokkan (1968) called, after the title of a book that they edited, 'quantitative ecological analysis.' By 'ecological' they meant studies of areal association. Geographical units, countries or electoral units, therefore, were to be lifted out of their geographic contexts and treated in isolation from one another. The assumption of independent observations that was at least implicit in the regressions of 'quantitative ecological correlation' was, in effect, accepted with grim earnestness. Absolute space trumped relative space; which was an intriguing development given that the spatial-quantitative revolution in geography was, at almost the same time, making the shift away from absolute space to more relative conceptions.

There was then a modest counter-movement. All of a sudden processes that breached the bounds of the nation state were discovered. The equating of society to the nation that had been taken for granted in the social sciences was challenged. Some of the notable names here were Gunder Frank, Immanuel Wallerstein and Anthony Giddens. Frank led the way in the '60s with his critique of the modernization theory on which so much comparative study had been based. Instead he reintroduced those metropole-satellite relations that comparative study, in a post-colonial era also marked by the relatively self-sufficient economies of fordism, thought it could ignore. He was then followed by Wallerstein and world systems theory; society, Wallerstein claimed, was defined by the market and the market was world-wide. States entered into a relation with one another in order to defend or challenge positions in a global division of labor. Giddens' theory of structuration then made its mark, processes of time-space distanciation knowing seemingly no bounds, and certainly not those of countries.

What is interesting though is the fact that despite these interventions, despite the globalization babble from the 1980s on, comparative study still enjoys a powerful cachet. Charles Tilly's (1984) influential *Big Structures, Large Processes, Huge Comparisons*, although focusing on theories of social change, does so through

---

5   Many of these took off from the modernization paradigm and focused on developing countries. An important series was published by Princeton University Press in the '60s under the heading 'Studies in Political Development' including, among others, books on education (James S. Coleman), communications (Lucian Pye) and bureaucracy (Joseph LaPalombara) along with a number of collections. A more programmatic collection was edited by Richard Merritt and Stein Rokkan (1966) with the title *Comparing Nations*. One thinks also of Almond and Verba's (1963) highly influential *The Civic Culture*.

a review of different approaches to comparison, only one of which can fairly be said to see countries in relation to one another rather than as isolated or to use the parlance of statistics 'independent' observations.[6] Equally influential in the social sciences was the 'how to' manual by Charles Ragin.[7]

For a human geographer this approach now seems not only empirically questionable, given the nature of the world as we experience it, but also difficult to defend theoretically. One of the major contributions of human geography to the social sciences over the last thirty or so years has been the development of a conception of space as relational: how people and other agents in particular places, whether a city or what we call a 'country', internalize through their social relations other places; how, that is, a place, in terms of its institutions, its position in wider divisions of labor, its class relations, its discourse, is composed by wider relations, that stretch out beyond what we take to be its boundaries. This conception is very evident in the work of Massey and Harvey, among others, even while they have not used it to critique the concept of comparative studies. It is a conception apparent in some of the chapters in this book. Kevin Ward examines the role of policy networks in the adoption of particular urban policies: how cities make each other rather than make themselves, in other words. Similarly the sort of dominance that the City has acquired in the economy of the United Kingdom, and as Delphine Ancien shows, makes little sense outside of the sort of adverse competitive environment faced by British industry in the closing years of the nineteenth century and a financial services infrastructure already in place in London at that time as a result of the growth of British investment overseas and the significance of the British merchant marine. Among other things, this is a conception that puts all theories of exceptionalism in doubt, including the sort of exceptionalism I implied in my discussion of the American state and the politics of local economic development.

How, therefore, might we re-imagine differences between countries and cities and so avoid the problems associated with comparative studies? How can the American politics of local economic development be situated with respect to broader forces, or for that matter the seeming exceptionality of Columbus's annexation policy? If we accept the global character of the accumulation process, then things become clearer. The institutional forms through which inward (industrial) investment is mediated differ between the US and the United Kingdom. In the US the gatekeepers are the gas and electric utilities (Cox and Wood 1997); they are the ones with the information banks on industrial sites. In the United Kingdom it is the larger jurisdictional entities comprising the counties, metropolitan and non-metropolitan that perform that function (Cox and Townsend 2005). In the American case the local dependence of the gas and electric utilities encouraged them early on to form their own economic development departments for that purpose. In the United Kingdom that local dependence was lacking.

---

6   This is his procedure of 'encompassing comparison.'

7   *Comparative Method* (1987).

Furthermore, it was only from the late 1970s and the contraction of the British regional planning apparatus that counties started taking a serious interest in local economic development rather than simply responding to inquiries from investors on an *ad hoc* basis. There is an important sense, therefore, in which the institutional forms through which inward investment is mediated in the American and British instances are functional substitutes for one another. There is some need to which they are a response, but a response influenced by national specificities, like those governing the provision of gas and electricity.

This, however, is insufficient. 'Inward investment' is itself a problematic category. It assumes firms prospecting for sites elsewhere and this cannot be taken for granted. Rather its status is historical. Inward investment only became significant with the growth of firms beyond a home base; the desire, pushed by competition with other firms, to gain access to new markets or alternative sources of components.[8] Likewise it assumes a locational discretion that would have been foreign to firms prior to the age of electricity, and the de-skilling of some industrial functions. None of these tendencies were limited to particular countries. Rather they were a more universal condition among capitalist countries: a condition which, when juxtaposed with national specificities, led to the formation of particular forms of mediating inward investment.

Countries and cities *are* different. Comparison is useful, even essential. It is important to know how places differ and what some of the correlates of that difference might be. Those differences though need to be understood in terms of wider sets of influences; as having emerged or been re-worked within the context of conditions and influences of a much broader geographic, or more accurately geohistorical, scope. As I argue in my own chapter in this book, through its contradictions accumulation generates constant change and agents try to deal with that change through the construction of new structures of relations as in the sorts of institutional infrastructures drawn on to facilitate inward investment. These infrastructures inevitably bear the mark of local specificity, even while they have been reworked in the context of the shifting challenges of the accumulation process.

Questions of Method

Some of the contributors to this book make reference to method, usually to my use of critical realism. There are also references to how I have engaged with dialectics. Alistair Fraser recalls how for his dissertation research in South Africa I emphasized that in his interviews of South African commercial farmers confronted with the challenge of land reform he should pursue the contradictions

---

8   That growth was itself predicated on the introduction of the joint-stock form, and therefore on the growth of stock markets and the sort of modern communication that allows the latter to function.

in which they found themselves and the strategies they saw as allowing them to resolve them from their own standpoint. I should also express my gratitude to Jamie Gough for bringing out this aspect of my approach, even while I might not have realized the dialectical character of what I was doing and certainly early on lacked a full appreciation of it. And indeed, when he says in his chapter about some earlier work that "At the methodological level, then, my criticism is that Cox does not take his dialectical approach quite far enough, to focus not merely on complexity and contingency arising *out of* abstract structures, but on *contradictions within them*" I can certainly agree. That is an adequate reflection of where I was at that time.

My earlier engagements with method were, of course, with the quantitative. This was my approach in empirical research into voting geography. Like many of my peers at that time, I was fascinated by what quantitative methods were telling us about spatial pattern in general and how they could be deployed in pursuit of spatial order in voting. During that period, methodological protocols were very clear: the continual search for models from elsewhere that could be spatialized, the reduction of data through factor analysis, the testing of hypotheses through regression and the identification of residuals in pursuit of evidence of yet more order. In this particular regard the historical materialism of the '70s left me baffled. The unity of theory and practice meant that there were no clear methodological signposts *per se*. I had difficulty coming to terms with that and it was in that context that, along with a number of others struggling with how to direct the research of their graduate students as well as their own, I was attracted to the critical realism that Andrew Sayer introduced towards the end of that decade and then expounded in *Method in Social Science* (1984).

In retrospect I was insufficiently skeptical. Rather I was lured by the numerous positive references in the critical realist literature to Marx and with some, at least, the view that Marx, quite unawares, had been one of them. I now realize the serious incompatibilities between critical realism and Marxism and I make some reference to them in my chapter elsewhere in this book. Critical realism is a philosophy of science and not a social theory, but it secretes a social theory, as any epistemological position must, and whether it is acknowledged or not, and this theory is quite contrary to how Marx constructed the social world and its dynamics. Through its mode of abstraction and its insistence on a sharp separation of the necessary from the contingent critical realism entails a pluralism sharply at odds with the totalizing character of historical materialism.[9] Marx's totality, moreover, is always one that is self-transforming through the way in which its different aspects necessarily enter into contradiction with one another. And at its center are the necessities of production which means, under capital, the accumulation process. Instead of the multiplicity of structures of social relations that exist alongside capital in the critical realist understanding,

---

9   Note that to refer positively to Marx's totalization is not to commit oneself to a social determinism.

therefore – patriarchy, race, the division of labor, the state – one is faced with the task of understanding them as production relations that while in some cases they might pre-date capital, they have been utterly transformed by it into an essential aspect of its functioning.

I cannot therefore share Kim England's dismay when she notes that I "tend to ignore other forms of exploitation and oppression, the non-economic and even non-capitalist ones (à la Gibson-Graham 1996). Class (in the Marxist sense) is the power relation that matters most to Kevin. Ethnicity and race (and presumably gender, sexuality, and other relations of difference) are reduced to merely 'complicating the issue' or modifications to class relations." In the past my refusal of this sort of pluralism was more instinctive and should have told me that critical realism was problematic in the social theory it entailed. As it was, I was always attracted to the work of the socialist feminists, like Brenner and Ramas (1984), who tried to situate the changing character of the gender division of labor with respect to the development of capitalism. I can now see more clearly why they were correct.

It is equally true, as Mark Goodwin notes, that critical realism nicely jibed with the comparative approach to which I was attracted:

> There is also a consistent thread of comparative work running through Kevin's work – whether between the local politics of different cities in the United States, or between urban politics in the US and those in other countries (most notably the UK and South Africa). This stems from his realist approach and Kevin's insistence to explore the way that the same broad processes can give rise to different outcomes in different places, due to the contingent nature of their empirical articulation.

I now think, though, that this sort of formulation is problematic. It relies on a notion of internal and external relations that fails to provide the traction on how things unfold in the world; a world that is constantly changing in which, as Harvey and Scott have made clear,[10] what seems to be external is constantly being transformed into something internal.

But as I make clear in my chapter, none of this means that critical realism has nothing to offer historical materialist research. Its concept of a structure of social relations remains highly pertinent. Structures of relations in the sense of mutually entailing conditions and practices which then empower have been, in their concrete expression, extraordinarily important in the capital accumulation process. Rather it has been through the introduction of new or re-worked structures that capitals have sought to successfully confront the contradictions that are inevitably thrown up by their actions in the same way that labor has sought out new structures of

---

10   "We need to show...how particular contingencies that on first sight *appear* as external and arbitrary phenomena are *transformed* into structured internal elements of the encompassing social logic of capitalism" (1989, 19)

relations through which to resist. As far as capital is concerned, these can occur at the level of the individual firm through structures like their spatial divisions of labor, or at the level of capital in general, as in the development of the joint stock form and the stock market. On the side of labor one thinks of obvious ones like the different institutions of the labor movement and less obvious examples like the working class family. Quite how these different structures come about often has a random element to it; Massey's chance juxtapositions are suggestive, as Alistair Fraser notes in his chapter in this book.

This means, however, that when drawn on in historical materialist research they are always situated with respect to the accumulation process. They are, in short, *capitalist* structures of relations and as such, they have a history. They come into being to meet the challenges of the contradictions of accumulation and as a result their study entails an historical investigation. In retrospect, and as I implied earlier, it was not enough for Andy Wood and I (1997) to identify what we called the local economic development network; that division of labor comprising gas and electric utilities, local chambers of commerce and local governments that came into being to mediate inward investment in industry. Rather we should have questioned the historical status of the idea of 'inward investment' and investigated the conditions that made it possible. Just what was it that resulted in firms seeking sites elsewhere? What did it presuppose in terms of locational calculi that were both enabling and compelling?

This also suggests new ways of thinking about countries that accord with my scepticism about comparative studies. Among other things, every capitalist country has an institutional fix, often underpinned by appropriate discourse, which embeds its position in a wider geographic division of labor, facilitates defence of that position but can also result in lock-in. South Africa is a classic case in point. Without the sorts of coercive labor institutions that came into being during the first twenty to thirty years of gold production there, profitability in the mines would have been seriously challenged. The Africans, who bore the brunt of those rules, would never have permitted their introduction if they had had the vote; so the colonial form of the state was an additional part of that structure of relations. The effect of apartheid was to reinforce those institutions and hence the country's role as a mineral producer; something that now, as it attempts to industrialize, presents major problems.

The territorial structures of the state and spatial entrapment referred to earlier can be interpreted along similar lines. Stratification is certainly subsequent to the accumulation process but it is also a structure of relations of which territory and territorial defence are necessary parts. Institutional structures that protect homeowner values and the integrity of desirable school districts are part of this. Meanwhile the territorial structure of the American state facilitates the formation of enduring and empowering relations between local growth coalitions and 'their' Congressional Representatives and state legislators.

These sorts of structures then need to be traced back to the contradictions which are their necessary condition in the first place. In human geography we need to be particularly attuned to how those contradictions get expressed spatially. David Harvey, of course, has been especially helpful here. He quickly saw the significance of the contradiction between a necessary fixity for capital and an equally necessary mobility. This lies at the heart of any capitalist geopolitics at whatever geographic scale. A case in point is the politics of urban growth coalitions and research into them has to take that contradiction into account as a necessary condition of its possibility. There are also the (overlapping) spatial tensions which are generated as the social character of production encounters the private form of appropriation of the product: congestion and the housing cost issues that Delphine Ancien has drawn attention to in the context of London in her chapter; the attempts of local governments to externalize their fiscal problems on to others, attracting in the uses that will allow them to 'export' their tax base while excluding those seen as a burden on public expenditure; or the resistance of land owners and developers to land use planning. The danger is, of course, that to the extent that these contradictions are apprehended as spatial in character, then the more fundamental nature of the class forces at stake is missed. Territory comes to trump class, as in the siren song of 'local economic development.'

*****

All these questions – local dependence, the territorial structure of the state, the status of comparative studies and method – are, for me, of major importance almost to the point of obsession. I hope that I have helped clarify what is at stake there and moved the debate forward. Needless to say, and like so much else in my intellectual development, none of this would have happened without the constant stimulation of peers and graduate students. It is a truism that intellectual labor is cooperative but it is also subject to a good deal of chance. I count myself extraordinarily lucky in the relations that I have been able to forge, including with all those people who have prepared chapters for this book. I could not have wished for better. What a wonderful group they have been and continue to be.

References

Adams, D., Leishman, C. and Watkins, C. (2012), 'Housebuilder networks and residential land markets', *Urban Studies* 49, 705-20.

Allen, J. and Cochrane, A. (2007), 'Beyond the territorial fix: regional assemblages, politics and power', *Regional Studies* 41, 1161-75.

Allen, J. and Cochrane, A. (2010), 'Assemblages of state power: topological shifts in the organization of government and politics', *Antipode* 42, 1071-89.

Almond, G. and Verba, S. (1963). *The Civic Culture* (Princeton, Princeton University Press).

Brenner, J. and Ramas, M. (1984), 'Rethinking women's oppression', *New Left Review* 144, 33-71.

Cox, K. R. (2004a), 'The politics of local and regional development, the difference the state makes and the US/British contrast', in D. Valler and A. Wood (eds) *Governing Local and Regional Economies: Institutions, Politics and Economic Development* (Aldershot, Ashgate), 247-76.

Cox, K. R. (2004b), 'Globalization and the politics of local and regional development', *Transactions of the Institute of British Geographers* NS 29, 179-94.

Cox, K. R. (2010), 'The problem of metropolitan governance and the politics of scale', *Regional Studies* 44, 215-27.

Cox, K. R. and Jonas, A. E. G. (1993). 'Urban development, collective consumption and the politics of metropolitan fragmentation', *Political Geography* 12, 8-37.

Cox, K. R. and Townsend, A. R. (2005), 'Institutions and mediating investment in England and the United States', *Regional Studies* 39, 541-53.

Cox, K. R. and Wood, A. M. (1997), 'Competition and cooperation in mediating the global: the case of local economic development', *Competition and Change* 2, 65-94.

Dogan, M. and Rokkan, S. (1969), (eds), *Quantitative Ecological Analysis in the Social Sciences* (Cambridge, MA, MIT Press).

England, K. V. L. (1993), 'Suburban pink-collar ghettoes: the spatial entrapment of women?' *Annals of the Association of American Geographers* 83, 225-42.

Gordon, I. (1995), 'Migration in a segmented labour market', *Transactions of the Institute of British Geographers* NS 20, 139-55.

Harvey, D. (1985), 'The geopolitics of capitalism', in D. Gregory and J. Urry (eds), *Social Relations and Spatial Structures* (London, Macmillan), 128-63.

Harvey, D. and Scott, A. (1989), 'The practice of human geography: theory and empirical specificity in the transition from Fordism to flexible accumulation', in B. Macmillan (ed.), *Remodelling Geography* (Oxford, Blackwell), 217-29.

Jessop, B (1990) *State Theory*. (Cambridge, Polity Press).

Jessop, B., Peck, J. A. and Tickell, A. (1999), 'Retooling the machine: economic crisis, state restructuring, and urban politics', in A. E. G. Jonas and D. Wilson (eds) *The Urban Growth Machine: Critical Perspectives Two Decades Later* (Albany, NY, State University Press of New York), 141-59.

Massey, D. (1983), 'Industrial restructuring as class restructuring: production decentralization and local uniqueness', *Regional Studies* 17, 73-89.

Massey, D. (1993), 'Power geometry and a progressive sense of place', in J. Bird et al. (eds), *Mapping the Futures: Local Cultures, Global Change* (London, Routledge), 59-69.

Merritt, R. and Rokkan, S. (1966), *Comparing Nations* (New Haven, Yale University Press).

Ragin, C. C. (1987), *The Comparative Method: Moving Beyond Qualitative and Quantitative Strategies* (Berkeley and Los Angeles, University of California Press).

Savage, M. (1987), 'Understanding political alignments in contemporary Britain: do localities matter?' *Political Geography Quarterly* 6, 53-76.

Sayer, A. (1984) *Method in Social Science: A Realist Approach* (London, Hutchinson).

Tilly, C. (1984), *Big Structures, Large Processes, Huge Comparisons* (New York, Russell Sage Foundation).

Topalov, C. (1985), 'Social policies from below: a call for comparative historical studies', *International Journal of Urban and Regional Research* 9, 254-71.

Wood, A. M. (2004), 'The scalar transformation of the U.S. commercial property-development industry: a cautionary note on the limits of globalization', *Economic Geography* 80, 119-40.

Young, K. and Kramer, J. (1978), 'Local exclusionary processes in Britain: the case of suburban defense in a metropolitan system', in K. R. Cox (ed.), *Urbanization and Conflict in Urban Societies* (Chicago, Maaroufa Press), 229-52.

Index

Note: references to illustrations appear in bold.

For Product Safety Concerns and Information please contact our EU
representative GPSR@taylorandfrancis.com
Taylor & Francis Verlag GmbH, Kaufingerstraße 24, 80331 München, Germany

www.ingramcontent.com/pod-product-compliance
Lightning Source LLC
Chambersburg PA
CBHW070401270326
41926CB00014B/2656

9 781138 268005